CREATIVE NONFICTION

Researching and Crafting Stories of Real Life

CREATIVE NONFICTION

Researching and Crafting Stories of Real Life

PHILIP GERARD

STORY PRESS

Cincinnati, Ohio

Creative Nonfiction. Copyright © 1996 by Philip Gerard. Printed and bound in the United States of America. All rights reserved. No part of this book may be reproduced in any form or by any electronic or mechanical means including information storage and retrieval systems without permission in writing from the publisher, except by a reviewer, who may quote brief passages in a review. Published by Story Press, an imprint of F&W Publications, Inc., 1507 Dana Avenue, Cincinnati, Ohio 45207. (800) 289-0963. First edition.

Other fine Story Press Books are available from your local bookstore or direct from the publisher.

00 99 98 97 96   5 4 3 2 1

Library of Congress Cataloging-in-Publication Data

Gerard, Philip.
    Creative nonfiction / by Philip Gerard.
        p.   cm.
    Includes bibliographical references and index.
    ISBN 1-884910-07-6
    1. Authorship.   I. Title.
PN145.G427   1996
808′.02—dc20   95-46303
                                                      CIP

Designed by Clare Finney
Cover illustration by Celia Johnson

for Tom Mikolyzk,
who is true blue.

ACKNOWLEDGMENTS

The author gratefully acknowledges the following writers,
editors, interpreters, translators, producers and organizations
for their assistance in preparing this book:

Bill Atwill, David Haward Bain, Lisa Bain, Jerry Bledsoe,
David Bristol, Dr. Robert H. Byington, Kevin Canty, Nancy Colbert,
Stanley Colbert, Ted Conover, Lawrence Criner, Jan DeBlieu,
Annie Dillard, Lee Gutkind, Katherine Hatton, Robert Houston,
William Howarth, Pam Hurley, Kathleen Ann Johnson,
Judy Logan, Paul Mariani, Anne Matthews, William Matthews,
Thomas A. Mikolyzk, David Nasaw, Michael Pearson,
Daniel Pinkwater, Jim Polson, Ron Powers, Bob Reiss, Michael Rozek,
Norman Sims, Margaret Low Smith, Terry Tempest Williams

The Associated Writing Programs
The Bread Loaf Writers' Conference
The World & I, National Public Radio
The University of North Carolina—Chapel Hill

Special thanks to Lois Rosenthal and Jack Heffron for their sound
advice and imagination, and to Robin Hemley and Jim Trupin.

The author is grateful to the University of North Carolina at
Wilmington for a research reassignment that helped
to make this book possible.

CONTENTS

A NOTE ON SOURCES . . .

In preparing this manuscript, I interviewed many writers and editors, some of them famous, some not, all of them passionate and working. I also attended panel discussions at writers' conferences, sometimes including people I also interviewed directly. Because of the awkwardness of continually having to explain the context of a spoken comment, usually I have chosen not to do so. Whenever a writer or editor is quoted without other citation, his or her words were spoken out loud. If I am quoting from a book or other published or unpublished written source, I have so indicated.

In certain passages, I have made points about the working process of certain writers in specific books, essays or articles. I have tried to limit my suppositions to those that can be reasonably inferred from the finished piece—what the writer actually wrote. Where such insight was provided by direct interview, I have so indicated.

P.G.

CHAPTER ONE

WHAT *IS* CREATIVE NONFICTION ANYHOW?

I t was late afternoon, the day before the close of the Bread Loaf Writers' Conference in Vermont, when Bob Reiss approached the lectern of the Little Theatre to give the final reading of an eleven-day marathon of readings. A warm, breezy day, with just a hint of fall in the lengthening mountain shadows. The Little Theatre was crowded. Writers and would-be writers craned forward in their folding wooden chairs. At the open screens of French doors along the rustic clapboard walls, other conferees leaned in as if watching a summer stock production of some new Eugene O'Neill play.

Behind Reiss clustered all the literary ghosts of Bread Loaf, the celebrities who had stood where he was standing now and read from their genius: among them Saul Bellow, John P. Marquand, Theodore Roethke, A.B. Guthrie, Jr., Richard Wright, May Sarton, Maxine Kumin, Toni Morrison and the patron saint of the mountain, snowy-haired Robert Frost. This was a place of repose, a place of poetry, a literary rendezvous.

Reiss was thin and drawn, just returned from the war zone known as the Sudan, where he had spent weeks behind rebel lines and survived mortar attacks, a harrowing unauthorized plane trip at the mercy of a malaria-ridden pilot, and being trampled to death by a famine-crazed mob of refugees.

In his open chambray shirt over black T-shirt, with his sunburned cheeks and raw lanky wrists, fighting off stomach parasites and the accumulated fatigue of weeks in the field, he didn't look like a guy who creates literature. He said amiably, "I'm not going to read fiction or poetry. I'm going to read some *non*-fiction for all you *non*-men and *non*-women."

The crowd laughed easily and then listened, intrigued.

He read, indeed, nonfiction: a tale of suffering and heartbreak and idealism. The arc of the story was simple: Altruistic men and women try to deliver food to the starving multitude of refugees in the Horn of Africa. The protagonists were idealistic young people, foreign service officers with a humane sense of duty, and bureaucrats doing the unglamorous fund-raising and paperwork of rescue. The antagonists were distance, red tape, bad roads, the rainy season, armed and irrational political factions, time running out, and the dark side of human nature.

The rebels made deals about food. Ordinarily peaceful people rioted over food. People stole food, shared food, killed for food, suffered without food. The conflict was compelling: Food was the prize, there were precious few winners, and it was a true story.

Creative nonfiction: timely, but also timeless.

His story didn't come out of a quiet country house or a private reverie. He'd gone out there into the dangerous world to find it, to recover it, to make it, and he had brought it back to us.

People listened hard, some of them holding their breath. In every line, there was an implicit courage, a moral and physical stand against what was wrong with the world. Not polemic, not prescription, not opinion or editorial, just clean, accurate description; real characters who leapt to life in a few quick strokes; an overwhelming and unsettling sense of a far-off, perilous place; deft connections between CIA analysts in Washington, sacks of grain tumbling out of the blue African sky, an airplane bogged down in a muddy cow pasture being hauled out by four hundred laboring Dinkas, malnourished babies being weighed to determine if they qualified for extra rations, food thieves prowling the deadly bush after nightfall, a few choice statistics, and a bunch of American kids in concert T-shirts trying to do the right thing far from home in the middle of a shooting war.

Nonfiction.

Creative nonfiction.

Literature.

THE RENAISSANCE IN NONFICTION: A HUNGER FOR THE REAL

These days creative nonfiction is enjoying an astonishing renaissance. Many of the finest writers in our literature, including eminent poets and novelists, are writing it. Even the National Endowment for the Arts recognizes the genre in its fellowship awards, and many state arts agencies are following suit.

"I think it is invariably a response to crisis. Nonfiction flourishes in times of great upheaval," theorizes William Howarth, who teaches nonfiction at Princeton University and whose articles and essays have appeared regularly in *National Geographic* and *The New York Times*.

David Bain, author of *Sitting in Darkness—Americans in the Philippines*, compares the present resurgence with the enormous popularity of reportage, factual stories, during the tumultuous days of the Second World War. "People needed something concrete that they could use to measure what was going on in the world," he explains. "Since we are again in a period of serious flux, without people knowing what's really going on or what they should believe in, that could call for it."

It's always seemed odd to me that *nonfiction* is defined, not by what it *is*, but by what it is *not*. It is *not* fiction. But then again, it is also *not* poetry, or technical writing or libretto. It's like defining classical music as *nonjazz*. Or sculpture as *nonpainting*. As Reiss himself says in his wry New York accent, "I feel like the Rodney Dangerfield of literature—nonfiction don't get no respect."

Historically, nonfiction was around long before fiction—at least in the form of the short story and the novel—ever came on the scene. But nobody called it that. Farther back still, nobody seems to have made much distinction between the two. Aristotle divided the literary world into History and Poetry, and, much to everybody's surprise, Poetry seems to have included literary nonfiction. *The Iliad* of Homer was long considered to be "only" myth by those who cared about such distinctions, until one reader, Heinrich Schliemann, used it as a nonfictional document to discover the actual remains of Troy. A real place, after all, even if it was fought over by mythical gods and goddesses. Poetry and History together.

Ron Powers, contributing editor of *GQ* magazine and winner of the

Pulitzer Prize for media criticism, says, "The novel is a way of creating a mythic truth from your own personal mythos. And the contract with the reader is that the reader is sharing your myth, and that's powerful simply because we're a storytelling species. We like stories. The non-fiction act is similar to that, except that it satisfies our hunger for the real and our need to make sense, make order, out of chaos."

TELLING STORIES, TELLING LIES

On the face of it, the term *nonfiction* doesn't make much sense. No other genre suffers under this metaphysical definition by negation.

The term is doubly odd when you realize that we're defining the factual, the actual, the things that really happened, with an explicit disclaimer that assures the reader we didn't make it up—as if *making it up* were the primary way to communicate the events of our world. As if, were any reader to come across a narrative of people, events and ideas—a *story*—he or she would assume, unless assured otherwise, that the story was fiction.

Well, it turns out that's not such a bad assumption. Our natural tendency in real life seems to be to tell stories: the story of what we did at the office all day, the story of how we met our husband or wife, the story of what happened at the party last night. And, in telling stories, we invariably surrender to the delicious temptation to make fiction—or, less politely, to lie. When we're kids, being accused by our parents of "telling a story" means being caught in a lie.

The nonfiction writer must always rein in that impulse to lie, in all the subtle ways we can shade the truth into something less than—or more than—the truth. The nonfiction writer must be more truthful than we usually require of ourselves or of each other.

We lie a lot. We don't mean to—not always, at any rate—but no matter how clear-cut or simple the events we're trying to relate, the minute we open our mouth or take up our pen we are delivering fiction. We embellish. We misremember. We inadvertently change what somebody actually said because we didn't happen to have our tape recorder handy. Or worse, we paraphrase their words, giving them a different emphasis, a sharper tone. We conveniently leave out details that make ourselves look bad and leave out other information because it seems irrelevant and leave out still more details because we just plain didn't see or hear them.

And what's left out can change the story of what happened—a lot.

We're limited by our point of view—from where we stand, we can see only so much of the action. Our vision is blocked, or crucial things happen in several places at once and we can be in only one place at a time. Or we assume a God-like objective omniscience that equally distorts pure fact. We make judgments about which character (we've already turned real people into characters) is important, which event deserves emphasis, which detail best conveys the feeling of the moment.

And we tell it all out of order—we want to establish suspense, after all. Give it a dramatic punch. But telling events out of order can be a kind of lying, of fictionalizing. Or it can be a better way of being truthful. It's a tricky business, but it's made less so if we remember always that our first obligation is to tell the truth. Every strategy, every dramatic convention, every selective choice must be employed in the service of making the story *more* not *less* truthful.

So when we label a piece of writing *nonfiction*, we are announcing our determination to rein in our impulse to lie. To test our memory more carefully, do a little research to fill in the holes in what we witnessed, draw clear lines around what we are offering as objective fact (as if such a thing exists—more on that later) and what we are offering as opinion, meditation, analysis, judgment, fancy, interpretation.

In the past few years, the lines between all the genres have blurred: Poetry and stories merge into the prose-poem, fact and fiction into "faction," the so-called nonfiction novels of Truman Capote or Norman Mailer. But there is a meaningful distinction between fiction and nonfiction, Powers says: "It's interesting to me that people who otherwise would say that it's *all* fiction, that there's no such thing as nonfiction, because truth is infinitely elusive—I happen to agree with that last part—they're the same people who would get very exercised when George Bush says that the wetlands aren't wetlands after all. They don't say, What a marvelous act of deconstruction or reexamination of the 'text.' They say, Let's impeach that so-and-so."

Expletive, of course, deleted.

YOU CAN'T MAKE IT UP

The hardest part of writing creative nonfiction is that you're stuck with what really happened—you can't make it up. You can be as artful as you want in the presentation, draw profound meanings out of your subject matter, but you are still stuck with real people and real events. You're stuck with stories that don't always turn out the way you wish they had turned out.

I once sent a piece to a producer at National Public Radio's *All Things Considered* who had used a couple of my radio essays in the past. The piece was a reflection on our American obsession with *things* from the point of view of a long-haul moving man, which I was for a summer. Most of what we trucked back and forth across the interstates of America was pure junk.

But one woman's belongings were all antiques, beautiful and probably priceless: lovely furniture, original paintings, heirloom crystal. We picked up the load at a warehouse in Florida, where we knew the crates had been damaged but had no idea how badly. When we unpacked them in Las Vegas, everything was destroyed. Completely, utterly smashed.

It wasn't our fault. A careless forklift operator back at the warehouse had probably dropped the container full of her crated belongings onto a concrete floor.

As we unpacked piece after broken piece, the woman cried, and I didn't blame her. We spent several hours taking inventory of the damage, filling out forms for the insurance company, and I sat with the woman while the driver made all the necessary phone calls. After awhile, somewhat embarrassed, the woman regained her composure, stopped crying, and told me, "It's not right to cry over things." As a parting gift, she gave me a paperback novel to read on our way west to Beverly Hills, our next stop.

The book was William Styron's *Sophie's Choice*.

The NPR producer liked the piece a lot, but she thought *Sophie's Choice*—a novel about a woman caught up in the Holocaust—was a pretty heavy book to drop into a piece about losing everything. Couldn't it be a different book?

Well, no, I told her. It happened to be that book. The woman was real, and when she was done crying she was a little embarrassed and oddly grateful to us, and she gave me a real book, and that book was *Sophie's Choice*. Not only that, but I read it on the way to Beverly Hills, and, reading it, I understood her remark about not crying over things: Styron's novel is about a woman who loses everything—and everyone—to the Nazi Final Solution. Reading it in the context of what I had just witnessed moved me beyond words. By the time I had finished reading it, I had developed a profound respect for that woman in Las Vegas and a deep curiosity about what—whom—she'd really been crying about as we uncrated the broken souvenirs of her life.

Too bad, the producer said. They didn't use the piece.

I really wanted them to use the piece. It had every natural irony real life ever offers—including Las Vegas *and* Beverly Hills in a piece about materialism. The problem was, the truth seemed as if I had contrived it. The ironies were too neat to be believed in real life. I could not fault the producer—she wanted the story to *sound* true as well as *be* true, and it may be that, in her experience, other writers took greater liberties with the form. Radio commentaries frequently tend toward memoir, which the reader or listener recognizes as inherently looser and less objectively reliable than other kinds of nonfiction.

But to me, such a change would have broken my contract with the listener. It was *non*fiction. That's the first good reason for the term *nonfiction*: to announce that, while every story tends toward fiction, *this* one at least owes an allegiance to the truth of events.

The second reason is simpler: Nobody has yet come up with a better term. Lee Gutkind, a writer and long-time faculty member at the University of Pittsburgh who founded and edits the journal *Creative Nonfiction*, explains why he avoided other terms, such as "literary journalism," in coining the name: "Because I thought the word 'journalism' would frighten away those in the creative writing program and the word 'literary' would frighten away those in the journalism department."

FIVE HALLMARKS

But what in the world makes nonfiction *creative*?

Five characteristics: First, it has an apparent subject and a deeper subject. The apparent subject may be spectacular or mundane. Unlike in a feature article, it is only part of what we are interested in.

John Steinbeck's *The Log From the Sea of Cortez*, for instance, is the chronicle of a voyage of exploration in the Gulf of California. But it is also a meditation on the creative process, especially for the writer using the facts of the world meticulously observed and recorded: "The design of a book is the pattern of a reality controlled and shaped by the mind of the writer," he confides to us in his introduction. "This is completely understood about poetry or fiction, but it is too seldom realized about books of fact." Again and again he returns to this implicit comparison between a voyage of discovery and a book of nonfiction.

But the apparent subject must itself be made fascinating—as Steinbeck makes fascinating the tidal pools and ports-of-call and beer-drunk companions of his maritime expedition. Gutkind says that the best nonfiction always teaches the reader something: "One important distinguishing factor is this teaching element—a reader reads on to learn something. It's not just personal experience."

Second, and partly because of the duality of subject, such nonfiction is released from the usual journalistic requirement of *timeliness*: Long after the apparent subject ceases to be topical, the deeper subject and the art that expresses it remain vital. That doesn't mean it isn't triggered by today's headlines—in fact, every great piece of creative nonfiction I've ever read seems driven by the writer's felt urgency to tackle that subject right now, not tomorrow.

But what captures the writer's attention is not just what everybody else sees—the current crisis. In today's headlines, the writer recognizes larger trends, deeper truths about the way human beings behave. The particular event offers an epiphany, a way of getting at the deeper subject. This ironic tension between the *urgency of the event* and the *timelessness of its meaning* keeps the writer firmly planted in particulars, in the concrete detail that will make the larger abstract truth come to life on the page.

Writers are passionate about different subjects at different times in their lives. They are attentive to the world and alert to the hinges of history—those great and terrible moments of promise, crisis, impending salvation or doom—and they are drawn to write about them in an effort to affect the outcome. Thus Bob Reiss writes about famine relief in the Sudan ostensibly because it is an urgent practical and political problem *right now*. We—our country, the world, private citizens—have some hard choices to make, and it's the nonfiction writer's job to make us face our choices.

And, to be practical, that's the moment when editors and readers are most likely to care about the subject. To assign the piece and publish it. To read it with at least a shadow of the writer's urgency.

The writer must not only write about what he or she cares about but must do so *at the time* he or she is most passionate about it. That sense of passion, of personal urgency, cannot be faked. And it endures.

All art seems grounded in paradox, and nonfiction is no exception. Triggered by the timely meeting of writer and subject, a piece may stand outside of time. Beyond the particulars of present-day politics, Reiss' story about famine relief is almost biblical in its archetype: Do you give the starving man fish, or do you teach him to fish? And what does he eat while he's learning to fish?

Third, creative nonfiction is narrative, it always tells a good story. "So often, it ends thirty minutes after it begins—something is happening in time," Gutkind says. It takes advantage of such fictional devices as character, plot and dialogue. "It moves," Gutkind explains. "It is action-oriented. Most good creative nonfiction is constructed in scenes." And, he says, just as in a good short story or novel, "There is always a magic moment. Your readers are waiting for that magic moment to occur, waiting for a change to occur, a lightbulb to flash, something to happen."

In Ted Conover's journal of riding the rails, *Rolling Nowhere*, the entire journey—and thus the whole story—moves toward that moment when Conover, a clean-cut college boy, will at last be initiated as a true hobo. And like the best magic moments, when it happens it brings surprising and dramatic consequences—once he has truly entered the world of the railroad tramp, he is terrified that he will never find his way back to the world he knew, the person he was.

The moment comes in the hobo jungle in Everett, Washington, as Conover watches his bickering alcoholic companions binge on cheap wine and sees one possible future for himself reflected in their violence, their incoherent babble, their broken teeth and ruined bodies. He searches out a gas station washroom, where he scrubs his teeth and washes his long hair, and then calls long distance to a college roommate. "In a complete turnabout from my earlier concerns, I wanted a guarantee that, while I could get close to tramps I could never really become one, and they would never permanently 'rub off' on me," he tells the reader. But of course there is no such guarantee. The roommate ironically congratulates him on having proved himself a true hobo—for Conover, at this stage in his travels, a truly frightening insight.

We anticipate that magic moment, we expect it, but some part of it is always unexpected.

Fourth, creative nonfiction contains a sense of *reflection* on the part of the author. The underlying subject has been percolating through the writer's imagination for some time, waiting for the right outlet. It is *finished* thought.

The purported subject of the piece, though it may seem like a target of opportunity, is actually one that has preoccupied the writer for some time. He has written about it before, in other ways and in exploring apparently unrelated topics. He has brooded about it, asked questions all his life about it, trying to make up his mind. He is building on what he has already learned, what he has already written, coming to ever more sophisticated insights with each pass.

Terry Tempest Williams, author of *Refuge: An Unnatural History of Family and Place*, says that it takes time for an experience to sink in, that the writer must meditate on what she has done and observed to discover what it means, how to write about it. "There's such a pressure to write fast, to get it done," she says. "But one of the most important things in writing nonfiction is to have patience."

In such a reflective piece, you'll see the writer making connections between the subject at hand and books he has read, between history and philosophy and a remark his fifth-grade teacher once made. So Conover invokes Jack London. In *Arctic Dreams: Imagination and Desire in a Northern Landscape*, Barry Lopez talks about early Arctic explorers. Steinbeck ruminates on a political stance he has been cultivating for years. Even in the context of a boat trip on the Sea of Cortez, he finds insight about the relationship between government and people in a democracy, one of his chief preoccupations as a writer in both his fiction and his nonfiction.

In other words, the piece reflects not only whatever immediate research was necessary to get the facts straight on the page, but also the more profound "research" of a lifetime.

"I tend to write about subjects I was born to," observes Anne Matthews, whose book about the landscape inhabited by eight generations of her family, *Where the Buffalo Roam: The Storm Over the Restoration of America's Great Plains*, was a finalist for the 1993 Pulitzer Prize in nonfiction. "It takes a lifetime to know a subject."

When I set out for Paris to track down the haunts of Ernest Hemingway for a piece on the twenty-fifth anniversary of the publication of *A Moveable Feast*, the memoir of his formative years in Paris as a young writer learning his craft, my journey was steeped in fifteen years of reading Hemingway's books and wondering about his marvelous, troubled life. We had shared an editor at Scribner's. Hemingway's Nick Adams stories had given me my first inspiration to try writing stories of my own. I wanted to go to Paris to find out what had been so special about that city to him—did the Paris he knew still exist, and could it still inspire a young writer to greatness? So that journey back to the city of *his* first inspiration was one I had been preparing to make for a very long time.

Fifth, such nonfiction shows serious attention to the craft of writing. It goes far beyond the journalistic "inverted pyramid" style—with interesting turns of phrase, fresh metaphors, lively and often scenic presentation, a shunning of clichés and obvious endings, a sense of control over nuance, accurate use of words, and a governing aesthetic sensibility.

Finding the writing is as important as finding the subject. Good writing is elegant—cleanly arresting rather than gaudy or merely decorative. It carries itself gracefully and falls rhythmically on the ear. It is artistic, and often informed by other art. "There's a certain voice, where the voice doesn't get in the way," explains Lisa Bain, senior editor at *Glamour* who learned her trade at *Esquire*. "Which is one thing with a lot of heavy stylists—you get caught up in the language, rather than having the language forward the story." Editors have a phrase for wonderful writing, she explains: They say it *sings*. "Good writing has a lyricism and a rhythm to it," she says. "It's very hard to put into words."

Look closely at this brief passage from Lopez' *Arctic Dreams*: "Winter darkness shuts off the far view. The cold drives you deep into your clothing, muscles you back into your home. Even the mind retreats into itself."

Listen to it. Hear the writing *sing*?

Or this sentence from *White Town Drowsing*, Powers' book about Hannibal, Missouri, a hometown he shared with Mark Twain: "I grew up in a town that seemed less a town to me than a kingdom."

The simple, unadorned writing opens an elegant metaphor.

THE ART LIES IN THE CRAFT

A good way to approach writing creative nonfiction, paradoxically, is to forget about the *creative*—the literary—part and concentrate on the *nonfiction* part. Pay enough attention to the craft of learning the story and telling it clearly, accurately and economically, and the art will happen when you're not looking.

Writing nonfiction is simple: You find out some facts, you figure out how to arrange them in light of a larger idea, then you do something artful with the arrangement. Simple, but hard. Like climbing a mountain—all you have to do is keep going up. The most important step is always the next one. That's the craft of it—paying attention to what's under your feet, what your hands are grabbing hold of, working against the gravity of all your bad habits.

"I consider myself a storyteller," says Reiss, author of seven novels and two books of nonfiction and a correspondent for *Outside* magazine. "And I distinguish between stories I make up and stories I find out." Creative nonfiction is the stories you find out, captured with a clear eye and an alert imagination, filtered through a mind passionate to know and tell, told accurately and with compelling grace.

CHAPTER TWO

FINDING AN ORIGINAL SUBJECT

Terry Tempest Williams was facing one of the most chilling threats a woman can know: breast cancer. Two biopsies, a small tumor between the ribs, borderline malignancy. Would she inherit the legacy of her female relatives? Her mother had fought the same disease and won, but only for a while. Both grandmothers and six aunts, like her mother, had all undergone mastectomies. The future looked dangerous.

Because she is a writer, and writing is how writers make sense of the world—especially the scary parts—she chose to write about it: "A person who is told she has cancer faces a hideous recognition that something monstrous is happening within her own body," she writes in *Refuge*.

The subject captured her attention, preoccupied her, focused her. "Perhaps I am telling this story in an attempt to heal myself," she writes in the prologue, "to confront what I do not know, to create a path for myself with the idea that 'memory is the only way home.'"

But had she written only about her personal struggle, or even her mother's struggle, while it might have been compelling in the way that TV-movie scenarios are compelling but ultimately forgettable, she would have written a one-note symphony—just a sad story we already knew by heart.

But she did something most writers would never think to do, something profound. She looked beyond her own predicament and found a larger parallel in the impending ruin of a migratory bird refuge threatened by the rising waters of Great Salt Lake. She set her own struggle—and that of her mother—in the context of a larger world of community, nesting birds, Mormon tradition, the desert West, theology and humane values. She chose beauty and meaning over personal melodrama.

Refuge takes the reader beyond easy sympathy to understanding— of a much larger chain of events, including nuclear testing, environmental caretaking, family duty, religious faith and personal responsibility. She gives the reader choices and so makes the reader participate in *her* choices. Her book is painfully accurate, poignantly sorrowful, yet also full of warmth, gentleness and hope. It is the work of a clear mind and a large imagination—not of self-pity or victimization or blame.

It is also a book of facts and figures—it even contains an appendix listing the birds who find refuge in the Bear River preserve. And Williams does the human arithmetic precisely, in a voice we can trust—the statistical balance of breeding species, the ratio of habitat to survival, the equation between nuclear testing in the 1950s and cancer rates in the 1980s.

Since we're talking about literary nonfiction and not plain journalism, it might seem that subject matter is irrelevant. The literary writer is, we agree, a stylist—a maker of literary art. So there's no need to do research, to pay attention to the mundane details of real life, to take notes, visit archives, go on field trips, interview interesting people. It all comes from the Muse, right? You reach inside where your art lives, and you tell the truth, right? You are inspired, and, being inspired, you write beautifully, the lovely words tripping off your pen?

Well, not exactly.

William Matthews' poem "A Night at the Opera" shows us two aging performers struggling mightily to pull off their operatic roles. Using makeup to hide their flaws, faking what their talent isn't quite fine enough to do naturally, enduring shopworn and gamy costumes, they manage, barely, to float their romantic illusion before the audience. It's a kind of magic show, really—a triumph of appearance over reality, of what *seems* over what *is*. During the poem, we pity them— we want brilliance, virtuosity, genius, not these journeymen actors. We even resent them for pretending so hard, for resorting to stagy tricks, for being such stubborn, veteran troupers.

Until the devastating last line: "Beauty's for amateurs." We realize, all at once, that they've been making art the only way art can be fashioned, through labor and craft, out of the imperfect things of this world.

WANTED: AN ACCURATE SENSE OF THE WORLD

There's no denying that some reflective writers write mostly about themselves, tracking their thoughts, exploring the whimsical workings of their own imaginations: Vladimir Nabokov. Nancy Mairs. Peter Matthiessen. Gore Vidal.

But notice also how their best work always depends on an absolutely accurate sense of the real world—not in some vague, generic way, but in all its astonishing particulars. They know the names of plants and animals—in Williams' book, each chapter is named for a migrating bird: western tanager, long-billed curlew, Wilson's phalarope. She presents each of them with a naturalist's living detail.

Such writers pay attention to what goes on around them and are curious about nearly everything. They have read not just American history but also Russian history. They can find Trinidad-Tobago on a globe. They're intrigued by Caribbean weather, suburban traffic patterns, how farm machinery works. Reiss speaks for all such writers when he says, "One of the great things about being human, one of the joys of being alive, is the understanding of things that are complex."

They listen to how new lovers talk, watch how they move their hands during an argument across the room. They touch the coarse fabric of an old army uniform jacket—and the broken knees of an old friend who once played football. They roll down their windows and stop the car so they can smell the night breeze outside of Deming, New Mexico. And even at that moment, when they are completely captivated by the moment, they are also outside themselves, inventing the words they would use to describe the aroma of dust, hot asphalt and sage. They can't help it. They are in the habit of noticing things through words.

When they go on vacation, they go off the tour. It isn't that they are not astonished by cathedrals, but they are more fascinated by the old women in black shawls drinking apéritifs at the tobacco shop next door at nine o'clock in the morning—in the looming shadow of a sacred Gothic architecture of light.

They find local monuments to suffering that aren't in the guide-books—in this forest clearing in Brittany, three local partisans were executed by a Nazi firing squad. At an Anasazi cliffhouse ruin, they are overwhelmed by the ghosts, real as tourists, going about their business across the centuries. At parties, they always wind up in the kitchen among people they've just met, very late, sitting on the counter drinking too much wine, not talking but listening.

When they go for a walk in a new city, their eyes gaze up past the first story to the signature architecture above street level, where the gargoyles live. They deliberately do things they've never done, go places they haven't been, even—especially—to places in their own backyards. They climb up into their neighbor's attic and watch their own house from a completely new perspective—briefly, irrationally thrilled, expecting some stranger to emerge from their own front door.

They make it a point to be where interesting things are liable to happen. And because they prowl the world with their eyes wide open and their ears pricked for sound, wherever they go interesting things are liable to happen.

REFINING THE SUBJECT

For example, in the closing chapter of Annie Dillard's autobiograph-ical gem, *The Writing Life*, Dillard describes the life and death of aerobatic pilot Dave Rahm. It's a thoroughly researched and precisely reported section. And, like all good literature, it's also about some-thing else: making art. Dillard spins a lyrical analogy between the airborne line of the stunt pilot through an imaginary box of blue sky—curving, dipping, rolling, falling and recovering—and the transcen-dent exhilaration that is the reason for art. And the dangerous life of the artist.

Then in a stroke, she closes the analogic distance and makes them one and the same: "When Rahm flew, he sat down in the middle of art and strapped himself in."

So creative nonfiction seems to need a subject at least as much as a newspaper story—more—because the subject has to carry itself and also be an elegant vehicle for larger meanings.

But Dillard reminds us that she didn't start with a fully realized idea for an essay that connected aerobatic flying with making art. She started out by going to an airshow in Bellingham, Washington, where she had recently moved, with, as she writes, "the newcomer's willingness to try anything once." In other words, having arrived at a new home, she was casting about her for interesting ways to pass the time. She was not herself a pilot or even an airplane buff. She did not go to the airshow for the specific purpose of writing about it, then or ever. The airshow just seemed more interesting than an afternoon at home.

Who knows—something might turn up.

What turned up—*who* turned up—was a living wonder. A pilot of amazing skill and daring named Dave Rahm. Like the others in the crowd that afternoon, Dillard oohed and ahhed in amazement. But then she did the next thing: She pondered what she had just witnessed and decided it was important enough to learn more about. She worked on it with her mind and imagination. She read articles, asked questions, even went flying with him, so she could feel his art happening in her stomach, in the pull of g-forces against her viscera, experience the vertigo, the liberating terror of tumbling through space under control, just barely. She began to understand what Dave Rahm was all about. The larger implications became clear.

This is important: Good subjects aren't just lying around waiting to be scooped up. The writer has to take raw data and somehow refine it toward meaning. Sometimes the interest is obvious, in a general way; other times it is not obvious to anyone, even the writer.

In this case, hundreds, thousands of people had witnessed Rahm's performance over the years without ever turning it into literature. Finding in aerobatics a worthy subject—beyond the pedestrian interest of the feature story, an ooh-and-ahh in print—took imaginative effort. Time and hard work. Reflection and phone calls. A willingness to invest herself, to take chances, to be scared. In this case, Dillard literally risked her life to discover her subject. Such aerobatic flying is very risky, as Rahm was the first to admit. Pilots routinely crashed. Every stunt pilot eventually crashed, including Dave Rahm—those were the odds.

Dave Rahm wasn't a subject until Dillard dared to turn him into a subject.

FIND THE HUMAN STORY

And there's a corollary lesson: One way or another, the focus of every really good story is a person. In a magazine, the human story often takes the form of a profile. The writer is intrigued by a particular individual—usually a celebrity, some newsworthy figure, or else some unsung hero of science, politics or art. The profile is a kind of portrait. It depends on intimate detail of a living personality—and, if the writer is not scrupulous, it can quickly devolve into sentimental hero worship or a gossipy ambush. It's easy to hold up a paragon of genius, virtue or worldly success, just as it is easy to bash anybody who has a high profile. Much harder is to present a portrait of a life in action that communicates the complexity, the contradictions, of a particular human personality.

Gore Vidal is one of the few masters of such portraits—he has given us such diverse figures as John F. Kennedy, Anthony Burgess, Eleanor Roosevelt, Ronald and Nancy Reagan, and Orson Welles. His profiles usually come in between the lines of his purported subject—a review of a new book, an analysis of a political campaign, an essay on popular culture. His portraits have provocative, unexpected titles: "Theodore Roosevelt: An American Sissy."

Vidal deftly blends objective detail with his own interpretive powers, and admits his biases both implicitly and explicitly. In "Barry Goldwater: a Chat," he first tells us that Goldwater's office is in the old Senate Office Building. "The corridors are marble with high ceilings and enormous doors which tend to dwarf not only visitors but Senators," he writes. So far, so objective. Then: "There is an air of quiet megalomania which is beguiling in its nakedness." And we haven't even met Goldwater yet.

When we walk into Goldwater's office with Vidal, we see that "The large desk was catercornered so that the light from the windows was in the visitor's face." We know at once who is in charge. By the time we are told that Goldwater keeps a small bookcase beside his desk, we already have guessed what it contains: a leather-bound set of the speeches of Barry Goldwater.

The biographer takes the human subject even further, trying to re-create a whole life and the mystery behind the accomplishment of that life, the reason the individual is worthy of a biography in the first place. As David Nasaw, biographer of William Randolph Hearst, puts it, "What the biographer does is try to figure out the riddle of creativity: how did it get there? Why did it get there? What the biographer tries to do is unravel the alchemist's mystery, to find out how, out of these mundane lives, great things are created—out of nothing, something appears."

FIND YOUR PASSION

Any story is a very complex transaction between writer and reader. It's useful for the writer to answer three questions about this transaction:

1. Who is writing this?
2. Why am I telling this story?
3. Who will be reading this?

The answer to the first question seems obvious to the writer: *I* am writing this. But it's a trick question, a two-parter. One part is, Who am I? in life. The second part is, Who am I to be telling this particular story?

Bob Reiss recounts the story of his first meeting with Walter Anderson, editor of *Parade* magazine. He managed to get an appointment with Anderson, even though he was just starting out as a freelancer, having left the *Chicago Tribune*. He had a list of eight ideas—story proposals—that he thought were original and interesting. As he ticked off his eight brilliant ideas, Anderson dismissed each one in turn. He'd heard them all before. Within half a minute, Reiss was out of pitches.

"And I figured, I guess I handled that wrong—it's time to leave," Reiss recalls. "Wrong again. Walter Anderson started talking, and he talked to me for thirty minutes. Started telling me about his life, about being in the Marines, about what he thought of stuff, and at first I was thinking, what is he trying to tell me? And then I gave up and just started listening."

When it was time to leave, Anderson shook his hand, Reiss says, and told him: " 'Write me a letter and tell me what you believe in.' He didn't ask me to write him a letter and give him any story ideas—he just wanted to know if I knew what I believed in."

Like most of us, despite years of newspaper experience, travel and witness, Reiss couldn't say at that moment just what it was he believed in—what he was passionate about. He went home and racked his brain for an answer to Anderson's challenge. At last he wrote him a letter containing two stories: one of a thing that had disgusted him, the other of an event that had moved him: "Disgust came from sitting in a courtroom in Washington and watching a convicted terrorist who'd killed a friend's wife get a reduced sentence at the prosecutor's request.

"And the thing that moved me most was standing in Madison Square Garden on the floor on the night Jimmy Carter got nominated, and the lights went off, and they played 'Fanfare for the Common Man,' and in a pure glorious moment I felt like I was in a room with all the people who had ever nominated any president, and experienced at least in my mind a sense of what democracy is supposed to be at its best and greatest, and started to cry. The lights came on, and everyone was crying.

"I just wrote him those two stories. I got a note back from him and it said, 'I guess we think the same way—and we'll have to live with it.' And I got an assignment." Time and again in his writing, Reiss returns in some fashion or other to those two essential subjects: justice and politics.

Find your passion, find the subject—because the subject begins with the writer.

Ask yourself, Where is my passion? What keeps me awake at night? What are the rules of conduct I set for myself as I make my way in the world? What makes me angry or lifts up my spirit? What am I willing to defend, and how far will I go to defend it? What do I really believe in? It's not enough to answer glibly, as one of my students did recently, "Family, God, and Country." The writer needs to discover a more exact answer than that.

What you believe in is a large part of who you are, and who you are determines your point of view on the world. That point of view yields subjects, and it will very often determine your approach to those subjects. So the Delphic oracle's admonition "Know thyself" is not just of lofty concern to the soul; it's of urgent, practical value to the craft.

DISCOVERING YOUR SUBJECT IN WHO YOU ARE

Start with a simple exercise. Each of us is a kind of multiple personality, playing different roles in public and in private. List ten different identities for yourself. For example, husband, father, college graduate, resident of Washington, DC, runner, veteran, guitar player, American, Catholic, Boy's Club volunteer. Write a short paragraph describing yourself in each of these identities.

As a veteran, you may have strong opinions about the role of the U.S. military in keeping peace around the world. As a father, you may be worried by the sudden transformation of your teenaged daughter into a nose-ringed monster in a black T-shirt bearing a death's head inscribed "Spawn Till You Die." As a Catholic, you're troubled by— or maybe tremendously reassured by—the latest papal edict on family planning.

As you write about what concerns you in each of these roles, some of the superficial subjects will bloom into something deeper, more profound, that isn't in the headlines but lies behind the headlines, between the lines of the facile stories in the news magazines. Between the lines of your own cocktail party opinions.

What began as a short paragraph may run on to the bottom of the page. Not for every identity—some of the people you are will be straightforward, easily summarized, roles you take on in clearly defined circumstances—and take off just as easily.

Others, though, turn out to be complicated. At some point, you may stop writing and simply reflect, letting your train of associations continue. You discover, for instance, that you learned profound lessons in the Marines about leadership and courage—not all of them pleasant—and how rare true leadership is and how difficult in a democracy. You see this everyday in Washington, DC, the place where you live.

You start to understand why you're troubled by all those offhand references to football stars as "American heroes"—because you have come to define courage in a very exact and complex way, and part of your definition has to do with moral fortitude.

You meditate further and it occurs to you that the problem with moral fortitude is that it depends on recognizing what is the right thing to do. And that's very hard, even for a faithful Catholic in America, who may disagree with the Pope from time to time. So leadership must begin in courage and courage must begin with a reliable moral compass, and while that may be helped by faith, faith may not be enough.

It's not that you walk around all day meditating on courage and leadership; it's just that your subconscious has been debating the definitions for years, and you begin to recognize hidden motives in your own everyday behavior. You're not sure any more whether you really believe the glib opinions you've heard yourself express at cocktail parties.

Now you meditate on those subjects openly, and it turns out a family is a kind of democracy and so are universities, while high schools are not. Is your daughter's behavior an expression of a will toward courage or a retreat from decision? How does leadership exercise itself in a classroom, or a parish or a family meeting? And is that why you run so religiously, to keep yourself fit for some kind of duty—moral leadership perhaps—you know is coming and which will test you? Do you eagerly await that test, or are you afraid of it?

Or do you run to have quiet time alone or to avoid the frightening implications of your own mortality—or merely because you like being outdoors at that hour of the day?

As you describe each of your identities in a paragraph, key words—potential subjects—will appear in all of them. Some of the key words will be abstractions, words you don't use in everyday talk: "courage," "leadership," "duty." Others will be mundane: "daughter," "parish," "classroom." They will likely—but not always—be nouns. Whatever their part of speech, whether an everyday word or a high-sounding abstraction, all the key words will have one thing in common: Each will name something you feel strongly about. Maybe you didn't know it before, but you do now.

Circle one key word in each paragraph. Connect the circles between paragraphs as connections—and their implications—become clear: "Leadership" as a father to your own "daughter" takes you into the realm of responsibility for the general future of your community— public "duty" to posterity—both of which are also addressed in your "parish" through teachings about morality and faith and in the academic "classroom."

With luck, you will find out two important things, both of them the same in essence: at least ten subjects you care about, and at least ten subjects you can write about—all about yourself, true, but about yourself *in relation to the world*. They will be the beginning of what *The World & I* magazine editor Lawrence Criner calls a "large, long view."

There are other ways to mine subjects from your own experience. Revisit your childhood and adolescence through photo albums, yearbooks and diaries. If you don't already keep a journal, start. Don't try for wall-to-wall coverage of each day's events, just scribble whatever is on your mind whenever you have a few minutes to write. Make notes on the books you're reading, the movies you're watching, the things your friends say that you don't quite know how to take. From time to time, reread your old entries. Words will repeat, patterns will emerge. You'll start recognizing your own preoccupations. You'll be astonished at the range of your own naivete and wisdom. Certain words will stop you. Certain ideas will snag your attention. Subjects.

Go through your drawers, your closet, the junk in the attic or garage. Each of the objects stored there is the artifact of a story, a story that somehow defines you. That's why you can't bring yourself to throw them out, even though the reasonable part of you knows you should: the old wooden crutches, the discarded sports jacket, the suitcase full of letters. Rummage through them. Pick up the baseball bat and take a practice swing. Open the dusty steamer trunk. Sit in the director's chair you were so proud of when it was the only real piece of furniture in your first apartment.

What was the story? What do you remember? What does it matter now?

Spend some idle time reminiscing, pen in hand, and test your recollections against those of old friends and family members, then marvel at the discrepancies. Go for long walks. Reflect for hours on who you used to be, who you are now, and how you got *here* from *there*. It takes time—but the fastest way to write is to pretend you have all the time in the world.

The late John Gardner, author of the controversial book *On Moral Fiction* and also a teacher of rare captivating power, maintained that his writing workshops at SUNY-Binghamton always turned out to be exercises in developing character—not story *characters*, but the writer's *character*. After fifteen years of teaching, I can't help but agree: Every workshop I've ever conducted tested my own character and taught me important things about myself, not always flattering news. And most of the failures I have observed in my students' writing have been failures of honesty, sincerity, fairness, effort, generosity of spirit, practice, thoroughness, precision, truthfulness, imagination, the ability to give and take criticism gracefully, and an accurate sense of beauty—all urgent matters of character that leave their greasy fingerprints on the writing.

Find out who *you* really are first; if you're not happy with the answer, do something about it.

And then be prepared to tackle the second part of the question: Who am I to be telling *this* story? The likely answer will be, I am a writer who will do honest, thorough and inventive research to find out what I need to know.

But the answer may also be, I am a father, a veteran, a Catholic with a fierce desire to know the answer. I am an aging athlete, a lesbian, the survivor of an automobile accident, a businessman, an environmentalist, a Republican, an amateur photographer, a sailor, a Jew, a black woman in a white neighborhood, a volunteer firefighter, a classic movie buff, a convicted felon, a suburbanite who owns a riding mower, a trumpet player, a widow.

The things you are, the scars you bear, the experience and insider's knowledge you bring to a subject—all are part of your credentials.

Then you become the Writer and apply all the mundane tools of your craft—you find out information, cast it in light of a larger idea, and create a piece of nonfiction. You take the large, long view.

THE SUBJECT IS A QUESTION THAT MATTERS

The subject is always a question, often a fundamental one: What's it like to be a hobo in late twentieth-century America? What will we find in the Gulf of California? What did young Ernest Hemingway discover in Paris that was so important he returned to it all his life? What does it mean that a man can dance an airplane through space and make us all feel better about ourselves? How will I survive my family's cancer— and what if I don't? Find the right question, and you have a worthy subject. Ask the right question, and the answer matters.

The answer matters. That's always the right answer to the second question the writer poses at the beginning of a project: Why am I telling this? He can look the reader in the eye in every sentence and say, *Because it matters.* It matters because the writer has found his or her passion, and every detail of setting, every quoted line of an interview, every fact shows the reader why it matters in particular and right now.

Passion is contagious.

Passion is also quirky. For reasons that seem utterly whimsical, we are attracted to certain subjects and not to others. And sometimes the subject transforms itself before our eyes. We thought all along we were writing about one thing, but it turns out our subject was really something quite different. We spotted it just in time out of the corner of our eye—we spotted it, had the guts to admit we were on the wrong track, and the courage and discipline to go back and do it right.

This is very often the case with subjects that lie outside our own experience. We may have a general sense of the topic, but we need to poke around a bit, do some undirected research, even before proposing the story idea to an editor. Even then, of course, if we really knew how the story would turn out, we wouldn't have to bother with a proposal at all. It's a Catch-22: If you know how the story is going to go, you can write a very accurate proposal and be faithful to it. But that kind of story is likely to be predictable, or downright wrong, because you didn't keep an open mind.

So you actually define a subject twice: once before you write, again as you are writing it.

One way to accumulate a stock of subjects from the world beyond your own personal experience is simply to indulge your quirky interests. Buy a box of file folders. Each time a newspaper story, an item in a museum brochure or theater program, or some other nugget of information catches your interest, label a folder and save it there. Each time a related item comes your way, simply file it in the relevant folder. You may not have any conscious intention of ever writing about any of these subjects, but if your interest ever begins to coalesce, you will have a whole file of background. A headstart.

And one way to cause your interest to coalesce into a focused subject is to review those folders from time to time. What intuitive connections can you make? A news story that disappeared three years ago may surface all at once in a new place. A social issue may take on an entirely new incarnation. A certain book may wind up being banned by both the right and the left. A public figure may go away and come back again—like the seemingly immortal Richard Nixon.

In the meantime, of course, you are busy living your life, reading your files in light of what you now know that you didn't know six months ago. Howarth says, "The way the imagination seems to work is that you are constantly constructing analogies out of something familiar to you."

METAPHORICAL CONNECTIONS

How then does a writer come up with a subject? How do you sharpen a general interest into the shape of a story?

David Bain tells this story about the genesis of *Sitting in Darkness*, a modern-day adventure story of an expedition he mounted in the Philippines, following in the footsteps of a little-known hero of a forgotten war: "It's something very strange and celestial for me. It may be laughable, but it always feels like a bolt of light out of the blue above. And I mean that quite literally.

"The idea for my book on the Philippines came one day when I was sitting in the New York Public Library reading room surrounded with all sorts of old musty books telling me about the forgotten Philippine-American War at the turn of the century. And I was planning to write a straight history thereof. And the sun moves through those high windows like spotlights and, literally—I'm not making this up—at the moment when one of those spotlights from the sun came in through one of the west windows, I had this blinding flash about a pivotal episode in 1902 in which an American hero, an American general, captured a Filipino hero and turned the tide of the war.

"And I realized in that same moment that the isolated stretch of the coast of Luzon where this had happened had not changed in eighty years, and furthermore I realized that I could go back and retrace those steps and I would have a book that would be both historical and contemporary—that would take the things that began happening with America's relationship with the Philippines at the turn of the century and bring it all the way up to the Marcos era. And that I could stairstep these chapters one by one, going from the past to the present, to the past to the present, and circle around that way. And all of that came in a flash. And I still have the scrap of paper that I wrote out the chapters on."

The result was a gripping tale of adventure as well as a cautionary political parable. As so often happens in the best nonfiction, several subjects are interwoven around the main arc of the story, and the lasting value comes out of the connections. Two or three subjects together form a complex subject larger and more profound than any single subject. One important reason for this is *metaphor*: Each element of the story reflects the other, offering insight that would otherwise be missing.

"Metaphor can be very powerful in nonfiction," Powers maintains. "Many people don't remember that."

So Bain's Philippine expedition to test the truth of Colonel Frederick Funston's heroism in capturing Filipino insurrectionist Emilio Aguinaldo becomes a metaphor for the writer's search for answers. The historical sections resound metaphorically on present foreign policy with other far-flung regimes—in Cuba, Haiti, Nicaragua, Vietnam.

In Terry Tempest Williams' *Refuge*, suspense over the fate of migrating birds mirrors the suspense about the future of the author and her female relatives as they come to terms with a biological legacy of cancer. And Great Salt Lake metastasizes like a giant cancer across the bird refuge, bouncing the metaphor right back. In such a feedback loop, meaning becomes charged, heated up; it picks up speed and power. One makes us understand the other in a deeper, more profound way—a way inexpressible except by metaphor.

The perfect subject doesn't always manifest itself in a flash of inspiration. But even if it does, that's not really so remarkable. What Bain experienced in the reading room of the New York Public Library was simply a recognition. Sudden, but not different in kind from other less dramatic recognitions. Good writing—and good writing begins with the intuitive choice of the right subject—is always a matter of timing, and timing is partly a matter of luck and accident. And partly a matter of being receptive to the wisdom of luck, to the insight provided by accident.

Dave Rahm happened to be the featured performer at an air show that Annie Dillard, who had just moved to Bellingham, happened to witness. By coincidence, Great Salt Lake began its flood as Terry Tempest Williams was struggling with her mother's cancer. Both writers were alert enough to recognize the metaphorical connections that became their subjects.

We write about certain things when connections start to clarify themselves. Out of the fog of our general interest, a definite shape starts to emerge. We watch it, squinting, trying to get a better look, trying to urge it closer. Or, preoccupied with what we thought we were going to write about, we glance up from our desk as the light strikes the high window and, all at once, there it is.

Lawrence Criner, the editor at *The World & I* magazine who worked with me on "Hemingway's Paris: A Moveable Feast Revisited," has definite ideas about what constitutes a good subject: "I would describe it in terms of new-ness. A person has a new approach to a common subject, or can blend different disciplines."

Criner was one of several editors I queried in writing. I knew other writers before me had toured Hemingway's Paris, some leaving behind an extensive trail of photographs. But none of these travelogues, I believed, had made any attempt to connect *style*—how Hemingway actually built his sentences—with his sojourn in Paris. It was a connection I had wondered about for years. That would be my underlying subject.

The apparent subject would be my search for three different Parises: the real Paris of the 1920s that so inspired the so-called Lost Generation; the literary Paris as it shows up in the stories, novels and memoirs of Hemingway; and present-day Paris—what it looks like, smells like, sounds like. As a novelist, I would ask of all three cities a question: In this nuclear age, does Paris still make a special claim on the artistic imagination?

Criner called me and asked a lot of questions, some aesthetic, some practical, and made a fast decision to commission the piece. It was important that it be done in a timely way, for two reasons. First, the twenty-fifth anniversary of the publication of Hemingway's *A Moveable Feast* was fast approaching. Second, my wife was in Paris for several months directing a college internship program. She had an apartment where I could stay without additional expense, and she could act as interpreter and guide.

I had no idea of what I would actually find in Paris, but that's always the excitement of a worthwhile project: the knot in the stomach, the dry mouth as the plane lands in a foreign place, the sense of having made a promise to a reader who doesn't even know it yet and being honor-bound to fulfill it.

In the end, Criner, my editor, was pleased with my discoveries and, more important, with the connections between the discoveries: "It was a travel piece, it was an introspective piece, it was a literary piece— it had all these different voices running through it and *connected*. That was what appealed to me. There aren't too many people who can pull it off, but when it's pulled off well, you know it."

YOUR PROMISE TO THE READER

On to the third question: Who will be reading this?

If you're writing for a particular magazine, you have your practical answer: the kind of people who subscribe to that magazine. A look at any three recent issues will usually tell you exactly who they are, by politics, age, geography, education, income, sex and so on. *The World & I*, for example, Criner describes as a general interest magazine that seeks to provide a bridge between scholarship and journalism. Its thirty thousand readers are upscale, intelligent and well educated but don't necessarily have any specialized knowledge about the range of political, cultural, artistic or economic subjects the magazine covers. "You certainly don't want the pieces to go too academic, because then of course it becomes an intramural discussion," he says. "And you certainly don't want the piece to become too fluff, because then you miss the substance."

Balance, he maintains, is the key: never writing down to your reader, but also never indulging in a personal ego trip, showing off what you know.

Gauging the potential readership for a book is trickier, unless yours fits into a neat category—nature writing, history, biography, sports. But of course these categories tell only a tautological truth: People who are interested in this subject may be interested in this subject.

Still, the question is worth asking. Rephrasing it might help: Why should anybody be interested in reading this? And if you can't answer it, your editor—your first reader—will have to. Your writing is just black marks on a page until it happens in somebody else's head. Ultimately, it seems to me we write for that reader with whom we share at least one of our many identities. We start on some small corner of common ground and try to show why the subject matters to us in hopes that it will begin to matter to the reader.

There are three kinds of reader:

1. The reader who will never be interested in what you have to say and will always disagree with your point of view no matter what.

2. The one who already pretty much knows everything you have to say and agrees with it.

3. The reader who neither agrees nor disagrees with you, indeed may never have given your subject much thought.

Reader #1 is a hopeless exercise in frustration. Reader #2 is already in the choir and needs no converting. I write for Reader #3, who occupies that vast middle ground between for and against, between belief and skepticism. I can win this reader. I want to persuade this reader, show him the world as I know it, the truth as I have discovered it.

I like to believe that the great majority of readers out there browsing through magazines and bookstores have #3 souls.

Criner maintains that the audience is an imaginary figure with whom writer—and editor—have a dialogue. "I'm always interested in somebody telling me something about a subject that I don't know."

So the writer must always take the subject beyond the obvious, beyond the truisms and conventional wisdom, into new territory. The reader recognizes the subject. It is familiar, comforting. But somehow it has been offered in such a way that the reader would never have thought of it without you, the writer.

When you announce the subject, you make a promise, and your task then is to deliver on that promise.

CHAPTER THREE

RESEARCHING

I had promised an editor at *The World & I* that I could go to Paris and bring back a useful truth about Ernest Hemingway and his mysterious stylistic connection to the City of Light, something nobody else had ever found, and put it into words that would sing for a reader.

Yet I was not a literary scholar. And I had never been to Paris.

But this is usually how it works out. Once you have defined your subject and made your promise, long before you know exactly how the story will evolve, you've got to begin to become an expert on it. You need to be able to tell the reader things he doesn't already know— surprising facts, intimate details, accurate impressions, all leading toward profound connections, a larger truth.

In short, you need to get it right.

This requires *research*—in its broadest and simplest terms, finding out what you need to know. The first phase of research usually takes place before you go where the story is, whether the story will happen in Paris or in your kitchen garden. You develop background. You build a platform of knowledge under you from which to work.

Before writing the proposal, I had reread *A Moveable Feast*. Once I had the assignment, I reread it four more times, the last on an American Airlines jet bound for Orly airport, on each pass flagging key passages in which Hemingway describes significant personal landmarks. I reread most of Hemingway's short stories and several of his novels, reread one biography and read for the first time two others. I sought out a Lost Generation scholar and left his office with an armload of books about Hemingway's life, Paris and the 1920s.

I called my wife, Kathleen, in Paris and gave her a list of places to reconnoiter—cafés, restaurants, monuments, street addresses, art galleries. I read passages from French novels, dictionary in hand, to sharpen my limited facility with that language.

Once in Paris, I bought a pocket map of the city by arrondissement or district, and, sitting around our apartment on the Rue Blomet, began literally to map out my story, listing the places I would visit, the order in which I would seek them out. And then the real "research"—the assignment—began: I was in Paris, a real city, chasing down a ghost.

Let me also mention the research I deliberately *did not* do, because what you choose not to do can be part of your active strategy for finding out what you need to know. I deliberately did not read scholarly analyses of Hemingway's style. I deliberately did not look at photographs of sites in contemporary Paris. Because those were the two main things I needed to make up my own mind about: How was Hemingway's odd prose style formed, and what was the actual physical city of Paris like?

The third thing I did not do was study plates of Cézanne's paintings, since Hemingway claimed Cézanne as one of his most influential teachers, providing a graphic touchstone for his style: "I was learning very much from him but I was not articulate enough to explain it to anyone. Besides it was a secret." I wanted my first impression to be the real McCoy, the actual paintings as he had seen them, not their pale reproductions.

I discovered that those inspirational Cézannes had been moved since Hemingway had spent "belly-empty, hollow-hungry" lunch hours staring at them in lieu of eating. They no longer lived in the cozy neighborhood Musée de Luxembourg, bordering the gardens and handy to Gertrude Stein's atelier, where he hobnobbed with the likes of Picasso and Ezra Pound, but at the Musée D'Orsay, a grandly renovated railroad station across the Seine from the Louvre and the Tuileries gardens: "You have to hunt for the Cézannes. Finally you come to them, half a room full—"La Maison du pendu" ("The House of the Hanged Man") at the end of a brown lane that puddles at the closed door, the stripped skeletons of two trees leaning into one another; the brisk vertical strokes of "Les Peupliers" ("Poplar Trees") like upthrust bones that hold the greens spattered with a cloudy light; all the paintings flat and vivid, detail suggested by splotches of color, reality disassembled and put back together again simply enough for any eye."

They were *my* Cézannes now, but the sadness I felt in them was different from the ache young Hemingway had known: "Somehow they are farther removed from the heart in this monumental place, less significant, too much objects of veneration and not active challenges to the restless imagination of a writer learning his difficult craft. No one in the jostling tourist crowd of Germans, Japanese, and Americans seems very hungry. No one seems curious to share the secret."

Research: background and foreground.

As much as possible, I wanted my first impressions to be genuine, unprejudiced by expectations. I didn't want to arrive in Paris thinking I knew the story, the answer. I wanted an open mind.

Before embarking on his Sudan journey, Bob Reiss called the public relations firm that handled the Sudan (yes—sovereign nations employ PR firms). "The guy said, 'What's your slant?'" Reiss recalls. "I said, 'I don't have one yet—I didn't go there yet.' The best attitude to have going into a story is, I don't know what's going to happen, but, whatever it is, it's going to be interesting. And as long as you have that attitude, you're going to find what's interesting."

I didn't know Paris or Cézanne, and I had no formal theories about Hemingway's style, and it was my very ignorance of all three that made me passionate to find out about them, and that gave me my strongest credentials for success.

The question was never, Should I do research? The question was always, What kind of research should I do in what order? Just as a story—a narrative—succeeds or fails in large part because you tell the events of it in the right or wrong order, the prewriting process is partly a matter of finding out what you need to know in the right order: each fact, each impression, leads you on to the next. The act of doing research takes on the exciting feel of a story.

You have to figure out what it is you need to find out, and you need to determine where to go to look for it. Because later on, when you get down to the actual writing, you don't want to be hobbled by ignorance—all the things you don't know, all the things you didn't bother to find out.

Reiss, among many writers I talked to, is adamant about this point: "Until the research is finished, you can always be surprised. Until it's finished, you don't know enough. If there's one more question to ask, you don't know enough, because the answer to that question—the fact that you *have* that question—means that you do not have a sense of the story yet."

Good writing is about all the things you do to prepare to write. All the nonwriting things are part of the writing, the craft that makes possible the art. I agree wholeheartedly with Reiss: "Nothing will destroy your piece faster than thinking that writing will be enough to overcome incomplete research."

Being a resourceful and smart researcher can open up your canvas, free you to apply to your subject the full sweep of your imagination. Remember Matthews' opera poem, mentioned in chapter one: Art is built on the shabby things of this world.

ARCHIVAL AND LIVING RESEARCH

There are two basic kinds of research: archival research and living research. Both are meant to ground your work in accuracy and truth; both can also inspire you with sudden insights about what else you need to find out. And often the two overlap.

Archival research—isn't that what your freshman composition teacher made you do for your so-called "term paper" or "research paper"? You hated it. It consisted of skulking around the library in the dead of night locating and copying onto index cards obscure passages by brilliant dead people to back up your so-called "thesis." But you were hazy then about what a thesis actually was, and research was something you could (and did) avoid if you had the right connections at the frat house or an older sister who had once taken the same course.

Too bad if you learned it that way, because it's much more exciting and unpredictable than that. It's detective work, investigation, piecing together the threads of a story that solves a mystery.

And a thesis is nothing very complicated, just a subject refined into an assertion *that can be proved wrong*: Living in Paris formed Hemingway's style. When you write your story, it becomes a question, a kind of mystery: *Did* living in Paris form Hemingway's style? Maybe it didn't. Maybe living in Cleveland would have had the same effect.

That's why I had to go there and find out. That's the risk—you have to be ready to change your mind.

Archival research is not meant to back up your thesis, in the sense of assembling heavy-hitting authorities who agree with you. It's not that blunt. Archival research is meant to help you formulate the right question to ask, and then to help you figure out where to go to find the answer. It helps to establish the history of the idea you are grappling with, setting your subject in a context over time. It yields facts and testimony, often contradictory, that may or may not be relevant, and that may or may not be true. It gives you insight into the people and issues you intend to write about.

Archival research starts with your own private reference library, useful for establishing a general background of facts. By my writing desk, for example, I keep the following:

• Several good dictionaries, including *Webster's New Universal Unabridged Dictionary* (nearly five inches thick and weighing eleven pounds), just to make sure the words I want to use mean what I think they mean. That fat dictionary also contains its own miniature reference library, in nineteen supplements, including the Declaration of Independence; the Constitution of the United States; a Dictionary of Biography; a Dictionary of Noted Names in Fiction, Mythology, Legend; Commercial and Financial Terms; a Dictionary of Foreign Words and Phrases; even the Charter of the United Nations.

• French-English and Polish-English dictionaries, bought specifically for particular stories. Any foreign language dictionary will help you learn what happens when ideas are translated between languages—they are always reinvented with spin.

• *Roget's Thesaurus*, not for fancy words but for simple words I know but can't remember ("daub"), including archaisms and exact professional jargon.

• A *Lincoln Library of Essential Information*, in which I can find everything from a brief history of the United States to a list of Nobel Prize laureates to basic theory of architectural design. *The New York Public Library Desk Reference* gives me ready access to even more facts and connections.

• Both the King James Bible—for the Old Testament archetypes, the New Testament parables, and the lyrical language—and an ancient leather-bound *Wilmore's New Analytical Reference Bible*, complete with concordance. A good bit of our tradition and literature has roots in the Bible, and it's useful to be able to find them easily.

• Daniel I. Boorstin's *The Creators*, an artistic history of Western civilization, for context.

• *The Reporter's Handbook—An Investigator's Guide to Documents and Techniques*, a primer for ransacking the public record for essential facts, especially those facts somebody would prefer to keep hidden— in a courthouse, federal bureau or vital statistics file.

• Three books of quotations: *The Writer's Quotation Book: A Literary Companion, Popular Quotations A-Z* and *The Oxford Dictionary of Quotations*, useful when tracing the provenance of allusions in public speeches, books, remarks made during an interview, etc. And for inspiration, as in "What is a writer but a schmuck with an Underwood?" (Jack Warner).

• *The Associated Press Stylebook and Libel Manual* and *The Writer's Law Primer*, for answers to vexing questions of fair use, privacy, permissions and contracts.

• *Sound Reporting—The National Public Radio Guide to Radio Journalism and Production*, for practical advice about writing out loud and for its excellent section on libel and privacy law.

• *Great Beginnings: Opening Lines of Great Novels*; *Practical Homicide Investigation: Tactics, Procedures, and Forensic Techniques* (don't ask); a *Chapman Piloting, Seamanship and Small Boat Handling* and a *Field Guide to Sailboats*; *The Ocean Almanac*; several world atlases, a current *Rand McNally Road Atlas* for the United States, Canada and Mexico; a globe; the complete works of Mark Twain in twenty-three volumes; biographies, novels, poetry and essay collections, and assorted books on first aid, history, geography, swearing, weather, navigation, birds, big game animals, archaeology, exotic cultures, music and song lyrics, movies, airplanes, backpacking, paleontology, physics, foreign policy, astronomy, early explorers, ghost stories, sports, art and war.

Every writer I know has his own favorite reference works and keeps them handy for generating ideas, cross-checking errant facts, making connections and just idly browsing.

David Bain, at work on a book about the building of the first transcontinental railroad, ran across the name of a functionary in the War Department who single-handedly managed to block legislation that would have made the railroad possible. Bain was trying very hard to bring the story to dramatic life as the struggle of ambitious individuals, not just as a catalog of dry facts. So on a whim, he cross-checked the name in one of his American historical dictionaries. "I thought to myself, I'll look and see who this guy is. I don't have anything on him. He's just a name. It turned out that he was the one who later became Walt Whitman's boss and who fired Walt Whitman for publishing *Leaves of Grass*—dirty, smutty book! By being able to add that, I could humanize this functionary and add another anti-visionary thing that he'd done."

ADVENTURES IN CYBERSPACE

You may not want or need your own reference library, especially if you move around a lot.

Or if you write using a computer.

I myself own a 1930s-vintage enamel Smith Corona portable typewriter with keys as big as pennies and a musical bell that signals a carriage return. I *own* it—it photographs well and adds a tony ambience to my crowded little study, but it also weighs twenty pounds and won't forgive my mistakes. So I *use* a notebook computer that weighs four pounds, fits in my briefcase, and has a built-in fax-modem. A lesson I learned from my grandfather, a poor man who was also a master machinist and carpenter: Don't scrimp on your tools.

Nowadays, even inexpensive computers come with modems, meaning you can work in the most remote location and still have at your desk a very sophisticated reference library. All you need is a telephone line and access to the Internet via America Online, CompuServe, Prodigy or some other on-line service. From my home, using my Internet access, I have recently done all the following:

• Searched the catalog of the Library of Congress for the writings of Thomas Jefferson.

• From an economist in Chicago located an economist in Hong Kong through electronic mail.

• Located newspaper and magazine stories from all over the country about the current controversy over flying the Confederate flag from Southern capitols.

- Read abstracts of hearings conducted by the Office of Management and Budget about the effect of federal policy on local government (bad news).
- Accessed the CIA World Factbook (Iraq, I learned, is about twice the size of Idaho).
- Found out the most recent State Department travel advisory for global hot spots (in Haiti, sporadic violence, although the airport is open; and Americans are having trouble crossing into the Dominican Republic).

If you don't have an on-line account, many libraries now provide electronic access to general periodicals and a host of other information through Infotrac. And many also have CD-ROM databases.

Don't get scared away by all the techno-jargon. The way most of these gizmos work is that you sit down at a keyboard in the library and choose from an on-screen "menu"—a selection of choices. Each choice produces a new menu, until you narrow your search to exactly what you want. Then by pushing a button—usually marked "print"—you print out what you see on the screen. So you leave the library with a printed "hard copy" of the information you need—or else you use the printed information to find what you need in the traditional print archive, microform archive, special collection, etc.

Card catalogs are obsolete. Nowadays you check a library's holdings via computer, and this is a good thing for the researcher. Not only can you search by title, author and Library of Congress subject headings—since all holdings are cross-referenced—but you can also perform a "keyword" search. In other words, you give the computer a word that describes your area of interest (for example, "Murder"), and it will search for related material. If you wind up with too many choices, you can then narrow your keyword by adding an adjective or other qualifier ("Serial Murder"). This lets you browse systematically.

A word of caution comes from reference librarian and bibliographer Thomas A. Mikolyzk, who routinely accesses more than seven hundred databases. "On the database—most people don't know this—you're at the mercy of some untrained or minimally trained $5-an-hour clerk who is reading through the articles or abstracts that were given to them, and they're picking out key words. *They're* deciding whether or not you want to see that article."

It's the same error built into any printed index, multiplied by the speed and power of technology. Never assume any index is complete.

LIBRARIES AND LIBRARIANS, SPECIAL COLLECTIONS AND MUSEUMS

If you don't know what your library has in the way of computerized reference tools, or if you don't have a clue about how to begin to use them, go straight to the other great (low-tech) research wonder available at the library: the Reference Librarian.

Now, realize that not all libraries are equal. Your local public library deals in numbers, and it's unfair to expect a public reference librarian to aid you in sophisticated research. For this you need an academic or research library. "At an academic library, they like research questions. They like to do in-depth things—it's more what they think they should be doing themselves," says Mikolyzk, who holds an M.A. in Library Science from the University of Chicago and has worked on the staffs of several college reference libraries. "And a good research library will keep things that a public library will not. By its nature, a public library weeds—vigorously weeds—its collection. An academic library sees itself as a depository for materials."

A public library expects 20-50 percent of its holdings to be checked out in a given year, while at an academic library 3 percent is the standard; most items are used within the library walls.

All the reference librarians I've ever met have two things in common: One, they are all highly trained, knowledgeable individuals; and two, they love a challenge. Many spend their days answering the same routine questions over and over. So when you walk in with a really sticky problem, their eyes light up and they smack their palms together and become, in a flash, your very high-powered research assistant.

Some libraries are U.S. or State Government Depository Libraries, meaning that they contain government documents. Depending on whether it is a partial or full federal depository, the library will have either only major documents, such as the *Congressional Record*, or additional reams of lesser documents. Once the government—any government—records a fact, it will always be kept on file somewhere. The government never throws anything out. This works in your favor.

For example, in preparing to go to Hong Kong and write TV scripts about the impending changeover from British to Chinese sovereignty, I went to the Government Documents section of our university library (a partial depository, which means it chooses which items to receive) and looked up every Congressional committee that dealt with the Far East. Congress had held a number of hearings, and I collected all the testimony and read it. It was heavy sledding, but in the end I understood the issues clearly and with some thoroughness—and I learned who most of the major players were.

Congress, by the way, holds hearings on an astonishing variety of issues, and its published archive of expert testimony can furnish up-to-date background that would take you weeks to track down interview by interview.

Once in Hong Kong, it was going to be crucial to interview key people in government, business, education, and in both the British and Chinese communities. But Congress had, in effect, done a good part of my job for me. It had hunted up experts and brought them to Washington, where they had talked extensively for a stenographer, whose transcripts I had in my hand. We were able to line up many of them for interviews long before we got to Hong Kong.

Another archival resource overlooked by too many writers is the Special Collection. Many university libraries are famous for their special collections, but too often we assume that only scholars or academic biographers have any use for them. But this is simply not true. Special collections contain letters, unpublished memoirs, diaries, period magazines and newspapers, even art, memorabilia, artifacts and photographs—all rare treasures for the essayist writing about the world.

And even private collections are more accessible than you might think. What does it take to gain access? "Just prove you're not some bum from the neighborhood," Mikolyzk says. "Once they figure you're legit, they're interested in you. The librarians who work in special collections normally are very knowledgeable, willing to share, provided you're smart enough to listen." They are professionals, and they expect a similar level of seriousness from you. The best strategy is to call ahead and find out what the particular archive requires in the way of credentials. A university affiliation can help, but equally useful can be a letter from you, or from your magazine or book editor. Sometimes a simple driver's license will suffice.

A phone call will get you a general list of their holdings (in many cases you can get this information on-line, through your local library). Then you fill out a simple form and they will locate the item you want and deliver it to you in a quiet climate-controlled room. Usually they will not permit you to take into that room anything other than a pencil and notebook, and they will require you to submit to a search of your materials on the way out—valuable holdings have legs, they say. Some will let you work with a notebook computer, and most will, for a fee, provide photocopies of documents unless the item will be damaged by the process.

Bear in mind that each collection operates a little differently, and some will be more welcoming than others. Persistence and courtesy usually pay off, and there is always more than one way to find out something.

Mikolyzk warns, "Don't go in there saying, 'Gee, I think I might . . .'—that's going to turn somebody off. You have to have very specific information you're looking for, even if it's in general terms: 'I want to research such-and-such a person'—you can say that—'I think he might have lived here or there.' Or a family. Or an incident."

But no one is going to do your research for you. "The librarian can't give you what you want," Mikolyzk says. "You have to find what you want." A good librarian will be a kind of human map, guiding you through the resources of the library. "It really is a team situation," Mikolyzk says. "It sounds so trite, but it is: You know what you want, they know how to get you to a certain area."

And you may have to be resourceful in figuring out where to look for the information you want. "Sometimes *not* finding something is an answer," Mikolyzk says. "Oftentimes, somebody says, 'What can you find on such-and-such?' Well, after eight hours, nothing. They say, 'Well, there has to be something.' Well, no, not really. 'Why not?' Well, because one, it may not have been important enough to write about. If it was written, it wasn't important enough to publish. If it was published, it wasn't important enough to buy. If it was bought, it wasn't important enough to keep."

In researching a historical novel about a racial massacre in 1898 in North Carolina, I visited the special collections at Duke University. Hugh MacRae, a businessman, had been a key player in organizing white supremacists to "redeem" the city of Wilmington from a coalition of black and white Republicans, and Duke holds the Hugh MacRae papers. I wanted to be as accurate as I could in portraying the real people and actual events of the time, just as if I were writing nonfictionally about them, though because I was taking liberties in creating dialogue and dramatic scenes it was only fair to call it fiction. The method of researching fact-based fiction and nonfiction is the same, even if the narrative ethics are different.

I found the papers, but there was a hole in the record, roughly covering the period I most needed to know about—almost as if someone had deliberately excised all the material directly related to the event.

But I already knew the particulars of the event. What I needed was the *person*. MacRae had written extensively about his views on race, as well as about many other issues. His business ledger told me he was meticulous; the letters he wrote and the ones he received told me he was shrewd, smart, ambitious and ruthless (he once hired a private detective to dig up dirt on his sister's fiancé, then threatened to expose the man if he went through with the marriage). Though a key part of his career was missing from the record, it was easy to read the arc of his life in the wealth of material still in the files.

A woman who had been married to another white supremacist left behind, in the Wilson Library Special Collections at UNC-Chapel Hill, her "receipt" book, which contained not only her favorite recipes for Lady Baltimore cake and Christmas goose but gossip about her neighbors and bitter poetry about her not-so-faithful husband, Alfred Moore Waddell.

At the local courthouse, after a skeptical clerk assured me they could not possibly have anything so old (but I knew different—as I said, the government *never* throws anything away), I found the Waddells' marriage record: She was his third wife (after a pair of sisters), and he had led the massacre on their second wedding anniversary. The man had his priorities.

Sometimes the most basic information isn't in the record—at least not yet. Mikolyzk, who spends Saturday nights answering the telephone for Night Owl, a call-in public library reference service, says, "The toughest question in the world I ever get—THE toughest question: Is so-and-so still alive? Can't prove it."

ARCHIVES WE DON'T THINK OF AS ARCHIVES

In researching the same book, again and again I stumbled upon references to a Gatling gun, which had become a sort of icon of white supremacy. The vigilantes hauled it from place to place in the bed of a special wagon as if it were the Ark of the Covenant, meant to inspire awe and terror in the hearts of the black masses.

But I had never seen a Gatling gun. So I called the most logical "archive" I could think of: the U.S. Army Ordnance Museum in Aberdeen, Maryland. Did they have a Gatling gun? Sure, they did, one used in the Cuban campaign of 1898, exactly the year of the massacre. I drove five hundred miles to Aberdeen and saw the gun—an awesome and fearful weapon. Not only did I look at it, I photographed it from many angles so I could describe it accurately later. Then I handled it, swiveling the four-hundred-pound drum with its ten rotating barrels, wrapping my fingers around the brass crank, sighting targets.

Research. Feeling the weight, smelling the gun oil, looking down the barrel.

Archives we don't think of as archives.

Museums constitute special collections. The thing to remember about museums is that most of what they own is *not* on display. The Smithsonian Institution, for example, keeps millions of items in warehouses all over the country. Dr. Robert Byington, former folklore curator at the Smithsonian, says, "What they have on exhibit at any given time is probably less than one tenth of one percent of what they actually have—and remember that an exhibit will remain in place for a long time, since it may take years to set it up."

Even small local museums usually have more artifacts in the basement storage room than in the exhibit hall, and, if the staff are doing their jobs, all of it will be cataloged and, if you're persistent, accessible to you, within reason. This may include paper and electronic archives as well.

In fact, many museums have libraries and archives already set up for visiting researchers. Some years back, I spent a week at Mystic Seaport Museum in Connecticut which houses, among its many restored period buildings, exhibit halls and historic ships, an excellent maritime library. I went there to research a novel about Joshua

Slocum, the first sailor to complete a solo circumnavigation of the globe, and I wound up also doing a nonfiction book for the museum press on the schooner *Brilliant*. During both projects, the Mystic library staff were energetic in finding information for me—not only from their own holdings of logbooks, photographs, films, monographs, maps, blueprints and letters, but from other museums and maritime archives around the country.

"A place like Mystic, that's a *special* special library," Mikolyzk says admiringly. "Those guys aren't reference librarians, really—they're more keepers of the flame of knowledge there."

MAPS TELL STORIES, TOO

Local and state historical societies, likewise, often have surprisingly sophisticated archives, often including such invaluable tools as Sanborn-Perris insurance maps, showing the architecture of a specific American town during a particular period. The detail on such maps is remarkable; they're color-coded to indicate the type of material used in construction, the placement of water mains and other utilities, and landmarks that may have disappeared or been altered over time. Even local libraries often have map rooms.

Maps in general are a wonderful research tool, displaying much more than simple geographical layout. Topographical maps indicate elevation, how rugged the country is, and a series of maps over time can lead to remarkable discoveries about how the land figured in the human story.

Political maps show us the evolution of nations—Poland disappears, reappears, disappears again, reappears larger, then becomes part of the Nazi Reich, then suddenly shifts westward as Russia steals the East and Germany gives up Silesia—and we visually grasp the ebb and flow of the European empire. The last fifty years of the history of Eastern Europe is written on its maps, as the Soviet Union gobbles up nations and then fragments into quarreling ethnic enclaves.

Communist-era maps of the USSR show blank spaces where cities actually stood, an absence of roads where highways existed, end-of-tracks where railroads actually crossed borders—a graphic metaphor of paranoia, of the obsession to keep even trivial secrets.

Navigational charts, weather maps, local street maps, hiking trail guides, topographic moonscapes, maps of the stars, all can inform your story. All narratives move through time and space. Time is only history, and space is only geography; a good map can show you both at once.

WALKING THE GROUND

Like maps, the built environment can offer exact clues about history and culture. You can read the entire Civil War in the garden of monuments at Gettysburg—every regiment is honored by a marker that lists not only dead and wounded but all the other battles in which it fought. The placement of the monuments—on two opposing heights with a mile of cornfields between—replicates the movement of the three-day battle. The figurative "high-water mark of the Confederacy"—the farthest point that General Pickett's men reached during the final disastrous charge that broke the back of the Southern army—is made literal by a stone obelisk.

The entire battlefield is an archive.

Throughout the South, thousands of historical markers demonstrate both a revisionist pride in the Lost Cause and the separate and decidedly unequal status of the black population, whose monuments are mostly invisible. In practically every village in New England, the town square features a statue of a Union soldier, a monument to those local sons who died putting down "The Great Rebellion." Even the terminology informs.

Want to understand a small town? Visit its cemetery. Oakdale Cemetery in Wilmington, North Carolina, for instance, unfolds exactly along the class lines of the old town: imposing sepulchres for leading families, modest stones for the middle class. The Jewish section is fenced off. The black section is across another fence in Pine Forest. The freemasons have their own prominent plots, as do other secret fraternities. The yellow fever epidemic of 1861 is recorded by rows of gravestones, as is the influenza epidemic of 1918.

In that cemetery I learned that my old friend Alfred Waddell, who led a massacre on his wedding anniversary, had buried his first two wives, sisters, under a common headstone. A thrifty man.

I spent three days skulking around that cemetery, for another reason: On the night of the massacre, hundreds of blacks fled the city and hid out among the tombstones. As I navigated the narrow dogwood-shaded lanes, climbed the berms and hummocks, spied on caretakers behind moss-hung live oaks, I began to understand why: The landscape itself offered safety, refuge, barriers to ranks of mounted riflemen hunting "blackbirds."

I was on the ground. I was doing the second kind of research—living research.

WRITING IN THE BORDERLANDS

Living research is not always done deliberately—hardly anyone, for instance, goes through childhood planning to write about it later, taking copious notes of important games of kick-the-can, recording verbatim conversations at Thanksgiving dinners, conducting formal interviews with Mom and Dad and Uncle Bilbo, the eccentric trumpet player.

Tobias Wolff, in *This Boy's Life*, the most moving and true account of boyhood I have ever read, reminds us that such a memoir is always struggling toward truthfulness, but ultimately makes an imperfect bargain with it. "I have been corrected on some points, mostly of chronology," he writes in a foreword, being clear about exactly what he is promising the reader. "I've allowed some of these points to stand, because this is a book of memory, and memory has its own story to tell."

If you keep a diary or journal or book of days, you are moving closer to deliberate research—recording impressions, actual conversations, physical details of your environment, observations made during your travels.

You may even establish yourself in a place and then keep such a journal, intending at least in a halfhearted way that the journal shall become art, the imaginative re-creation of your experience there. Edward Abbey's *Desert Solitaire: A Season in the Wilderness* is such an account—of a lonesome but not lonely man, keeping lookout atop a fire tower in the Arches National Monument in the canyonlands of Utah, lyrically recording and reflecting upon his season in the wilderness. So is Jan DeBlieu's *Hatteras Journal*, written in a storm-battered cottage on Hatteras Island, on the most vulnerable stretch of coastline on the Eastern seaboard: "To me, a newcomer to the coast, the storm was exhilarating, bracing, good material for stories—but only as long as I kept a grip on my imagination."

Nonfiction writers often seek out the extreme environment, the marginal place, the no-man's-land between safety and danger, the edge between familiar ground and terra incognita. "My personal interest is in borders," explains Reiss, who has written of the Amazon, Antarctica, and the origin of manned flight. "Geographical borders, human borders, the gray area between where things are established and things are unknown."

The genre of nonfiction itself reflects this tendency, borrowing from journalism, fiction, even technical writing, to achieve the art of the real. Researching along these borders can be dicey and full of challenges— physical, aesthetic and emotional.

Jerry Bledsoe has ventured into the borderland between law and crime, between the light and dark sides of human personality, in such books as *Bitter Blood*, *Blood Games* and *Before He Wakes*—all real-life tales of particularly heinous murders committed by relatives of the victims. His research begins with access. "To do a book like that, you need two things," he says. "One, the cooperation of the police. And two, the cooperation of at least one of the families. If I don't have both of those things right up front, I don't proceed."

His research then meanders through thousands of pages of trial transcripts, arrest reports, depositions and media accounts. He interviews everybody he can: arresting officers, paramedics, coroners, detectives, lawyers, friends and family of the victim, neighbors, colleagues, former employers and teachers, ex-wives and husbands, high-school sweethearts—anybody who can help him get at the whole truth. The police are interested only in solving the case, he explains, and the prosecutor is only after a conviction. Oddly enough, the writer is the only person seeking the whole truth in all of its human complexity.

For this reason, those closest to the victims are often eager to talk to him, because no one else has satisfied their craving for justice, which can come only with the telling of the whole story. The research typically covers many miles and takes years.

Bledsoe, a former staff writer at *Esquire* who, despite his easygoing, countrified manner, is dead serious about good writing, worries about being typed as a "true-crime" writer—a kind of subgenre that for some critics carries sensationalist overtones. But his intentions are as literary as those of Truman Capote (*In Cold Blood*) or Norman Mailer

(*The Executioner's Song*) whose books deal with murder. He is delving into the mystery of the human personality gone awry: "It all comes down to the question of evil—does it grab you from without and take control of you, or is it something inside, a question of character?" he says of his latest book, *Before He Wakes*, in which an outwardly loving woman murders her husband in his sleep.

And there is another cost to exploring this territory of violent death and bitter grief. "The psychological burden of it bothers me," he says, his voice going quiet and reflective. "I just get so involved with the victims' families."

Biographers, too, must deal with emotional issues as they research a dead pubic figure and try to re-create him or her as a living personality on the page. "It's a terrible thing to die and leave behind people who have loved you and, in some cases, may not have resolved their anger, and who are left in possession of the myth that they don't want violated," says Powers, whose biography of Muppeteer Jim Henson ran aground on legal opposition by some Henson family members. "Often the biographer becomes the messenger who is persecuted for carrying an unpleasant message."

Hearst biographer David Nasaw agrees: "I think every family begins by wanting a full, truthful account. No family, few literary executors, set out to ask for a censored, partial view. On the other hand, *none* are ever happy with what they get."

To conduct the research necessary for his biographies of poets John Berryman, Robert Lowell and William Carlos Williams, Paul Mariani needed access to their literary estates—archives controlled by family or literary executors. Depending on how the deceased was treated by other biographers, it may take some time to arrange such access. But that is only one source. "We speak about the archives as though they're going to be there and we just have to wait," he says. "Well, that's not always the case. I mean, it may be that we have to generate those archives. We have to have those interviews—they then become part of the archive. We have to generate that pressure with the living voices, the living witnesses."

So developing the archive itself becomes living research—interviewing people, visiting the landmarks of that vanished life before they disappear.

And then, of course, there's the problem of interpreting that archive, distilling the truth from conflicting accounts, or finding it between the lines—all the things nobody will speak about directly, that leave no trace in the record. Nasaw cautions, "The archives always lie."

THERE'S NO SUBSTITUTE FOR BEING THERE

Not all living research is so emotionally taxing, but all research usually requires patience, ingenuity, a keen sense of observation, a willingness to follow the story wherever it leads, and more time than you expected. It may require travel or experience specifically designed to yield a story (see chapter five, "On Assignment"). It will almost certainly require interviewing (chapter four), both background telephone interviews and face-to-face conversations with all sorts of people, many—but not all of them—forthright, willing, articulate and amiable.

When Dillard went flying with aerobatic pilot Dave Rahm, she was doing essential living research—her subject was no longer abstract but viscerally real. Probably no other kind of research would have yielded the insight from which she wrote such a powerful and beautiful piece. Her experience in the air lends the piece an authenticity that can't be faked.

How could Ted Conover write convincingly about how it *felt* to be a hobo—hungry, lice-infested, looked on with suspicion by honest citizens, bullied by kids and cops, lacking in ambition, goals and confidence—except by becoming one?

How could Terry Tempest Williams use a flooded migratory bird refuge as a way of understanding the emotional cost of cancer if she didn't visit it frequently, as the waters rose higher and higher, recording the changes but also experiencing them in the way sound vanished, the way the mud sucked at her boots, the disappearing nuances of a landscape that was becoming all one watery thing?

There is just no substitute for being there, for doing it—whatever "it" is.

So if you're writing about the anti-gun control stance of the National Rifle Association, go out and shoot a pistol on a firing range. If you explain your purpose, your local police department may accommodate you, or else recommend a bona fide shooting club that can. Then you can understand the experience, the atavistic thrill of power and control, that underlies the abstract argument about individual freedom and self-defense. Visit a hospital emergency room where gunshot victims are wheeled in bloody and screaming, and your stomach will quickly teach you the other side of the argument.

If you're writing about a place, see it in all weathers—watch time move through it. Watch it move through time. A view that was obscured by thick foliage in summer is now an open vista in the leaf-stripped moonscape of winter. A tranquil beach turns into an other-worldly nightmare during a hurricane.

If you're writing about history, go there and walk the ground. In researching a radio essay on the Gettysburg Address, I read the speech aloud several times, to hear it. Then I went to Gettysburg and walked the route of Pickett's charge against the Union lines on Cemetery Ridge on the last day of battle, describing the landscape into a tape recorder as I walked. Halfway across, the ground turned from firm soil into a muddy bog—it had rained heavily the night before, as it had before the battle. It slowed me down. The feet of fifteen thousand marching men would have turned it into a mire. At certain points, I could no longer see Cemetery Ridge at all—the ground rolled like the waves of the sea—and I had the peculiar impression of being swallowed up by the earth.

When I listened to the tape later, I was surprised at how out of breath I sounded. Then it hit me: for almost a mile, I had been walking uphill. And, with no cannonade of explosive shells coming at me, no sharpshooters, canister shot, or volleys of musket fire to slow me down, no sprawled bodies or shell craters to step across, no fear to overcome, it took me fifteen minutes to cover the ground to the low stone wall where the Yankees had waited that July day in 1863. So it had not been a quick rush to glory—the men who survived were under constant massed fire for at least thirty minutes: fifteen minutes across, and at least that long to stagger back across the field of bodies to the spot where a monument now stands honoring General Robert E. Lee, who ordered them to charge.

Standing at the gate of the cemetery early in the morning, staring across the battlefield I had just walked where the mist was smoking up from the tree line, I was overcome by reverence and a fierce sadness—as Abraham Lincoln must have been when he gave his little speech.

The emotion was different from book-facts: It came from *being in that place*.

Farther down the stone wall, just within earshot, a squad of modern infantry were finishing their charge at a run. They vaulted the wall, then stood at ease in a circle around their sergeant, catching their breath and listening to a lesson in tactics and strategy. In the background, from a gunnery range somewhere behind the trees, I could hear the crackle of automatic rifle fire. In the clipped voice of the sergeant, the earnest questions of the young men and women in camo fatigues, the stuttering *pop-pop* of distant gunfire, the gray mist along the tree line, the solid, heavy garden of white monuments, the mud of the battlefield caked on my boots, past and present converged into something larger: an arc of story, resonant, real and moving.

In college I once took a class in primatology—the study of monkeys, apes and our hominid ancestors—from a very gifted and uncompromising professor. We read monographs and textbooks, looked at slide shows and movies, listened to her maddeningly thorough lectures on stereoscopic vision, opposable thumbs and upright bipedal locomotion. One day she announced that, on Saturday, we were all going to go to the zoo. Why? we asked. Because, she told us, that's where all the other primates are. It was time to visit our relatives in person. That was her lesson: You have go where the other primates are. You have to see the thing itself, not merely a representation of the thing.

You don't have to be a manic thrill-junkie—seeking out risk, always riding the razor's edge, high on the adrenaline-rush of danger. In fact, you don't want to be. There's a line that, as a writer, you don't want to cross. As soon as war correspondent Hemingway started toting a tommy gun on the road to liberate Paris, he stopped being a writer of the story and became the hero of it, and the story became less true—and more a self-aggrandizing fiction, stagy and posed. He and his band of "irregulars" went about looking for Germans to fight, creating drama so he would have something interesting to write about later.

It's not that you must stay completely out of every story. But the writer fails, I believe, who skews the story, distorts the crucial focus of truth, by mistaking for candor the celebration of his own ego. You're not there to *make* things happen, only to *see* what happens, to witness with the clarity and judgment of a well-trained imagination.

Still, a lot of the joy of writing nonfiction comes from having an honorable excuse to go out into the world and find out interesting things, lay your hands on the stuff of the world and feel its heft, its weight of meaning, to meet fascinating people and talk to them about the things they care about most deeply.

Don't write too soon—before you write, ask the last question you need to ask.

But the converse word of caution comes from Bain, who spent months in the library and many more months humping through the Philippine jungle to find the story that would capture the essence of a century of imperial foreign policy in the Philippines: Don't fall in love with your research. "Just because you get obsessed with something," he warns, "you figure everyone else will. But you can't include the world."

Remember always, you're researching to prepare *to write*. The writing is the hard part. Research can be seductive, partly because it satisfies your curiosity, but also because it postpones that moment when you have to *deliver*. A project too long pursued can grow stale, and you can easily fool yourself into thinking you don't yet know enough, when in fact you know too much.

Your genius as a researcher lies in discovering—and recognizing—the part of the world that matters to your story—then writing it.

CHAPTER FOUR

THE ART OF
THE INTERVIEW

We sat in the office of the manager of Lenpol, a flax factory in northern Poland, my interpreter and I. Solidarity's revolution had succeeded beyond anybody's wildest dreams—*Komunizm kaput!* confirmed graffiti all over Warsaw and Gdansk. But what now? That's what I had come six thousand miles to find out.

Across an imposing desk, the young manager shouted repeatedly into the telephone, his face flushed with anger or frustration at whoever was on the other end of the line, or maybe just at the telephone system itself, which alternately worked perfectly or not at all. I couldn't tell, since I could not speak the language beyond a few pleasantries and proper names.

My interpreter, a dignified old gentleman who, during World War II, had survived both Nazi labor camps and Soviet gulags, as well as sustained combat in a Free Polish brigade on the Eastern Front, was nervous, rubbing his big hands together and glancing about this way and that, as if looking for a way out. Like most of us, the one thing that really unnerved him was genuine rudeness.

The manager kept shouting belligerently into the phone.

Against the interior wall stood a glass display case full of samples of raw flax and finished linen goods—some of the finest in the world. Behind the manager, the wall was covered with a poster of a nude woman, her pendulous bare breasts looming just over the man's bobbing head—a glaring trophy of the new, decadent capitalism.

Every time my interpreter would ask him a question, the phone would ring, and he'd spend several minutes shouting into it. This had been going on for at least half an hour. Then a severe young woman entered, some kind of public relations assistant. Her status never did become clear, but she immediately launched into a shrill tirade at my interpreter, and before long the two of them were shouting back and forth at each other, gesticulating wildly, the director was still shouting into the phone, and I was trying not to stare at the leering pinup poster, tune out the two shouting matches in Polish, and figure out what to do next.

The interview was not going well.

That's the first lesson about interviewing: It's a human encounter, and however carefully you plan it, the event will take on a life of its own. You and your subject may hit it off wonderfully, or the conversation may take on an immediate edge. You may find your rhythm, or you may not. Factors you have no control over may interfere. Don't get thrown. Roll with the situation.

The free-for-all continued for a few more minutes, then all at once we were asked to leave. No, we would not be allowed to tour the factory or interview workers. No, we would not be permitted to take photographs, and we would please not use the manager's name. As he gave us the bum's rush, he did pause in the doorway long enough to harangue his workers for their laziness and bad attitude. "The saying is that the state factory is the factory that belongs to nobody," he complained. "A man owns a hammer, and it serves him for twenty years. In a factory such as this, it lasts three days or less."

On the way to the car, my interpreter filled in some blanks, since he had understood much of what had been said on the telephone. The factory was losing money. The manager was disgusted with his workers, and my guess is they were equally disgusted with him.

I came away with some brief quotes. But more important, I had experienced the poisoned atmosphere of a company that had no clue about how to operate in a suddenly free market. In that sense, the interview had been a success. By living in the moment and being forced to discard my agenda—a list of questions about wages, costs, flax and linen products—I had found the real story. All over Poland, all across the newly liberated countries of eastern Europe, factory managers were suddenly accountable for production, for quality, for making a profit; but for two generations their employees had been trained according to the old communist joke: We pretend to work, and you pretend to pay us.

They could not be instilled with ambition and pride in their work overnight, especially when mass layoffs were sending thousands into unemployment lines every day. Everybody expected to be fired. The new order was fraught with danger.

Before I was through, I would interview dozens of workers, union organizers, managers and unemployed young men and women, and in their voices would emerge the human story behind the abstractions of "revolution," capitalism" and "free market economy"—all couched in a blood suspicion of Germans and Russians. "The Germans are bosses—they like to give orders," my interpreter explained. "The Russians are brutal. The Poles are somewhere in between."

REAL PEOPLE, REAL VOICES

That's what an interview adds to a true story: real voices of real people. Just as in fiction, these people become "characters," and what they say gives texture beyond the writer's style, deepens the meanings of the story. Their words make it true.

Creative nonfiction is always about people.

Even when the story seems to be about an issue or an idea or a phenomenon, somewhere at the center of the action are people. People talk. An interview is just a conversation between a writer and somebody who knows something the writer doesn't, and, filtered and edited, it comes out as a kind of dialogue—a narrative device that personalizes a story, that lends immediacy and authenticity to bare facts, that brings those people to life on the page and invites the reader to share their experiences.

"The voices in creative nonfiction are people's voices," Lee Gutkind says. "That is to say that real people have to appear, like characters in a novel, like voices in a poem. And they're real in the sense that a good novel makes characters real."

Quoted lines in a nonfiction piece do much of the same work as in a piece of fiction: They illuminate personality and character, establish the subtleties of character, move the piece along, add credibility to other claims in the piece, establish tone (including irony or humor), convey information, provide variety in point of view (often contradicting the governing POV of the author), even provide tension between subject and interviewer.

And even when the spoken words of the subject do not appear in the piece, the interview yields facts, impressions, leads, insights, truth.

Not every piece of creative nonfiction relies on interviews. And very often the interview functions as a tutorial for the writer—who needs to find out information—and the *subject*, or interviewee. Such an interview is simply a shorthand way for the writer to get on top of complex information that would take years of law school or graduate work in astro-physics to learn. The subject's exact words may never appear in the piece.

But you might be surprised to learn just how many "introspective" pieces take on spin from other voices. Annie Dillard's work, for example, is full of other voices, quietly adding an opinion or a fact or a way of saying something at exactly the right moment—the moment when the reader needs a counterpoint to the author's tone. You hardly notice them—they slip in and out of her prose like highlights in a painting, adding depth here, a touch of shadow there, humor, emphasis and color.

Sometimes they are the voices of the people about whom she is writing. Dave Rahm, the aerobatics pilot, lends a down-to-earth and slightly ironic perspective to Dillard's intricate, lyrical vision of his aesthetic. He says laconically, "I get a rhythm going and stick with it."

Other times, they are the voices of people almost tangential to her story, except as they illuminate it by utter, unstudied sincerity.

PRE-INTERVIEW ANXIETY

One of the instincts that drives the writer who is fascinated with a topic is to find out what other interesting people have to say about it. Even when we're not actively writing about something, most writers I know are conversation junkies, always asking questions of people who just might know something we don't, eavesdropping on conversations that intrigue us. We like hanging out with people, enjoy arguments and speculation, the sound of voices talking for its own sake. So it may seem a short step between that and a deliberate interview. But in fact most writers I know are just as timid around strangers as the average nonwriter—some even more so.

After all, we writers are used to spending long stretches of solitary time in small, isolated rooms, with only the company of our word machines. We hate to bother people. If the person in question is famous, we feel a bit like impostors and are reluctant, even apologetic, about taking up that person's valuable time. You would think that practice would make it easier to approach complete strangers and ask questions, but in my experience, at least, it never gets easier.

So you wind up sitting by the telephone, pencil tapping, going over the questions you want to ask, checking your tape recorder again and again to make sure it's working, then taking a deep breath and mashing the numbers, part of you stupidly hoping that the person you're calling will be out.

Or else standing outside a closed door (the most intimidating thing in the world is a closed door) and taking that same deep breath.

But it's just human nature to be anxious about a first meeting with a stranger. Once past the awkward introductions, you stop being strangers, and as the interview goes on you're feeling more and more comfortable with each other, and the questions and answers become just conversation.

Even when you are about to interview someone you already know, the artificial nature of the planned interview can put you both under a certain tension that would be unthinkable during an ordinary, spontaneous encounter.

For instance, I first met Ron Powers years ago and have seen him half a dozen times since then at the Bread Loaf Writers' Conference. But when we sat down to do a "formal" interview for this book on subjects we had discussed informally in workshops and dinner conversations, suddenly I felt very nervous. The place we had decided to meet turned noisy and we left, seeking a quieter venue. And as we sat down on a secluded porch to talk, I realized I had left behind my notebook and pen. My microcassette tape recorder turned cranky and wouldn't record, despite the fact that I religiously change batteries before I start any long interview. Powers lent me paper and pen, gave me a patient few minutes to fix the glitch in my recorder, and we both had a laugh and relaxed. Then he said wonderful things about writing.

Any initial awkwardness is not a disaster but simply a matter of course, a moment to get past as gracefully as you can. And if you feel nervous—and you've done this before—imagine how your subject may feel.

A TYPICAL INTERVIEW

There is no such thing.

The whole premise of interviewing is that people come in an amazing variety. Just when you think you've heard it all, you'll hear something astounding.

But as writers we live by our habits, and like many writers I try to follow a template for interviewing. Naturally, it varies a lot based on the situation and the person, and other writers do it differently, but it's a useful starting point for a formal, set interview.

To prepare for the interview:

1. Ask yourself *why* you want to interview this person. This is the question to ask before you ask any others. Is it to get background information? Is this person a main character—maybe the only character—in my piece? Or am I interviewing him or her in reaction to another interview? Am I interviewing this person as a way of getting a chance to interview the person I really want to talk to? Until you know why you're talking to somebody, you don't know what you want to take away from the interview. Which means you don't know what to bring into the interview, or what questions to ask during the interview.

2. Establish basic background facts—a resumé that includes vital statistics such as age and nationality, education, occupation and job title; key credentials, achievements and honors (and dishonors—if the guy is a convicted murderer, I want to know that, too). Bear in mind that the object of the interview may be to elicit such a resumé, especially in the case of a noncelebrity, so don't take the above too literally. Sometimes it's as simple as reading the author's bio on the back flap of a book jacket. But if there's background I can reasonably find out before I sit down face to face, I want to make the effort to learn it. I want to have some precise sense of whom I'm talking to— that will partly determine what questions I ask him.

How much should you know about a person before you sit down and ask her questions? That depends. If the person is a celebrity— Henry Kissinger or a Nobel laureate—it pays to do your homework beforehand: You don't want to waste precious time, theirs or yours, on basic background you can find out from *Who's Who* or *Time* magazine. Partly it's a question of how much time you can spend with them, and partly it's a question of why you want to talk to them in the first place.

Shooting a public television documentary in Hong Kong, I was asked to write interview questions for Sir Jack Cater—who wasn't one of my sources. All I knew about him was that he was on the board of a nuclear investment company in China. Why in the world would we want to talk to him for a show about the reversion of the colony to Chinese rule? The producer said he'd been told this fellow was someone we should talk to, but he didn't know anything about him, either. So I wrote up some boring questions about investment and atomic energy, figuring the interview would be a throwaway.

Chatting with our narrator while the camera and lights were being set up, Sir Jack mentioned offhandedly that he had been in Hong Kong since the end of World War II. It turned out he had helped rebuild the colony after its devastation by the Japanese, and that he had gone on to become the founding commissioner against corruption in the civil service. Both foreign occupation and communist corruption were important themes of the show. So we asked him about the war and about anticorruption, and he gave us a fascinating and emotionally charged interview, full of living memory and anecdote, not facts and statistics, but vivid stories about a place and a people he loved.

Most interview subjects are flattered when you obviously know their work and accomplishments—it's a measure of your seriousness as a writer and also of how seriously you take them. Showing that you have done your homework sets a baseline for the interview. The subject does not feel compelled to explain basic background and may feel freer to move on to more interesting matters.

3. Decide *where* you want to conduct the interview—you may or may not have control over this, but it's a factor.

4. Decide how best to record the interview—using notebook, tape recorder, or only a good memory. This is not a trivial matter, so we'll cover the choices in more detail toward the end of this chapter.

5. Write a very brief list of the questions you really want to ask. And I mean *brief*. I usually go into an interview with three to five absolutely essential questions that I intend to ask no matter what. Sometimes, I have only one question. This does not always mean I ask them all—or ask any of them. But having the list gives me a starting point that reinforces the connection between this interview and the larger piece, and keeping it brief allows me to invent other questions on the spot in reaction to something that's been said in the

interview. To follow up. Or to repeat the question, if the subject thinks he's answered it but I don't. It means, even if time runs out, I usually get answers to the most important questions on my mind.

6. Review your notes on other interviews, on your research in general—so you can cross-reference, inform your conversation, elicit responses to what others have said about the same set of facts, set the stage for a kind of dialogue among your sources.

7. Read what's already been written about your subject, and what he or she has already said in print. This is not always necessary or possible, but especially with celebrities it can help you avoid triteness. It can also give you qualified (because they may or may not have been quoted accurately, or may have changed their mind since) access to their opinions and attitudes.

The writers I quote at length in these chapters are all writers whose work I read before I asked them for insights about writing. I didn't want to insult them or embarrass myself, and I wanted to make sure I admired their art enough to trust what they had to say about the act of making it.

It's an enlightening—and unsettling—experience for a writer to be interviewed. Try it yourself. We are so accustomed to questioning others and then implicitly asking them to trust what we do with their words, that we are too often surprisingly ignorant of how it feels to see your own words go in *there* and come out *here*. Persuade somebody to interview you and write their version of it—then see how well it jibes with your recollection of the interview. Even when I've seen myself interviewed on television, I am always convinced that I didn't really say all those things—surely I'm smarter, more poised, more articulate than that.

If you can't find anybody willing to interview you, interview yourself with a list of questions using a tape recorder. The playback will be an eerie reminder of the degree of trust your subjects are placing in you the interviewer, and of their vulnerability, of the power you have over their words.

To conduct the actual interview:

1. Begin the interview with an open mind—prepared to listen. You are not the star of the interview, your subject is. Out of nervousness, or ego, or maybe just because we like the person we're interviewing

and feel drawn to confide in him or her, we can inadvertently dominate the conversation. But when you're talking, you're not listening, and when you're not listening, you're not learning anything you don't already know.

2. Ease into the interview. Break the ice. Chat. Warm up. You may both be nervous, especially if you're using a tape recorder. Again, if you're interviewing on the fly, these niceties may be moot. William Howarth says he once interviewed a subject while clinging to the back of a speeding motorcycle—hardly the moment for small talk. And some interviewers deliberately open with a tough question, just to catch the subject in a candid moment—not my style. I prefer to begin with questions that help set the subject at ease, then get more and more pointed as I establish trust. I want the subject to forget I'm an interviewer and just talk to me from the heart.

3. Be prepared for the interview to generate some heat. You don't want your subject to stalk out in a fury thirty seconds into the conversation, but allow some latitude for emotions. Let him be angry. Let her express her feelings about her critics. One or both of you may end up in tears. But part of you must always be standing back from the process, emotionally disengaged, keeping track of the encounter.

4. Pay attention to what your subject is saying. Gratuitous advice, right? You'd be surprised how your mind can wander. You thought it would be terrific to interview the Pope, but now all you can think of is your next question, how bright the glare is from that window, and look at the funky costume on that guard standing next to him. And what in the world is the right name for that big hat he's wearing? Keep your eye on the ball. *Listen.* Even if it means you stop writing for a minute. For the duration of the interview, your job is to make your subject think he is the most fascinating person in the world. Don't insult him by acting bored or distracted.

5. Pay attention to the physical surroundings, the tone of the conversation and other cues. The glare from the window and the funky costume of the Swiss guard may wind up in your story. What are you picking up between the lines? What isn't the subject saying? And why won't he look you in the eye? There's a lot going on in an interview— it's a complex, dynamic event. Paying attention to the context *while* listening is an acquired skill—practice it. See the later arguments about the usefulness of a tape recorder to help capture it all.

6. If you missed something the subject said, if he spoke too fast for you to write it down, if you're not sure you heard what you think you heard, ask him to say it again. Slowly, so you can write it down accurately. Most people I've interviewed are pleased to see you making an overt attempt to get their words right on paper. But be careful not to turn it into a dictation session.

7. After you've asked all your questions, ask him what he would like to say that you haven't asked him. Such open-ended comments can turn out to be the heart of the interview—you thought it was winding up, but it's just starting. *Now* you know what questions to ask. Remember that you may listen for a long time before the subject says anything worth quoting.

The interview will either come to an end arbitrarily—the appointments secretary will arrive on cue and show you the door—or you will decide to end it. You can't think of any more questions to ask. There's an awkward pause. You're losing interest. The subject keeps looking at his watch. Maybe it just *feels* over.

That doesn't mean it *is* over: It may be only the first of several encounters. Or you may want to follow up with a telephone call after you've had time to review your notes—either to check a quote for accuracy or to ask that last question that never occurred to you until you were halfway home. So:

8. Before you leave, make sure you know how to reach your subject for a follow-up interview.

ASKING GOOD QUESTIONS—AND LISTENING TO THE ANSWERS

A good way to learn what *not* to do in an interview is to watch local TV news reporters at work. Again and again, you'll hear startling admissions, tantalizing hints, clues about important directions in which to take the interview—and the TV reporter, following a list of set questions, will merely move on to the next question:

REPORTER: So, what brought you to Milwaukee?

SUBJECT: Well, after we kidnapped the Lindbergh baby, things got a little hot for us in New Jersey.

REPORTER: And how do you like living here?

Because he or she is simply not listening.

"A good interviewer has an interesting mixture of qualities. A good interviewer is absolutely relentless," Bob Reiss explains. "You're absolutely relentless in driving toward your goal. At the same exact time, you're prepared at any second to abandon your goal—because what happens if you find out you're going in the wrong direction?"

The key to any interview is to listen.

Good questions open up the field of discussion, give the subject range to tell you what he or she knows. Those local TV reporters always interview children the same way—by asking "yes" or "no" questions. Unless you're trying to pin down a politician or a crook, a question that can be answered with one word is probably not a very interesting question. And questions do not always have to be phrased as interrogatives. Mild, leading statements can elicit "answers," and the interview can flow as a relaxed, enjoyable conversation.

So what makes a good question?

While preparing for the interview, think of all the obvious questions everybody else would ask, then ask something different, unexpected, something for which the subject has no canned answer. Some characteristics of a good interview question:

- The subject hasn't been asked it before—at least not the way you're going to ask it. As the subject speaks, he actually discovers what he thinks.
- It can't be answered in one word (Exception: when you want a specific affirmation or denial of fact, as in, "Did you steal the money?").
- It opens up rather than closes down possibilities for revealing character.
- It can't be answered with the same authority, wit or nuance by anyone else.
- The question engages the subject's passion—he cares about the answer, so the answer matters to you.
- It is responsive—to the mood, the setting, the subject's words and actions. If he is constantly toying with a small statuette on his desk as you talk, ask him about it. If he has just volunteered that he'll spend next weekend with the National Guard, ask him where and doing what.

Reiss admires the technique of Oriana Fallaci, who is renowned for her books of direct interviews with such notable public figures as

Golda Meir, Yasir Arafat and King Hussein of Jordan. "The *best* question I think anyone ever asked she asked Haile Selassie, the Emperor of Ethiopia, when Ethiopia was in turmoil," he recalls. "He was in the waning days of his rule. It was the 1970s, but the country was still running as if it were medieval times. Hundreds of thousands of people were dying of famine. . . . Students were being found in the morning in doorways, strangled with piano wire by the secret police."

Fallaci was there to learn about the student disturbances. "Her question to him was, 'Did you ever disobey instructions when you were a kid?' Now, she could have asked about numbers, about students, how long the university is closed this year. . . . And the answer, which was—he used the royal 'we'—'We do not understand the question,' pretty much summed up the whole situation in Ethiopia and the distance between this old man in a palace and students who were being killed every day."

Very often, no matter which question you ask, a subject will stubbornly get around to telling you what he wants you to know—or what he thinks *you* want to know. Your job is to hear that, but also to coax him beyond what he is prepared to tell you. Often it's not a matter of willful antagonism. It's just that the inexperienced subject will assume you are interested in the cathedrals, when in fact you are interested in those old women next door—which may seem absurdly mundane to his sense of the world.

OTHER KINDS OF INTERVIEWS

What constitutes an interview? An informal chat over a drink. A technical blackboard briefing with a nuclear engineer. An adversarial question-and-answer session in a senator's office. You could argue that remembered conversations constitute a kind of interview—and realize, too, that very often we write about things we never intended to write about, drawing on everything we know, including remarks people made in our presence that we never planned to use in a piece.

Anthropologists, folklorists and social historians long ago perfected the nondirected interview, really a series of monologues by "informants," which doesn't carry the connotation of "snitch" in this context, but means rather someone who is willing to talk on the record about his or her culture. Usually such interviews are tape-recorded or stenographed in the same manner as testimony at a court trial. In a very real sense, they *are* testimony. And like courtroom transcripts, they can run to hundreds, even thousands, of pages—and the challenge is to find the coherent story in the mass of information. An interview itself is not a story until it is shaped into one.

Studs Terkel's *Working*, long a staple of college anthropology and sociology courses, is a first-cousin to this category of nondirected interviewing. Terkel disappears into his interviews, which are artfully edited from transcriptions of answers to triggering questions. He talks to steelworkers, stockbrokers, waitresses, bus drivers, janitors, hookers, teachers, athletes, secretaries, cops, nurses, and a multitude of other people who all tell the stories of their working lives.

"If you're a real good salesman, you can put 'em in the car that *you* want and just forget about the car *they* want," a car salesman confides. "You can sell 'em the Brooklyn Bridge." A supermarket checker brags, "There isn't a thing you don't want that isn't in this store." A dentist admits something we always knew was true but hate to hear him say out loud: "No matter what you do, sometimes things just don't go right."

Wallace Terry's *Bloods: An Oral History of the Vietnam War by Black Veterans*, is an album of interviews that also demonstrates the power of the nondirected interviewing technique—allowing subjects to speak at length about their experiences, free-associating, in effect telling a story rather than answering specific questions. The voices of the men he interviewed are so diverse, honest and eloquent that the combined effect is far greater than any single point of view could provide. And for each man it was a different war—we can hear it in their voices, unfakably real, unabashedly emotional:

"I could smell the hate," recalls an electronics warfare officer, shot down and captured by Vietcong. "I had come half a world away from Fayetteville, North Carolina—the son of sharecroppers—to die in North Vietnam at the hands of peasants."

A Marine rifleman, to whom the My Lai massacre was unremarkable, says, "When you're in combat, you can do basically what you want as long as you don't get caught. You can get away with murder."

Like so many experiences in our culture, the war came in two colors, black and white: An Army captain who recalls that the enlisted ranks of combat platoons were always full of blacks says, "I was an absolute rarity in Vietnam. A black West Pointer commanding troops."

Because *they* say these things, the words take on immediacy and power: They were *there*. In such interviewing, the questions may or may not end up in the finished piece—and there's no telling how long they rambled on with pointless reminiscences and clichés before they said the things Terry found quotable. But good questions provoke good answers.

INTIMACY AND ATTITUDE

Most people are surprisingly forthcoming with interviewers. They tell you amazing and intimate facts. Even when you expect them to lie, the confessional impulse often grips them and they tell you the truth instead. And if they lie, and you find out they're lying, all you have to do is present their remarks in a context that shows up the lie—their nervous manner, documentary or eyewitness evidence that disputes their "truth," logic or common sense that is at odds with what they say.

Assuming an adversarial relationship can be a big mistake. The writer who comes on full of bluster and self-importance, or who immediately strikes a defiant and suspicious attitude, is not likely to establish the delicate human chemistry that results in good talk. Likewise, pretending to know too much—because you're afraid to look ignorant by asking a stupid question—will keep you from learning the complex truth. There's no such thing as a stupid question, only a stupid article. Check your ego at the door.

Also, it's not uncommon to strike up a friendship in the course of an interview—another reward of the craft.

But an adversarial attitude can be a tool, like friendliness. "The point is, attitude is a choice," Reiss says. "I always go in friendly. But I'll try something else if friendly doesn't work. Many successful interviewers go in tough. Their belief is, in that first moment, break through the defenses."

He cites an example from his experiences while researching his book about the rain forest, *The Road to Extrema*. "In Brazil, forest police were on strike. They'd barricaded themselves in their barracks and refused to talk to anyone. I took my reluctant translator over the barrier and walked up to four or five guys, who were playing dominoes. I was friendly. They refused to talk. I told the translator, 'Say to them'—and this was a lie—'that I only wanted to talk to them because I heard they were bribed to go on strike.'

"The translator was afraid to say it. I said, 'Go ahead.' When the cops heard it, they blew up and started shouting the answers to my question: 'We weren't bribed! We're on strike because it's dangerous. We could get killed. Because we don't get paid. Because . . .' And on and on."

And while we tend to think of an interview as a single episode, a question-and-answer session recorded in a notebook or on tape, that's only one kind of interview. More often, an interview will take place over days, even weeks or months, of face-to-face conversations, callbacks and simple companionship. Particularly if you're doing a personal profile, it may be useful to keep yourself from writing any notes at all until you have had time to take the measure of the person you are profiling.

THE HUMAN FACTOR

At the height of his success as a freelancer for such top-drawer magazines as *Esquire*, *Sports Illustrated* and *National Wildlife*, Michael Rozek became disenchanted with the way he saw many magazines routinely treating nonfiction—editing quotes, heating up the style, distorting the facts. "If you put the writer's name on a story in a magazine, there is a public trust," he maintains.

In his view, most magazines had begun to discourage long, accurate pieces, humanely reported, on people who mattered—not celebrities, but people who were out in their communities doing the work of the world—in favor of "highly opinionated, cynical, flimsily researched, shallowly realized pieces about empty celebrities and other societal flavors-of-the-month." So he started his own newsletter, *Rozek's* (using his own name only to avoid an expensive title search), entirely devoted to the extended personal profile.

Rozek's profiles are unusual in that he frequently quotes the subject for twelve to fifteen full paragraphs without intervening as author. "Not only is my interviewing technique helping me get *the* story," he says, "but it's helping me get a particular *kind* of story, a story where quotes are most of the story." Why? "Cause I believe, I truly believe, that there are nuances when a person says it themselves that are not present when you or I rewrite it."

Rozek is passionate about bringing integrity to his very meticulous interviewing technique, which involves many hours of close companionship with his subject over a period of time. "I will usually start an interview with basic questions, just because you've got to start somewhere. And I will find that, as people see that I listen to their answers to those basic questions—we'll have five to ten minutes where I'm not saying anything—I think that immediately builds trust on their part, that I care.

"And they begin, I notice quite often, to get on a roll. . . . You know, you're asking me about *me*—hey, let's go, all right! Everybody loves to do that, talk about what's important to them. So the more I let them go on, the more head of steam they build up, almost as if a vibe has been created. An atmosphere is created by this talk. It's like their talk is money in a little bank—it starts adding up."

Only when Rozek has established a relationship of genuine trust does he delve into deeper, more intimate matters. "You move from the *when* questions and the *what* questions to the *why* questions," he explains. "And the *why* questions are perfectly appropriate because they've been confessing. So if someone's confessing—it always works if they're really confessing—they don't mind you saying, 'Why did you do that?' If you open up with, 'Why did you do that?' I notice people are very put off."

He places great value on his humane way of pursuing his craft, and usually his profiles result in a kind of collaborative satisfaction: "They begin to feel really complimented by the process, so that in the end we are close in a structural sense. We may not be close in a personal sense, but we are two people who did it together."

Remember three facts about human nature:

1. People love to talk about themselves to someone who seems genuinely interested.
2. If someone talks long enough, he or she will inevitably tell you something they didn't intend to tell you.
3. People have a strong natural aversion to long pauses in a conversation.

If you pause long enough, without even asking a question, they will usually talk to fill the silence. It would be discourteous to let the silence continue. They weren't raised to endure awkward pauses, so they will do their best to take responsibility for the conversation. This can draw out otherwise shy, reluctant subjects—especially after they've just given you a one-word answer.

This doesn't mean your aim is to trick people into telling you embarrassing secrets. But people are complex and wonderful creatures, and they rarely reveal the most telling truths about themselves to a person they have just met in the first five minutes of talk. Conversations tend to range naturally, and one of the things that makes writing interesting is the element of surprise. Your subject may be delighted to have remembered something, or to have said something in a new way, or to have finally revealed a bit of personal truth he himself can use. Of course, the person you're interviewing might also admit to the Kennedy assassination—oops. Here's where you get into that slough of situational ethics, the on-the-record-or-off debate (see chapter eleven, "Law and Ethics").

THE RELATIONSHIP BETWEEN INTERVIEWER AND SUBJECT

"One of the sad things about this craft, and Janet Malcolm put it most brutally, is that even when you're trying to be scrupulous, you know that you're likely to end up hurting people's feelings," says Ron Powers, a writer with a deep sense of morality who, like all conscientious writers, struggles with the constant tension between truth-telling and honoring the trust of individuals who have confided to him their secrets. "We take advantage of the trust of the people we interview, and they always assume that what they say is going to reflect well on them. They don't realize the self-revelations that come up in conversation."

Malcolm's book, *The Journalist and the Murderer*, examines the relationship of writer Joe McGinniss and Dr. Jeffrey MacDonald, convicted of murdering his wife and children—though MacDonald always has maintained his innocence. McGinniss was offered the chance to become part of the defense team in order to have access to all the inside details of the case for his book, which Dr. MacDonald and his lawyers hoped would publicly exonerate him. But in the course of the trial, McGinniss concluded that MacDonald was indeed guilty—and wrote it that way in *Fatal Vision*, which became a best-seller and a made-for-TV movie. MacDonald felt betrayed and sued him—not for libel, but for fraud. McGinniss, MacDonald claimed, had gotten intimate information under false pretenses—the pretenses of friendship and sympathy.

The case struck at the heart of the interviewer's relationship with his subject. As Malcolm relates the dramatic trial, political columnist William F. Buckley and former cop turned crime novelist Joseph Wambaugh both testified on McGinniss' behalf that it was common and accepted practice in the profession to mislead subjects to get information—though there was some disagreement about what constituted an ethically unacceptable "lie" and an "untruth" told merely to urge a subject to talk. In the end, the jury could reach no unanimous verdict but was leaning toward MacDonald, so outraged were some of the jurors about his treatment at the hands of the writer.

It was clear that many of the people involved in the trial, including jurors, had only the murkiest notion of how writers interview real people and what professional standards govern their behavior as interviewers and their use of the material learned in an interview. And unfortunately the writers who testified didn't throw much light on the matter.

To keep from having to go through the ordeal of a new trial, and without admitting any wrongdoing, McGinniss agreed to pay MacDonald—a man convicted of butchering a pregnant wife and two children—$325,000. Apparently, in the eyes of at least some readers, there are things more reprehensible than multiple murder.

Malcolm's remarkable and disturbing book opens: "Every journalist who is not too stupid or too full of himself to notice what is going on knows that what he does is morally indefensible. He is a kind of confidence man, preying on people's vanity, ignorance, or loneliness, gaining their trust and betraying them without remorse."

Strong words, and I know many writers who would disagree with them wholeheartedly. But, in a qualified way, Malcolm's point is well taken: The people we interview often expect us to tell *their* story, when in fact we are using them to help us tell *our* story. The two may dovetail nicely—but then again they may not.

Malcolm's cautionary tale is required reading for any writer who aspires to tell the truth about people as an interviewer, using their own words, especially since she herself was sued by an interview subject, psychoanalyst Jeffrey Masson, who claimed she had invented or doctored quotes for a controversial *New Yorker* article on Sigmund Freud. Lower courts dismissed the suit without ruling on the question of whether she had indeed put words in her subject's mouth, but an appeal survived all the way to the Supreme Court. According to a *Newsweek* exclusive, five major news organizations were asked to sign amicus curiae (friend of the court) briefs supporting Malcolm, but all refused—a signal of just how uncomfortable straight journalists are with any suggestion of writerly tampering.

"Interviewing is a transaction in which both sides want something," says Anne Matthews, who has written for *Forbes*, *The New York Times Magazine* and *The New Yorker*. "It's like snake-handling—the lure of danger is on both sides, and it's fun."

Especially in a long profile or a book about a life, the tension between interviewer and subject can be palpable: The subject wants something from the writer—notoriety, good publicity, vindication, a sense of importance, the relief of confession, or even the altruistic satisfaction of having told a helpful truth to someone who cares. And the writer obviously wants something—insight, information, the "true gen"—from the subject. The person being interviewed has no particular allegiance to the writer. Why should he? And the writer's true allegiance is to the story.

Should it be otherwise? Most writers I talked to say their first responsibility is to the truth of the story, yet many also say that, under some circumstances, they hedge that position out of decency, respect for privacy or friendship. In her book, even Malcolm admits this. It's a judgment call of the most troubling kind. But I am reassured whenever a writer has such a nettling conscience—it can moderate the worst excesses of ego and sharpen his or her sense of exactly what is necessary for the "truth" of the story.

It's not always right to tell everything you know, just for the sake of telling all.

It's the same situation true-crime writer Jerry Bledsoe, author of *Bitter Blood*, alludes to when he speaks about how eager the family members of murder victims are to talk to a writer, who, they believe earnestly—or perhaps it's only that they hope—will tell the whole truth and nothing but the truth, but the truth as they see it. The truth that will prove their point of view.

WHO SEES THE INTERVIEW BEFORE PUBLICATION?

One way around this thorny problem is to let your subject know how you will quote him—read quotes back to him over the phone. Some writers share the entire piece with the subject, especially if the subject is a close friend or family member. Other writers, particularly those pursuing stories with a controversial edge, are adamant about never showing the piece to the subject: Announcing how you intend to write about someone can lead to a nightmare scenario—the subject's lawyers move to block publication.

After he left office as Secretary of State, Henry Kissinger for a time guarded his privacy. Reiss was the first writer to be granted an interview—with the proviso that, prior to publication, Kissinger be allowed to review his quotes for accuracy. "Kissinger made a statement while we were walking between buildings and the tape recorder was off," Reiss recalls. "We were walking to the World Bank and he made a statement—a critical statement—about critics of the Vietnam War. And I remembered it word for word, and I knew I remembered it, and I wrote it down as soon as we got to the World Bank, and put it in the piece. And later Kissinger's guy called up and said, 'He didn't say that, and we want you to take it out.'

"And I said, 'He did say it.'

"And he said, 'No the agreement is, you have to take it out.'

"And I said, 'No, the agreement is, he was supposed to review this for accuracy, and you're telling me he didn't say something that he said, and I'm not taking it out.'"

Reiss and Kissinger's people argued back and forth. "What I really cared about was doing the right thing," Reiss says. "It's not what's on paper, it's not the agreement, you know, how you tricked anyone. It's doing the right thing in the end."

Finally, Kissinger's people admitted that he *had* made the remark in question, but objected to the wording—an inconsequential change, as far as Reiss was concerned, that did not affect the accuracy of the piece: "As happens in 95 percent of these cases, the change was a comma and a preposition, which for some reason in Kissinger's Machiavellian mind eliminated some sort of potential ludicrous error that he might have made, and which to me made the quote emotionally seem exactly the same, made them happy, and made me feel like I'd kept the thing."

But checking your piece for accuracy with the interviewee is not always practical if you've interviewed dozens of people over time, or if they are not easy to find again. By the time I had returned to the

States and begun writing my post-revolutionary Poland piece, there was no way to get in touch with all the people who had spoken into my notebooks. And even if I could, we did not share a common language—I was relying on my interpreter's version of what they had said in the first place. I trusted my interpreter—I had spent sixteen-hour days with him. And I trusted my notes. So I simply tried to be as accurate and fair as possible.

Even when it is practical to let your interviewee preview your piece, is it a good idea? The conventional wisdom among newspaper journalists is *never*—in fact, usually the rules they work under forbid it, though it is also standard practice to phone the subject of a story and read to him or her allegations or comments made by other sources, to solicit a fair reply. Informally, especially in less volatile stories and when a source seems to have misspoken, reporters sometimes call back interviewees to check important quotes for accuracy or clarification.

Such *New Yorker* notables as Joseph Mitchell (*Up in the Old Hotel and Other Stories*) writes about sharing proofs of profiles with the people he was writing about. Rozek considers this stage of the writing process essential, not only to the integrity of the finished piece, but to the relationship of trust between writer and subject: "First of all, this is *their* life, so this gets back to the first thing I said: Nonfiction is a sacred trust. This is not only their life to the rest of the world— so I have a responsibility to make sure the rest of the world is reading an accurate account of their life—but this is their life to *them*. And if I've worked with this person so much, and they know me, we've spent time, and I went ahead and didn't show this to them and got something wrong, I've ripped them off totally. It's just the most ridiculously unfair, unfeeling, wrong—morally wrong—thing to do. It's unforgivable. And it's done by journalists all the time."

What if the subject insists on changes, is that a problem? "Almost never," Rozek says. "They see by how I comport myself throughout this process the level of integrity that I'm bringing to the process. And they become very respectful of that—not of *me* as much, but of the *process*. They suddenly realize that the two of us are involved in something bigger than ourselves, which is the presentation of truth to the outside world."

If you're interviewing government officials, self-important people, or if your topic is fairly sensitive—and you'll always be surprised at what your interviewee finds sensitive—you may be asked to supply questions in advance. Go ahead. Give several fairly basic questions. In the actual interview, use follow-up questions. One way or another, get around to asking what you came to ask.

Occasionally, a subject is too eager. I once showed up with a video documentary crew to interview a bank official in Hong Kong. He greeted us by saying, "I didn't know what you were going to ask, so I took the liberty of typing up some answers." I thanked him and we politely asked all our own questions anyway.

THE TAPE RECORDER

Whenever the topic of interviewing comes up in my writing classes, students are always eager to know whether or not they should use a tape recorder. As I said, it's not a trivial question: It cuts to the heart of how we take human conversation—spoken fact—and turn it into an artful story without distortion. What they're really asking for is a basic definition of their relationship to their subjects and to the act of "creating" factual conversation—how we record the real words of actual people and how we represent them on the page. It's as much a question of philosophy as of practice.

The tape recorder offers the advantage of total accuracy. Using it, the writer can capture in the exact words of the subject the entire conversation, then transcribe it at leisure, picking and choosing the pithiest quotes. It can protect the writer from claims of libel and can make you a lot less nervous about quoting celebrities, statesmen, accused criminals, lawyers and anybody else who may later take issue with how you portray them in print.

The tape recorder can preserve the sound of the subject's voice, the inflection and tone, the audible attitude he brings to the answers. This can be extremely valuable if you're working on a long project, or if weeks or months will elapse between the interviewing and the writing, when memory will intrude its tricks upon your research.

But even a notebook can come between you and a candid interview, and one sure way to spook a shy subject is to waltz in and plunk down a tape recorder.

No matter how you record an interview, as a writer you always apply art to what the subject says—in Janet Malcolm's phrase, you owe it to the subject "to translate his speech into prose." In practice, this means interpreting extemporaneous speech into presentable language that does justice to the truth of what the subject is *trying* to say.

When the interview finds its way into your piece, it will make the transformation in pieces—selected, edited for sense, truncated, all out of the original order.

But, as near as you can make it so, *accurate*.

You listen. You record—in memory, on paper, on tape. Then you exercise your best story sense and fashion a piece of artistic truth, a true story. This requires sound judgment and the craft to capture truth in the exact words of another person—exact, but not entire and not verbatim. Not the whole truth, but at least nothing but the truth.

Because you're not a stenographer. You're a writer.

CHAPTER FIVE

ON ASSIGNMENT

P aris.
Autumn.
Late afternoon.

I'm sitting alone inside the Closerie des Lilas on the barstool where Ernest Hemingway used to write away the cold gray days with a stubby pencil he sharpened using a pocketknife. His name is engraved on a brass plaque screwed to the lacquered bartop. In front of me stands half a warming *pinte* of Alsatian lager, amber-colored, frothy, strong and bittersweet. I've been sipping it for twenty minutes or so.

If you were passing by and looking in on me, you would not say to yourself, "Now there's a writer hard at work!" You would figure I was one more American tourist hanging out in a café while his wife went shopping on the Champs Elysées.

But you would be wrong.

At that very moment, hunkered over a bar, I was also hunkered over a book, and I was about to make two useful discoveries—one of them trivial, the other profound.

First, the trivial discovery. All through *A Moveable Feast*, Hemingway refers to the statue of Michel Ney, a field marshal of Napoleon's army. Ney is one of those famous historical bit-players who show up in every dictionary of biography—next to his name is usually the ignominious, cryptic notation, "Napoleonic hero, executed for treason in 1815."

If you can figure out how a man chooses his heroes, you can learn something important about him. Maybe his statue would hold some clue—an inscription, a poem, an epitaph. I'd already looked up Ney in a history book: Fiercely loyal, physically courageous, and a daring leader in battle, he was Napoleon's right hand. He rallied to the emperor during the Hundred Days of his comeback reign and almost carried the day at Waterloo. Napoleon blamed him for losing the battle; the new government convicted him of high treason for standing with Napoleon in the first place and had him shot by firing squad. I had no idea where the statue was, or why Hemingway should be such an admirer of Ney.

Then I had to use the restroom, which, like many Turkish toilets in Paris, is in the basement. To get there, I had to pass by the window looking out onto the enclosed cloister (the *closerie*) where in warmer seasons patrons drank at marble-topped tables in the shade of hedges, then descend a flight of stairs. As I started down the steps, I turned. Out the window, looming over the hedge, I could glimpse a statue— an upraised arm with a saber. Could it be? I walked into the garden and got a closer look: *Maréchal Ney*, beyond the hedge, on the Montparnasse where it comes together in a triple intersection with the Boulevard St. Michel and the Rue Notre Dame des Champs, the street on which Hemingway lived in those lean days.

So when he was sitting here at an outdoor table, all he had to do was look up from his drink, and there was the hero-traitor. He had a lot of drinks on a lot of afternoons, and he must have come to regard Ney as just another regular. The statue, then, was not an icon but merely a neighborhood landmark—a small portent of the ironies of fame, perhaps, to a writer who as yet had published almost none of the stories that were to make him such a literary lion and then, when fashion turned, such a universal target of parody.

The second discovery: The book I was reading was *Paradis Perdu* (*Paradise Lost*), a collection of short stories in translation. The author's name was written the same way as on the bar plaque: E. Hemingway.

I'd picked up the paperback at a used book dealer who'd set up an outdoor table on the Montparnasse—an accidental find. I knew Hemingway's books had been translated into many languages, but it had never occurred to me to read him in translation. I revisited such stories as "Dans un Autre Pays" ("In Another Country") and "La Grande Riviere au Coeur Double" ("Big Two-Hearted River") and

"Un Endroit Propre et Bien Éclairé" ("A Clean, Well-Lighted Place").

The stories—like the titles themselves—read more naturally in the French. They didn't sound *translated*; the originals, by comparison, sounded translated.

I'd come to Paris to find the touchstones of Hemingway's mannered style, and here was an important one: living in a foreign city, a place of strict social codes, he had written these stories *as if he'd been translating them into English*. As if, like Joseph Conrad—who shared Hemingway's mentor at *Transatlantic Review*, Ford Madox Ford—he'd come to English only as a second language. The stories' minimalist quality, though the opposite of Conrad's lushly over-modified and circuitous sentences, shared a similar strangeness. A self-consciousness, as if the sentences had been labored over almost too formally. An essential foreign-ness.

I was learning something important now, which I never would have stumbled on had I not strolled down a boulevard in a foreign city looking for a certain café and, along the way, passed by a sidewalk bookseller's table.

That's the value of going on assignment: You find the things you know to look for and find out whether they matter as much as you thought. You also find things you weren't looking for—and those discoveries often turn out to be the crucial ones.

TIME-TRAVEL: CHASING FAMILIAR GHOSTS

The assignment can take you far afield geographically, and it can also remove the reader from the present and become a kind of time-travel.

To write *White Town Drowsing*, Ron Powers journeyed into the past, sojourning in his boyhood town of Hannibal, Missouri, for weeks at a time, walking its streets, visiting its churches and town meetings, talking to residents and visitors, reading the spirit of the town, coaxing out its nuances and testing them against his own memories, at a time when the town as he had known it was on the verge of vanishing into a theme park.

"I wanted the reader to inhabit Hannibal as I knew it as a child," he says, reminiscing on a Vermont porch miles and years away from the place that still tugs at his affections. "I wanted the reader to live there with me for awhile in the 1940s and 1950s. So that if I was good at what I did, if I made that habitation real, the reader would feel indignant along with me and feel a sense of accountability for what happened in 1985, when Mark Twain turned 150 and the town fathers invited all of the theme park experts, the guys dressed up in Mark Twain suits, to come in and mount the sesquicentennial."

Though he could have found the history he needed at the library and conducted all his interviews over the telephone, the soul of the book was born during the time he spent in Hannibal, breathing air redolent with past associations, feeling a gut suspicion about the new boosterism that was all hype and image and precious little substance. As often happens, *being there* triggered long-buried memories and allowed Powers to discover the governing metaphor for the experience, and the story: "In the case of the Hannibal book, it became the Mark Twain Bridge over the Mississippi, which started out as a concrete object in the opening paragraph and became at the end, in the last paragraph, a metaphor of my suspension between past and present—'It is on the bridge where I belong, perhaps, with my invisible father, watching the President cut a ribbon to let the future in.'"

A STRANGER COMES TO TOWN

Frequently, a successful piece of creative nonfiction is the result of a deliberate experience—going someplace specific to do something special, to talk to particular people and observe certain events, to discover a story out in the world and bring it back on the page: going on assignment.

Typically this means traveling to some far-off locale where the story lives—for a few hours, days, weeks, even months. And perhaps making several trips over time. It would seem that a writer coming to a new place would be the last person in the world to be a reliable expert on it—especially if the assignment is relatively brief. You'd think local knowledge, years of studied insight, would be more helpful than a quick immersion in a new scene. And sometimes that's certainly the case—Powers' account of the theme-parking of an American town would lack a crucial resonance were Hannibal not the town of his boyhood.

On the other hand, he *went away and came back*.

That's one of the truths meant by the old saw "Travel broadens." It's not just that dipping into other cultures and geographies opens the mind; whenever you leave a place and come back to it, the place has changed—and so have you. You gain a perspective, a sense of proportion and context, that is nearly impossible to have about a place you have never been far away from, in space or in time.

You become the outsider, the stranger coming to town. Returning home, perhaps, but seeing things in a whole new—often amazing— light.

Thomas Keneally, best known for the novel *Schindler's List*, which straddles the precarious, fascinating no-man's-land between fiction and fact, writes of a similar resonance he found in Colorado, far from his native Australia, while gathering material for his reflective travel memoir of the American Southwest, *The Place Where Souls Are Born: A Journey to the American Southwest*: "A town like Leadville was fed from the same immigrant impulses and dreams which made the Australian frontier town. To visit the Leadville Catholic church, a hushed environment in itself, doubly silent amidst the snow, is to step back into the church I knew as a child in Kempsey, New South Wales."

He continues, "There is for me therefore a sense of being both at home and abroad in a town like Leadville.... It is as if similar passions have run through the earth's crust and core and made an organic link between the two places."

On assignment, you are always the stranger coming to town. Bob Reiss, whose assignments have taken him onto every continent, says, "The first thing you go with is an attitude that says this place is *not* where you live. You're in another place with its own rules. And the more you fit in with those rules, the more you're going to be able to work."

The outsider can frequently notice things, discover insights, grasp truths that would never occur to people living among the routine camouflage of their own place—seeing what they expect to see, judging it from their narrow vantage point, experiencing it according to their personal routine. This is not a slam on "locals"—all of us are locals somewhere. And in our locale, whether it's New York City or Leadville, we tend to trudge along in the same rut, driving or walking the same streets, visiting the same restaurants and stores, invited to be guests in a select few homes among people who are mostly pretty much like ourselves.

But the writer on assignment becomes a kind of temporary expatriate, a spectator of lives in which he does not participate. He comes to the task not as an expert but as a witness—alert and conscientious, without loyalties or agendas—and in witnessing becomes expert enough to write honestly and knowingly. If he gains trust, it may be only provisional. The writer always remains on the margin of the party. If he makes friends, they may disappear when the story is done and the door closes on that episode and the writer goes on to a new assignment.

MAKING THE EXPERIENCE WORK IN TIME AND SPACE

Making the experience work is one good way of making sure the piece will work. In important ways, preparing for the experience parallels the prewriting stage of writing the piece itself, and sometimes how the experience unfolds can be a template for structuring the story that will come out of that experience.

We'll get into structure in much more detail in chapter nine, but it may be useful to get ahead of ourselves just a little here, since, while you're on assignment learning the story, it's impossible to postpone your intuition about how you will structure that story.

The two simplest templates, just as in fiction, are based on time and space: a chronological "diary" of the experience—what happens first, second, third, etc., as the writer pursues the experience; or an account of a journey as it unfolds through space—the train stops here, then there, then at the next place.

John Steinbeck's *The Log From the Sea of Cortez* is exactly that—a logbook, a kind of ship's diary, a travelogue the reader can follow on a calendar and a map. So is his *Travels With Charley*, an American quest aboard Rocinante, a truck named, not accidentally, for the horse that carried Don Quixote off to tilt at windmills.

Richard Shelton's elegant memoir, *Going Back to Bisbee*, is structured around a simple drive between Tucson and Bisbee, Arizona, the mining town where he settled after leaving the army and where he fell in love with the Sonora desert, which helped form his aesthetic and provided him a subject emotionally complex enough to inspire a lifetime of poetry.

Sometimes the template is time or space, but not explicitly expressed as such.

In the case of the Hemingway piece, the template turned out to be an episodic journey, told out of order in a literal sense but moving in a figurative way further and further into the past, each part anchored in a specific place he had frequented, beginning with the resumé of the missing author—a kind of verbal wanted poster: "He has been called, variously, a man's man, an incorrigible bully, a natural genius, a hack with a great editor, a shameless adventurer, a repressed homosexual, a homophobic womanizer, a great liar, a real-life hero, and the father of the modern American novel. . . . Who was this premier American novelist—a career expatriate who almost never wrote about America?"

And ending with an imagined encounter with him at Harry's New York Bar: "I imagine he'd knock me down with a right cross, then give me a firm hand up, buy me another scotch, and tell me a tall story of war and love and older ghosts."

Because by then I felt I really had tracked him down. He'd gotten under my skin and joined me in the eternal present tense of stories. Except for a few superficial details—the style of overcoats worn by the men at the bar, the date on the front page of the *International Herald Tribune* hanging on a rod in the window—inside Harry's that night it could have been 1922.

But you can never be sure in advance what the structure of the finished piece will be, though sometimes you can make a pretty good guess. The most reliable way to ensure the integrity of the structure of the piece is to do your best to ensure the integrity of the experience, listening as the experience tells you how to tell the story. You can't wall yourself off from the milieu you're investigating, or your experience will be false. At the same time, you must reserve a private sanctuary—even if it's only a hotel room, a tent or a sleeping car—in which to catch your breath, record your impressions and regroup for tomorrow's sortie.

COMING UP WITH AN ASSIGNMENT

Mostly writers create their own assignments and then talk an editor into bankrolling the experience, which is how I got to Paris.

The big glossies will pay reasonable expenses, along with a fee for the finished piece, all negotiated in advance—and a kill fee, usually up to 25 percent of the story fee, in case the magazine can't use the finished piece, even though the writer has delivered. But smaller magazines don't operate on the same scale. An editor may offer you a single fee and expect you to be able to cover your expenses out of it.

And literary quarterlies pay little or nothing. If you're an unknown quantity to an editor, he or she may agree to look at your finished piece "on spec," that is: "You write it and we'll take a look at it, but no promises."

You have to be honest about why you are writing a piece, how badly you want to go on assignment to learn what you need to know, whether you are expecting an immediate payoff in the form of a short, publishable piece, or just laying the groundwork for a longer work that may be years in the making, that may indeed never see the light of day. And then you have to be resourceful about getting there—making use of frequent flyer miles, a friend's vacant apartment, a cooperative government agency that will let you ride along in its van or helicopter, family or college connections, a grant from a foundation or local arts council, whatever it takes to get you on the ground to do your work.

Michael Pearson, comparing his situation as a nonfiction writer to that of John McPhee, whose projects are supported by *The New Yorker*, observes that, like many other less famous writers, he knows the tension of gambling time and money on a project that may or may not work. Unable to commit to long-term assignments, such writers must make do with "brief forays into the world and with writing memoir," what he calls a mix of "guerrilla warfare and narcissism."

Sometimes an editor will approach a writer whose style he admires and broach an idea for an assignment. Editor Lisa Bain, who over the years has commissioned hundreds of pieces first for *Esquire* and now for *Glamour*, says, "Part of the process when we have an idea is really trying to find somebody whose skills will match it. Is reporting the big thing? Is voice the big thing? I mean, we really have to figure out what it is that we're looking for and how do we match it up."

She cites by way of example a piece she has been developing under the working title "Inside the Mind of a Rapist" and her choice of Stephen Fried to write it. "I wanted a piece that really got inside the mind of somebody who isn't an acquaintance-rapist but is an actual stranger-rapist. I wanted somebody who could write—not in the other person's voice, but really get inside somebody's head. And I needed somebody who was a good reporter—because he had to find the guy. And it was something that was going to be very heavy on style. I mean, I didn't want it to read like a newspaper. I wanted it to be very vivid and alive."

Like other editors who are always on the lookout for interesting writers in regional magazines, she had followed Fried's work in *Philadelphia Magazine* and later in *GQ* and had already been developing a professional relationship with him, figuring that sooner or later the right project would come along. This one seemed a perfect fit.

While most magazine assignments don't turn into literature, notice how high Bain has set her expectations: In conceiving the piece and trying to match it to the ideal writer, she is creating at least the chance for it to go beyond journalism into something more lasting and timeless. The rest depends on execution. It's like matchmaking a romance—there's no guarantee it will result in true love. All you can do is set passion loose in a promising arena.

ON YOUR OWN HOOK

Plenty of times the writer goes on assignment without any editor waiting to receive the finished piece, without any guarantee of recouping expenses or seeing the thing in print someday. Sometimes it's because the writer is just starting out. Ted Conover wrote his first book, *Rolling Nowhere*, without a contract but with a passion to follow the hobo railroad and see where it led. Other times, the writer just wants to see how the piece will turn out, whether it forms itself into an essay or a whole book. Novelists and poets who turn to creative nonfiction are used to writing first and worrying about what to do with the literary product later. Or the writer simply may not want the pressure of a deadline.

"I've done it all three ways, and it really depends on the piece," says essayist David Bain, whose passion is often rooted in "the unpredictable consequences of national acts"—a phrase he borrows from political historian Sir Herbert Butterfield. "I've done things by proposal. I've gone in and talked and worked on shaping something, if I trusted the editor. And just last spring I interrupted everything I was working on because I had to write an essay about an unrequited love affair with a two-hundred-year-old abandoned house."

The house, in Barnard, Vermont, once owned by Sinclair Lewis and Dorothy Thompson, had burned down, but it found new life in Bain's essay of ninety-one pages—a length that he admits makes the piece practically unpublishable in a magazine. "But," he says, "I had to get it done."

Passion again. Unpredictable, not always practical, but always essential.

If the assignment is self-imposed, the writer must ask two questions: Can I write this story? Can I afford to do it right?

The first is a question of access and ability. The second is about costs: time, money, danger, emotional investment. How much are you willing to risk? Whenever you go on assignment, there's a small stirring of terror in the pit of your stomach—you're venturing into unknown territory, and you're putting yourself on the line: Will you be able to find the story? There are no guarantees.

If the assignment comes from an editor, the writer has to answer a third question: Do I *want* to do it?

Life is too short to be thrashing around in places where you'd rather not be talking to people you can't wait to get away from about subjects that bore you catatonic.

EXPLORING YOUR OWN BACKYARD

David Bain is a native New Yorker who deliberately left the big city behind to live in the Vermont countryside, and his passion for an old house in his adopted state raises an important point: Going "on assignment" may mean going next door, or a few miles down the road. It may mean not leaving home at all—the physical dislocation is a way of altering perspective, and that perspective may be altered right at home.

Elizabeth Marshall Thomas writes about her home town of Cambridge, Massachusetts, in *The Hidden Life of Dogs*. But what she's really doing is exploring familiar territory through the eyes of Misha, a Siberian husky she volunteered to care for while his owners were in Europe. Curious about where Misha roamed, how he eluded danger and dogcatchers, she began to follow him two or three nights a week—and continued to do so for three years.

"Who could resist the appeal of this notion?" she writes. "No money, no travel, no training, no special instruments were necessary to probe the mystery—one needed only a dog, a notebook and a pencil." Following Misha's lead, she discovered a Cambridge she had never seen before—Cambridge viewed through the eyes of a roving dog. Like any good writer, she was able to infiltrate another perspective and so enlarge her own. She learned how Misha navigated past human and natural obstacles, jaywalking safely across busy streets to avoid complicated intersections, bypassing bigger dogs by ruse and feint, finding food and shelter in unlikely places.

Misha's map of Cambridge was very different from Thomas', and it was populated by an extensive circle of friends, human and canine. Her curiosity turned to passion about the astonishingly complex inner life of Misha and his canine companions—their emotions, their personal attachments, even their morals.

Maxine Kumin's blurb for the book is instructive: "The thought of her pedaling out at night through the back streets of Cambridge keeping track of her dog is so delicious visually and emotionally that it makes me rejoice in her art and her pragmatism." Art *and* pragmatism. Doing the practical work to make beautiful sentences happen on the page.

Try Thomas' approach yourself. Tour your backyard with a botanist. Patrol your town in the shotgun seat of a police cruiser. Explore your campus as if you were wheelchair-bound. Make the rounds of local restaurant kitchens with a health inspector. Spend twenty-four hours in your hometown—outdoors. See the familiar through a new lens.

It's not just *being there* that counts; it's your attitude about being there. One of my students who had suffered a traumatic riding accident had vivid, nightmarish memories of the hospital emergency room. Now recovered, she revisited the ER on assignment and wrote a fine, reflective piece on the way the whole place was divided into lines—organized into zones of access, lines that could be crossed only with certain credentials. On her previous visit, naturally, she had been too preoccupied with her own pain, too concerned with getting attention to her problem, to notice the larger, organizing metaphor.

ATTITUDE—LISTENING TO THE STORY

Attitude—an assignment always turns on attitude.

A big part of that attitude is being willing to listen to your story develop. If you've got definite expectations, if you've prejudged the world you're entering before you enter it, you're liable to miss the point. A number of writers I interviewed say they will often force themselves *not* to write anything in the first hours or days of their assignment—they just want to pay attention, get the feel of the place, let it work on them. They want to leave themselves open to a leisurely first impression, remain alert to subtleties, not jump to conclusions.

As Steinbeck reminds us in his opening to *Travels With Charley*, "A journey is a person in itself; no two are alike. And all plans, safeguards, policing, and coercion are fruitless. We find after years of struggle that we do not take a trip; a trip takes us. Tour masters, schedules, reservations, brassbound and inevitable, dash themselves to wreckage on the personality of the trip. ... In this a journey is like marriage. The certain way to be wrong is to think you control it."

Not every assignment turns into *Deliverance*, but most assignments go in surprising directions. Interviews evaporate. The visa you expected to get is, at the last minute, denied. What seemed fascinating a thousand miles away in your den turns out to be boring up close. Warring parties make peace. The rainy season comes early and you can't get to the interior for six more months. The trains go on strike.

You lose access to the person you meant to focus on.

When Gay Talese set out for Beverly Hills to do a piece on Frank Sinatra, he expected to be granted an interview. But Sinatra had a cold—no small matter for a singer—and wouldn't talk to him, so Talese was forced to find his story elsewhere. For six weeks he followed Sinatra from movie set to recording studio to nightclub, interviewing the people in his entourage, and came up with a telling, multifaceted portrait, a departure from the usual celebrity profile, called "Frank Sinatra Has a Cold." In his introduction to *Fame and Obscurity, Portraits*, in which the piece is reprinted, Talese writes, "I gained more by watching him, overhearing him, and watching the reactions of those around him than if I had actually been able to sit down and talk to him."

Reiss once had a similar problem with access to singer Linda Ronstadt and shifted his focus onto fans so obsessed they waited hours for an autograph or fought security guards to fling bouquets onto the stage while she played. The piece was chosen for the *Best of the Washington Post* collection.

It's exactly the unexpected, the thing you never counted on, the problem that inspires an inventive solution, that can carry a fairly predictable piece to a new level.

"I realize I sound like I know what I'm talking about in these stories," Reiss is quick to point out. "But these stories came out of the most profound sense of panic—they didn't come out of some cool, collected knowledge. In each case, I was desperate and convinced that the story was never going to work out, and just beside myself trying to figure out how, how can I conceivably pull this thing out of the fire?" Other writers echo his sentiment.

THE LAST THING

And then there's The Last Thing. It may be a phone call you've been putting off to double-check a fact. It may be having a nightcap with a local source. It may be visiting one more shrine, ruin, archive or monument. It may be taking one last stroll through the hotel garden.

It's the one last trivial piece of unfinished business, and it would be easy to avoid. But you make the call. You do the last thing.

In Paris, the last thing was pleasant: a return to the Closerie des Lilas, this time on a warm afternoon, to sit outdoors and contemplate the statue of Marshal Ney over the hedges. In Poland, the last thing was harder. I returned to the Grand Orbis Hotel in Warsaw the night before my flight home, having not slept in a bed for two nights running. I had never been more exhausted. But I went downstairs to the lobby bar and interviewed the German businessmen accumulating there—they were investors, the new hope of Poland, I had been told, and the new enemy. I needed their side of things.

Or I thought that was the last thing. The real last thing turned out to be a trip I made on my return—to Ellis Island, the old immigration port in New York Harbor. On the second floor of the great hall is an astonishing exhibit of actual *things* brought to the New World by immigrants like my Russian and Polish grandfathers: a lacy wedding dress, a potato-bug mandolin, a meerschaum pipe, a silver crucifix, a baptismal certificate, a carpenter's plane, an ivory comb, a key to the front door of a house.

A key. That was the end of the story. They had come across the ocean to stay, but they'd brought along a key to the house they'd left behind, clean and locked.

Because someday, years into an impossible future, one of their children's children's children—the old language lost, a strange new language in his mouth, a tribal memory of a distant land in his blood—would go home.

On assignment.

And write the story.

CHAPTER SIX

WHAT FORM
WILL IT TAKE?

So now you're ready to write.

You've crawled through the library stacks, carried out midnight raids on the Internet when the tourists had all pulled off the information superhighway; you've tracked down fascinating people and interviewed them till they said extraordinary things; you've got full notebooks, legibly kept, dated and labeled; your memory is crammed with images, sounds, smells, recollections of places and people's faces and odd remarks made in passing; you've gone wherever the story lives as often as you had to to get it right; you've reflected on what it all means and who you are to be writing it and what caught your passion in the first place; and now you're hungry to get it down on paper.

You've done all the parts that weren't the writing but that were crucial to the writing, and now you have to do the hardest part, the only part that ultimately matters: the writing. It's time to plant yourself in a chair and tell the story you found out.

What form will it take?

Probably you have either made an arrangement with an editor or you have envisioned the form before you ever started on the research—at least in a general, vaguely realized way, you knew the piece was going to be approximately so long, focused in a particular way, and addressed to a certain kind of reader.

If you were lucky, even as you were learning what you needed to know and meditating on what you discovered, the piece started to form itself in your imagination—you were *listening* to the story, putting aside your preconceptions, allowing the interesting facts you found out to nudge you toward the shape of the piece. Possibly you had already begun making notes toward the finished piece; more likely it was working on you subconsciously by a kind of osmotic process—a "soaking up" of your milieu. You began seeing connections, episodes, an arresting image to open on, or the punchline of an interview that would close the piece and send it soaring.

In other words, you've been conceiving of it structurally, which is related to form but is different. The *form* is the larger shape of the piece—the boundaries, if you will—and the special requirements of that shape. The *structure*, which we'll consider more fully in chapters seven to nine, is the internal arrangement by which you satisfy the demands of form.

Form is a slippery word. So is *genre*. Both are used loosely in several ways, sometimes interchangeably. Strictly speaking, creative nonfiction is a literary *genre* distinct from poetry, fiction and drama. Within the literary genres, there are subgenres, also referred to as *forms*, as in the *long form* and the *short form*.

In fiction, the long form would be the novel; the short forms would include the short story, the sketch and the short-short. The novella would occupy the intermediate ground.

Likewise, in nonfiction the long form is the book, and the short forms include the article and the essay. These can be broken down further into sub-subgenres—kinds of books, articles or essays. At any level, we talk about subgenres simply as genres. Don't let the terms confuse you. They're just ways of breaking down the big sprawling category "nonfiction" into workable smaller categories, some of them more limiting than others.

The categories are never as absolute as textbook writers would have you believe, and sensible people disagree about exactly how many there are and what defines each one; they are conveniences that make it possible to talk about differences. They weren't invented by an international convention but rather evolved out of long practice—writers and editors trying things and staying with the ones that seemed to work, tinkering and fine-tuning them.

That means they will keep evolving, which is fine, and that every really good piece of nonfiction will stretch the boundaries of whatever genre it falls into.

If you balk at writing to satisfy formal constraints, believing that only absolute freedom of length, subject and structure is necessary to produce art, you'll find yourself at odds with most of the greatest writers who ever lived. Limitations are common in all art forms: Sculpture is limited by physical material, painting by surface, music by the capability of instruments. Drama is often limited by human nature (how long will people sit still to watch this?) and economics (how much will it cost to produce the play?).

Limitations can force the writer to be more inventive, more economical with language, more intense in focus.

Before we go any further with this, realize that while it's convenient to talk about these matters in this book as if they happen in discrete, orderly stages, in real life things tend to happen out of order: We get an idea, we do some research in the library or have a chance encounter that turns into an interview, we talk to an editor who helps shape the idea, we go someplace to really find out the facts and wind up finding out things we never anticipated, we do more interviews, and the people we talk to send us back to the library, and the whole thing starts to find a context in something that happened on a family trip we took when we were six years old but forgot until now, and so on. We backtrack, follow leads that turn into blind alleys, re-interview, revisit, rethink. Tear it up and start over.

But since, at the moment, you're not writing but instead reading this book, it's useful to pretend as if we have arrived here methodically, and to consider these points one at a time at leisure, without the pressure of a deadline.

Just leaven all your expectations, all your ambitions for the piece, with the reality that writing is an inefficient business. You can rarely go in a straight line from here to there, doing everything exactly according to plan. That doesn't mean you don't want to plan—only that you have to be prepared for what happens when careful plans get mangled by real life. It's like Steinbeck's notion of a journey, which takes *you* more than you take *it*. The best you can hope for is to organize your facts and try to relate them always to the central passion, the organizing principle of the piece.

So in reality you will have been asking the question from the beginning: What form will it take? The simple answer can be gotten by asking three fairly obvious questions:

1. Will it be short or long?
2. Where will your audience encounter your words?
3. What is the subject—the apparent subject, the deeper subject?

THE LONG FORM

If the piece is going to go long—about 25,000 words or longer (one hundred pages and up)—you're really talking about a book. In unusual circumstances, a magazine will publish such a piece in one chunk (John Hersey's *Hiroshima*, for instance, narrating the atomic bombing of Japan in 1945, was first published in its entirety in a single issue of *The New Yorker* magazine) or in several installments (*The New Yorker* again, with John McPhee's work, including my personal favorite, his Alaskan odyssey, *Coming Into the Country*).

So the answer to question #1 above actually helps to answer question #2: Since it will be a book-length piece, your reader will find your work between covers on a bookstore or library shelf.

The form it will take, then, is a nonfiction book, with possible serial publication.

Whether you think of your nonfiction book as belonging to a (sub-) genre or not, as a practical matter your publisher will almost automatically consider your book in terms of its genre. "It's the curse of the computerized inventory," says independent bookseller David Bristol, who owns Bristol Books (two stores). "Every book has three little letters that tell us exactly where to find it," he adds, referring to the category code by which Bristol Books keeps track of its twenty thousand titles, 30-40 percent of which are nonfiction. "For any book, the publisher gives you a list of four categories—the audiences they think will enjoy it. Then when it gets here, we sort of decide where it fits best."

Standard publishers' categories include Literary Criticism/Literature; Studies, broken down into Women's, Men's, African American and Native American; Current Events/Politics; History, broken down into American, World and Military; Psychology/New Age; Self-Help; Autobiography/Biography; Philosophy and Religion; Nature; and Travel.

These categories or genres are organizational conveniences that implicitly define audience expectations. A bookstore may break them down even further to appeal to specialized or local interests—adding Southern History, for example.

Visit several bookstores and you'll see what I mean. Make a list of all the categories you find and compare them. This will give you as exact an idea as you need about the established niches in nonfiction publishing. You may find, too, that all those books that are hard to classify wind up under the heading "literary nonfiction" or "creative nonfiction."

Your publisher has to figure out not only who is likely be interested in reading your book but how to pitch it to booksellers so *they* can talk about it to customers, and how to describe it in the publisher's catalog in a way that will arouse interest. The sales reps require a shorthand way to talk about your book in the very brief time (seconds—minutes, if you're lucky) they will have to do so.

These categories within the long form "book" are largely based on subject matter and *usually make no distinction based on literary merit*. So Edmund Morris' masterful *The Rise of Theodore Roosevelt* will be lumped in with the latest gossipy exposé of a matinee idol. Hersey's *Hiroshima* is often found under "Military History," along with the pragmatic *Enlisted Soldier's Guide*.

But such designations do carry with them at least general expectations: A reader expects a biography to offer a fairly thorough and interesting version of a famous life, including surprising facts not generally known; the reader may even expect a standard cradle-to-grave chronology—you don't have to write it that way, and most first-rate biographers know that stories are rarely best told chronologically, but you have to answer the expectation somehow. (Some biographers offer an abbreviated chronology separate from the body of the text.) Likewise, the reader will expect a travel book to take him someplace special and show it to him in convincing "insider" detail unavailable to the ordinary tourist.

It is in "answering these expectations somehow" that craft rises to art.

To learn what these expectations are—since there are too many categories to go into here—spend some time in bookstores. Pay attention to the way books are organized. Ask yourself what seemingly disparate titles have in common that they should be placed together on the same shelf. Put yourself in the reader's place: What is he expecting?

The genre designation reassures the reader that he is on familiar ground, and once the writer has met the reader on that ground by satisfying the apparent conventions, he or she is free to challenge the reader, to explore and create within that framework.

These are relatively easy expectations to meet, given the leisurely limitations of the book form. The genre designation, reinforced by the title (and often a subtitle) make a kind of promise to the reader about what he or she will find between the covers. The more specific or ambitious the promise, the greater the demand on the writer to make good on it, and the more limited the writer is in straying into other territory: *How to Turn $5 Into $5 Million* (a title I just made up) nails the writer to a very narrow promise, allowing precious little wiggle room.

And because it promises a formula to guarantee a specific outcome—like a cookbook or a shop manual for a used car—it is unlikely to provide either the raw material or the opportunity for art to happen on the page. But notice that even such a mundane title teases the reader: Inside these covers, it says, there's a valuable secret.

All book titles are come-ons.

The subtitle can be one strategy for broadening the reader's expectations right up front (literally), claiming the right to a large territory. Richard Hawley's thought-provoking *Boys Will Be Men* carries such a subtitle: *Masculinity in Troubled Times*. We know we are in for a book about male issues, though we don't know the specific context or narrative. It turns out to be a headmaster's eloquent memoir about boys he has taught at a private school in Cleveland, enlarged by his own wise reflections on the difficulties boys face maturing into good men.

An intriguing subtitle can open up the possibilities of what the reader will encounter in the book, reinforcing the subject but also allowing the writer range.

In fiction, referring to a book as a "genre" novel may be considered insulting to its literary merit. Serious writers often resist being dismissed as "mystery writers" or "historical novelists." Either they want to claim importance for their genre ("Writing mysteries is an art form that few can do well"), or else they want to escape the pigeonhole altogether ("A good mystery novel is a good novel, period").

Fortunately for nonfiction writers, no particular literary onus seems to attach to most genre categories, with the possible exceptions of "True Crime" and "Self-Help." A book that shows staying power, some core of style or wisdom that raises it above the general run of the genre, can jump categories.

"Current Events" carries a different liability. "Current Events has a lifespan of about two weeks," Bristol says, a life determined by promotion on talk shows and other media.

But genre remains largely a marketing convenience for publishers rather than an artistic concern for writers. The good travel writers I know, for example, are happy to have their books appear in the travel section, but are equally content when their books turn up on the nature or political science rack. The merit of their work—as lasting literature or quick throwaway reads—doesn't really depend on their genres. For nonfiction books, the genre is very blatantly a subject category, and that means it is always somewhat fuzzy—does a biography of Jesus belong in the biography section, or with the other more doctrinaire books about Jesus in the religion section?

Some bookstores recognize "Literary Nonfiction" as a commercial category, though their definition is narrower than mine, and they will frequently shelve even very literary books by subject category. But all good books of creative nonfiction transcend any particular genre. They have to, by definition. Since each, as we discussed earlier, has an apparent subject and a deeper one, it will cross into at least two genres. But more important, it will reflect a large imagination, delving into diverse corners of human experience, uncontainable by any categorical designation.

Rather than spend your time and emotional capital arguing that your book is one of those rare publication events that renders genres archaic, the most useful thing you can do is to pretend it fits a genre and spend a little time meditating on which one it fits best. Not a lot of time. Keep it far to the back of your mind while you're writing, and discuss it with the publisher when the time comes, so you'll understand how the sales reps plan to market it and you'll be able to offer suggestions. But if you're passionate and serious, you're going to write the book you're going to write, regardless of categories, and worry about pigeonholing it later.

The amateur writer often makes the mistake of proceeding backward—first casting the movie of his book, then imagining the terms of the movie deal, the paperback deal, the hardback deal, the reviews, the dust jacket blurbs, the design of the cover, the title and so on, and only then turning to the work of actually writing the book. Cocktail parties all over America are swarming with wannabes who are "working on a book"—by talking about it, daydreaming about it, fantasizing the celebrity it will bring them, doing everything except attending to that one niggling detail: *writing* it.

The book comes first.

BUT WHAT'S IT ABOUT?

There is one way that working backward can help you in the actual process of creating book-length nonfiction: It can help you decide what the book is really about. Imagine yourself sitting all alone in a bookstore behind a table stacked with newly printed copies of your book, as a timid prospective reader approaches, hefts a copy in her hand, riffles through the pages checking for clues, and asks warily, "What's it about?"

The best, truest answer to that question I've ever heard came from an old literature professor of mine who said, "It's about everything I've learned in my whole life. It's everything I know."

But of course that answer won't do. Just as it won't do for you to become indignant and claim that your book is *literature* and literature can't be summed up in a glib sentence and how dare this reader suppose that it can be and. . . .

The question is an honest one—and important. The reader is about to fork out $21.95 for your book and is trying to decide what she'll get for her money. She'll pay attention to the flap copy, the subtitle, the category stamped on the spine by the publisher, trying to decide if your book will offer her an exciting and thought-provoking experience, rather than one that will upset her stomach or bore her. Will it tell her what she wants to know?

But the question is even more important to you, the writer. You should be formulating your answer to that inquisitive, skittish reader with every chapter, every sentence, as you write it. Every morning when you sit down at your writing table, ask yourself: What is this book about?

Whenever you get bogged down, leave the trail, find yourself blocked, offtrack, at a loss for what comes next, ask that question. Refocus yourself.

I am fond of telling my students that every great book can be described in a short sentence. They find this absurd. What about the *Odyssey*, they ask?

"Guy comes home from work," I say. They all laugh, but it's true: Odysseus is a warrior by trade. His army has finally won a ten-year-long war with Troy, and it's time to go home. He longs for his wife. After another ten years of harrowing adventures, he arrives home just in the nick of time: Suitors have sacked his estate and are about to ravage his wife, Penelope. He declares his true identity ("Hi, honey— I'm home"), slaughters the suitors, takes Penelope in his arms, and they live happily ever after, more or less.

I am always deliberately flip in explaining this to make a point: It is not the great writers but the amateurs who hide behind a gauze of complexity, whose writing is deliberately difficult and unnecessarily obscure. Who over-intellectualize, who indulge themselves in every fancy that occurs to them, who make the reader work way too hard for far too little. The *art* of the craft of writing is to make it seem effortless, transparent as window glass, to make the difficult look easy. That's why a good writer labors over sentences, rewriting them again and again—to make the sentence read elegantly, easily, clearly, and in a way that lends forward movement to the piece (more about this in chapters to come).

The writer labors so the reader won't have to.

And every book I've mentioned so far has at its core a strong, simple narrative or thematic line. That doesn't mean any of them lack complexity or nuance, or that in some other way they are simple-minded. On the contrary, it is precisely that straightforward line that makes all the other intricacies of the writer's vision possible: metaphor, resonant truth, humor, wordplay, irony, counterpoint in plot and point of view, the exploration of large and complex ideas and all the rest—describing isn't the same as summing up.

All the fantastic adventures Odysseus and his crew endure—from Cyclops to the Sirens—relate always to the central, driving passion of the hero: to get home to his wife.

Moby Dick? A sea captain chases a monster white whale. That's why many readers skip the tedious whaling industry chapters in the middle of the book—they interrupt the obsessive chase after the white leviathan.

Huckleberry Finn? A white boy and a black man go down the Mississippi on a raft toward freedom. From time to time Huck and Jim leave the raft and have adventures ashore, but occasionally they stray too far from the raft, and the story starts to unravel. Whenever this happens, Twain—a writer who knew how to keep an audience— always hurries them back to the river. His book is about racism, boyhood, romance, coming of age, double standards, moral paradoxes, the meaning of civilization itself, but he gets us there through the simplest, most compelling device he can manage: a float trip down the river.

It works for books of nonfiction that tell a single story, too, even when that story has lots of real-life characters in it, moves from place to place, and addresses complex issues (not essay collections, which by their nature are usually disjointed—but we'll get to those).

Ted Conover's *Rolling Nowhere*? A young man deliberately becomes a hobo to find out what it's like. Steinbeck's *Travels With Charley*? A successful writer who feels a bit out of touch drives around America with his dog to find out who these "Americans" really are.

This takes us all the way back to asking the question that got you started (chapter two), defining the subject, focusing your interest— and by extension your reader's.

While it is rare (though not unheard of) to sell a novel based on a proposal, it is routine in the world of nonfiction book publishing. In this sense, the use of genres helps the writer, because the publisher can use the genre designation, the pure subject interest, to gamble on buying a book before it is written—which typically means paying half the advance-against-royalties on signing, with the other half due upon acceptance of the finished manuscript. A successful nonfiction book editor is successful in large part because he or she already has a pretty reliable sense of what the audience is for books about certain subjects.

Some books depend on good timing. An analysis of the Gulf War or the Clinton campaign, however well written, will cease to be "hot" as the event fades from the headlines and the public memory—the curse of "Current Events." Other topical events—usually those with a public mystery at their core—have a longer shelf-life: the Kennedy assassination, the Lindbergh baby kidnapping, the disappearance of Amelia Earhart.

Other books depend on a new approach to an old subject, connecting several subjects that aren't apparently connected, or in some way offering original insight that elevates personal experience and ordinary events to the level of general interest.

Books about people usually depend on who those people are: Harry Truman, Robert E. Lee, Amelia Earhart, P.T. Barnum, Frederick Douglass, or some obscure figure who will not remain obscure once your book makes the case for the importance of his or her life—a harder sell, and one that may require the entire manuscript.

And the way you get a book editor to back your project is to answer for him or her the question of what it's going to be about, the future tense of the question the wary reader will ask later. In both cases you're trying to communicate your passion—to make it first the editor's, then the reader's. A book editor may want more up front than a magazine editor—after all, a book is a greater investment for everybody concerned: a proposal of twenty pages instead of two; an extended face-to-face conversation instead of a telephone call; published evidence of your ability to write convincingly and see it through—but the principle is the same. You're offering a promise—an approach, a narrative line, a strong, defining focus.

You're answering question #3: What is the subject?

THE SHORT FORM

A short piece—500 to 6,000 words (two to twenty-four double-spaced manuscript pages)—cannot ordinarily be published all by itself. It will almost certainly appear in a magazine or literary journal—if it is published—and so will have to be consistent with the format and expectations of the particular journal. It will be a magazine piece. (Alert readers will have noticed a gap of several thousand words between the short and long forms. We'll get to the in-between forms later.)

It may even have to fit into a particular "department" in a magazine—the "My Turn" department in *Newsweek*, for instance, which always occupies a single page and addresses some issue of pressing topical interest. It will also probably fit more or less into one of the established subgenres of magazine writing: expository article, how-to article, nature piece, science or technology piece, review, essay of ideas, issues piece, public event narrative, political analysis, investigative exposé, personality profile, arranged interview, personal essay, memoir or adventure narrative.

You've answered question #1: The piece will be in the short form. And question #2: Your reader will encounter it in a magazine, and you know at least what sort of magazine, if not the actual one. Again, subgenres are not the same as formulas, and a good piece will overlap categories, though it will probably be more one thing than another. The subgenre—the specific kind of piece you write—will be determined by a combination of three factors: the subject (question #3 above), your approach to it, and the magazine's format, including the style it favors.

Again, all this talk about genres and subgenres makes it sound as if writing creative nonfiction is a paint-by-numbers enterprise, and it is anything but that. Because of the practical necessities of publishing, though, you should be aware that, to be successful, your piece has to somehow make it out into the world where your reader can find it. Editors must be able to figure out where it fits into their formats— they can't go reinventing the magazine every week or month, and space is limited. They know the kind of people who subscribe, and they can't afford *not* to be aware of their audience. Everything I have to say about genres is observation, not prescription. Just pay attention to how a piece gets from your imagination to the reader's.

In-flight magazines such as *American Way, US Air Magazine* and *Aboard*, for example, publish lots of reasonably short (around 2,500 words) "destination pieces"—tourist-oriented features on cities to which the airline flies. They're apt to be light, noncontroversial and upbeat. There's nothing wrong with this—airline passengers experience enough anxiety already without being troubled or outraged by what they are reading while captive at thirty-five thousand feet. But it can limit your range as a writer and make it hard to move beyond formula into "creative" nonfiction—the flip side of the relationship between limitations and art.

A writer I know did a piece on rafting the Colorado river for an in-flight magazine. She beautifully described the breathtaking landscape, portrayed convincingly the passion and independent spirit of the "river rats," as well as the various personalities of the passengers, and vividly captured the essence of the experience. It was much better than the typical feature. But she had one problem: In the course of her trip, one of the river guides was killed. In a wrenching twist fiction would never allow, the man who died happened to be the father of another guide on the trip.

Because of the vehicle in which the story would appear, she had to downplay this extraordinary event. Nobody wants to read about violent death while strapped into a metal tube hurtling along at four hundred miles an hour six miles above the planet. And dwelling on a fatal accident on the river was not going to convince readers to spend their vacations aboard a raft. If you read her piece quickly between the beverage service and the snack tray, you might have missed the guide's death altogether.

Had she been writing for a different kind of magazine, she could have followed where her experience, her assignment, and the resulting story wanted to go, rather than be reined in by the requirements of format. The piece could have taken a fascinating and ominous turn—as the river trip did—and the landscape, the campfire conversation, the whole experience might have been heated up, made more profound, in the context of sudden violent death and the grief of the river guide whose father had been killed.

On the other hand, *Outside* magazine also publishes what could be called travel pieces, but the format encourages the writer to be more daring: It routinely prints long, in-depth adventure narratives with an environmental or political edge. It will take on the ethical and historical dimensions of the treaty governing Antarctica, or the reintroduction of predators into federal wilderness.

You shouldn't attempt to mimic the style of a particular magazine. The writing will sound false, pretended, even to you. Instead, search for those magazines that seem natural vehicles for *your* style, *your* passions. And that will give you enough range for your ambitions.

From long editorial experience, Lisa Bain advises, "The most important thing—and this is very basic, but many writers don't do it, even established writers—is to do your homework." Read the magazines for which you want to write.

YOUR APPROACH—DOCUMENTARY OR PERSONAL?

Your approach will reflect, among other things, how much you the writer are in the piece—whether you are attempting to document some factual person or event in the world or writing the piece from the inside out, relying heavily on your own memory, insights, reflections. As you prepare to write, it may be helpful to consider this broad distinction between *documentary* and *personal* nonfiction.

"The documentary is the researched nonfiction piece that still involves all of that footwork involved in interviewing sources, going to the library, looking up the historical records, sifting through the competing versions," explains Bill Atwill, author of *Fire and Power: The American Space Program as Postmodern Narrative*. In his book, he reflects on how authors such as Norman Mailer (*Of a Fire on the Moon*) and Thomas Wolfe (*The Right Stuff*) have written about rockets, astronauts and moon landings in a highly novelistic way, yet from a solid grounding in extensive factual knowledge as well. "Then what they do is, rather than foreground that research the way a history scholar would do with footnotes and citations, they somehow overlay a surface narrative that's more interesting. That would be one form—a kind of documentary journalism with style."

Atwill notes that a different approach relies much less on journalistic skills: "The memoir, the highly personal essay, becomes a representative anecdote for a larger issue in the culture that might not involve as much research but more meditative thought. You read it and you're interested in the author's story, but you're also thinking, what's my story? How would I tell my story?"

As always, we're really talking about a tendency toward a certain approach rather than an absolutely rigid adherence to one or the other. While you, the author, may be completely absent from the events and people you write about, or else intimately involved in all that you tell, the odds are you will wind up somewhere in the middle range, tending toward either a documentary or a personal approach. Just because you use the first-person ("I") narrative voice, that doesn't mean you can't cite facts and figures. Indeed, the distinctive, human voice of the writer can make those statistics, scientific facts and historical ironies all the more compelling to your reader. Nearly all nonfiction, even some newspaper journalism, has in recent years moved away from a pretense of strict objectivity.

One last observation: Writing a short piece can actually be harder than writing a book, because it will require tremendous concentration. The challenge is to make it large—significant—without making it long.

GENRES WITHIN THE SHORT FORM

The following list cites the established genres that regularly appear in mainstream and literary magazines. Bear in mind that each category gives an editor a way to handle the story in the context of the magazine, and that the best writers are always refining or even reinventing the form, so that the best writing will always somehow be an exception to the "rules."

Article—A general term for any piece that presents facts and information, tells a story, or explores an issue in terms of real-world experience.

Essay—A general term for any piece that argues issues or reflects upon ideas. Every short piece can be thought of as being either an article or an essay, and often have elements of both.

Essay of ideas—An exploration of intellectual or philosophical ground. In a column for *Esquire* called "Ethics," unfortunately now discontinued, Harry Stein used to investigate all sorts of moral quandaries that cropped up in everyday life, from adultery to flattering your boss to get a raise.

Travel—A broad category ranging from a straight destination piece meant to arouse the interest of potential tourists to a reflective piece that uses the details of the outward journey to portray an interior one. Any story that relies on a journey motif is, in a sense, also a travel piece.

Expository or informational article—A more or less documentary piece that introduces the reader to a subject in some detail; a basic journalistic feature story.

How-to—A step-by-step primer for accomplishing something: training your dog, building a wooden boat, buying real estate. A growing number of these pieces could also be cataloged under "health and fitness" or self-help in general.

Nature—A fairly broad category that includes any writing about the natural world for a general audience. As in a travel piece, its close kin, *place* may take on the status of a character. Bill Atwill observes,

"The landscape becomes an analog for the interior consciousness, the narrator or viewpoint character's relation to the place."

Science or technology—A piece requiring a technical writer's expertise: to be able to digest complex scientific or technical material and present it in a way comprehensible to a general reader. Some nature writing shades into science or technology writing. Stephen Jay Gould, a Harvard paleontologist, for example, regularly deciphers complex evolutionary issues in *Natural History Magazine*.

Issue—Any piece that explores a topical issue, such as Bob Reiss' article on famine relief in the Sudan.

Public event—The detailed story of a public happening, such as Hersey's account of the atomic bombing of Japan in *Hiroshima*, or *New Yorker* editor and baseball fan Roger Angell's accounts of the World Series for *Sports Illustrated*.

Political analysis—An idea piece that explores a political issue or some aspect of political life. Joan Didion, for instance, wrote about Michael Dukakis' disastrous presidential campaign.

Investigative exposé—A piece that offers heretofore unrevealed truth about a public person, issue or event. Such writing demands exceptionally dogged reportorial and research skills and usually relies far less on melodramatic "Deep Throat" style meetings than on endless hours in the library and the hall of records.

Review—A reasoned and informed critique of a book, play, movie, concert or other public document or performance, frequently using it to discourse on the art in general. See John Updike's *Hugging the Shore: Essays and Criticism*, a collection of book reviews he wrote for *The New York Times Book Review*, which not only offers eloquent analysis of specific books but also stands as a history of contemporary writing.

Personality profile—Just what it sounds like. The focus is a person, usually a celebrity or other public figure. Think of it as a short biography of a living person, narrated in anecdotes and scenes, most often making extensive use of the subject's own words, usually during a limited time. The aim is to capture an interesting personality, to make the reader feel as if he or she has met the subject in an intimate way, and that the meeting mattered. Atwill observes, "These pieces sometimes seem dated, because if it's about somebody living they go on to be somebody else within a year or two after that." See Gay

Talese's profiles collected in *Fame and Obscurity*, or Joseph Mitchell's, collected in *Up in the Old Hotel*. Talese presents celebrities such as Joe DiMaggio and Peter O'Toole, while Mitchell favors the local "characters" who prowl old New York. Though both authors' profiles are frozen in time, they seem anything but dated.

Arranged interview—The aim is similar to that of the personality profile, but the bulk of the piece is told in the subject's own words, either as a brief introduction followed by a straight question-and-answer session, or a question-and-answer session interrupted at strategic places so the author can make telling observations of the subject's physical demeanor, the setting, past events, etc. The term "arranged" is used because in either case the interview will not be presented verbatim; rather the writer will select from notes or tapes those portions that best capture the subject, and then artfully arrange the questions and answers, often out of order, for effect. See Oriana Fallaci's interviews, collected in *Interview With History*.

Personal essay—A piece that offers one or more firsthand experiences from the writer's own life, then endows that experience with a meaning that transcends the reader's personal interest in the author's life. The classic example offered in college textbooks is George Orwell's "Shooting an Elephant," in which he describes his actions as a colonial official in India; the events that culminate in his being obliged to shoot a rogue elephant in front of an unruly crowd provided him with a functional metaphor of colonialism—he had to do what he knew was wrong in order to maintain face (and therefore power) with the natives, who vastly outnumbered him.

Memoir—Memory in words, and very closely related to the personal essay, although the meaning may be implicit in the memory. Or the meaning may derive from the glimpse it offers of a famous personality in an intimate moment. Sometimes the memoir takes on significance because the writer was a private witness to a historical event, such as the Holocaust. We'll deal more with this form in chapter eight.

Adventure narrative—A dramatic true-life story. Often this includes nature writing and shades into the personal essay.

Try this: Study several issues of a magazine you admire and derive the genres of writing it usually prints. Be specific about subject, length, focus, style and the writer's approach. Now do the same with a magazine you've heard of but have never read, and compare the magazines to each other and to the list above. You'll see firsthand how genres are fine-tuned for specific publications, how rigid or flexible they are, and how good writers cross them.

THE NOT-SO-SIMPLE ANSWER

Sometimes a book just doesn't pan out. The risk of undertaking any sustained project is that none of us can predict the future. The longer a piece of writing will take, the more things that can go wrong with it. You lose interest. Your editor leaves the publishing house and the new editor thinks it's a dumb idea. The trips don't work out, the research turns up nothing very interesting, you lose access to the people and events and places that were to have been the focus, or else you just plain lose the focus. Your money runs out. Or legal problems intervene. Or somebody else just published the book you are trying to write—to rave reviews.

There's not much you can do about any of it, except to take a calculated risk, try your best to write the book you have to write, and do your damnedest to see it through.

More frequently, a book begins to evolve from what you thought was going to be a short piece. When I signed aboard the schooner *Brilliant*, a sail-training vessel out of Mystic Seaport Museum, I intended to do an article on the boat itself—a lovely vessel built during the Depression for a cousin of P.T. Barnum. But once aboard, I got caught up in the experience: the eerie peace of sailing fast through fogbanks, relying on the "starscope"—radar—to avoid the trawlers on the Grand Banks; the late-night camaraderie in the cockpit, as crewmembers traded sailing stories over steaming cups of coffee held in mittened hands; the rush of physical joy from feeling the big hull sweeping powerfully along under you; the exhilaration of tacking into a crowded harbor under full sail, then at the crucial moment, lowering sails smartly and easing up to the mooring.

The voyage became an evocative interior voyage as well, calling up memories and insights and personal connections, and I knew on the first day out of Halifax that it was too much to contain in a slim article. It wanted to be a book, and so it became: *Brilliant Passage*.

So you may be wrong about what form the piece will ultimately take. This is not a problem. It is one of the great joys of writing—

watching your subject enlarge. Feeling possibilities open, discovering depth and breadth, realizing that a subject has captured you and you are on for the long haul. "I started out writing about the bird refuge," Williams recalls of how *Refuge* began to form itself. "I don't think I really found the confluence until I had a conversation with my mother, and then I saw the landscape I was working in."

This doesn't mean you don't write the shorter piece. In fact, writing the shorter piece is a good way of testing the durability of the subject, laying out the premise for the book to come, suggesting the direction in which the book will go, and helping incidentally to convince an editor of the promise of the book. Remember that one hallmark of a great subject is that you find yourself returning to it, sometimes years after your first encounter. Be alert when you find yourself captivated again and again by the same subject—it means you've been meditating on it even when you weren't aware of doing so, and it may be that you need to open up your approach, enlarge your thinking, reassess its scope.

Also, books accumulate. "This is a collection of personal essays, the distillation of what has seemed truest and best through a decade of reporting on the Maryland environment," writes Tom Horton in the preface to *Bay Country*, a portrait of the Chesapeake Bay so stunning it won the 1987 John Burroughs Medal for nature writing, and an illuminating example of how even newspaper journalism can aspire to literature: Horton covered the bay and related environmental issues for the *Baltimore Sun*.

Though each of the "chapters" in his book was originally written to stand alone, together they present a coherent narrative, a biography almost, of the Chesapeake Bay. Horton brings abstract issues, such as the depletion of the shad fishery, and inanimate objects, such as skipjacks and bridges, to life through the voices of the people who live and work on the bay—the fishing captains, the oystermen, the crab-pickers, the duck hunters, the scientists who are trying to save the bay. Like a tile in a mosaic, each piece is a discrete work of art in itself, and the book arranges them into a larger picture.

Other collections of essays offer looser connections—the book is a convenient way for a writer to sift through the accumulated work of years and retain the best in a more durable form. The best such collections offer the reader a chance to watch a first-rate imagination and intellect at work. Gore Vidal's *United States, Essays 1952-1992* offers that kind of experience, the chance to live within a brilliant and opinionated writer's mind. The cumulative value is not only that we see how his thinking develops, how he circles back again and again on favorite themes from different angles, but also that we get to know him by his distinctive voice. Along with his thinking also unfolds the mystery of his personality, and the satisfaction is close to that intimate connection the reader feels reading a candid autobiography.

BETWIXT AND BETWEEN:
TOO LONG, BUT NOT LONG ENOUGH

It sometimes happens that a piece comes out betwixt and between— not long enough for a book, but too long for a single magazine article. Anything over 6,000 words—twenty-four manuscript pages—is pushing the envelope (to borrow a phrase Tom Wolfe purloined from test pilots) for most periodicals.

That doesn't mean some magazines won't publish very long articles—*The New Yorker* is famous for its long pieces. But the odds go down. By 10,000 words (forty manuscript pages) you're really on the edge. At some point, you need to reassure yourself that the piece needs to be that long—you're not just indulging yourself, throwing in every thought that occurs to you. Consider breaking it down into a two-part series, or simply two or three separate pieces, each with a different focus. Give an editor a way to make it work. And remember that in some distant future you may find the rest of your book.

Remember, too, that you may be confusing superficial connections with *subject*. The same assignment may yield several different, and different kinds of, pieces. I went to Poland in 1990 to find distant family who had been separated from us by two world wars and a revolution, to find out how their future had been different from the future of those who had emigrated to America. That was one story.

I also wanted to investigate the allure of the Cult of the Virgin in Eastern Europe—the widespread belief in the miraculous intervention of the mother of Christ in history and everyday life. I interviewed many of the same people, visited many of the same places, explored many of the same historical circumstances for both pieces. But they were separate. I kept them separate in my mind even as I was asking questions, and the first thing I did upon returning home was to divide everything—photos, interview segments, impressions, notes—into two different piles. Both pieces were destined for the same magazine, and in any case I was careful not to overlap content.

If you plan to "double-dip"—to write more than one piece from the same assignment and publish it in different magazines, which freelancers often do to recover costs—talk it over with your editors. Beware: It's bad practice—and bad ethics—to use one magazine to bankroll an assignment for another. Nothing will get you blackballed faster than betraying an editor's trust. Make sure everybody is clear about the terms of what you are doing, and if possible arrange the terms ahead of time. Obviously, if you've done a piece on your own time at your own expense, your obligation is less—usually you just want to make sure you're not doing pieces that are too similar for overlapping readerships.

Still, be alert to the life your subject takes on even after you've written and published the piece in question. Long after I returned from Poland, I found myself writing a short story about the night train from Warsaw, and the experience yielded several public radio essays about the discoveries I made while doing the pieces. And the assignment provided general background for a novel, now in an unsightly first draft.

WRITING OUT LOUD—A NEW GENRE

Once a week for the past four years I have been writing—and reading for broadcast on WHQR, our local public radio affiliate—essays of 500-700 words. The word count matters less than the time it takes to read them, between three and four minutes. Any longer, and they can't fit into the "hole" reserved for them in network broadcasting. Occasionally they wind up with a second life on National Public Radio's *All Things Considered*, and some of them have found a second life in print. Most, but not all, are personal essays—stories with a point. Stories it had never occurred to me to write for any other medium.

Oddly, it was easier for me to tell personal stories and explore their meaning over the air than on the page. Radio is a strangely intimate medium. You speak into the microphone as if you are talking to one person who is listening intently, rather than to some generalized, anonymous audience.

This genre—called the "commentary" or the "radio essay"—is

relatively new and is no longer confined to public radio. "Commentators" as diverse as Daniel Pinkwater, an author of children's books, Robin Hemley, a short story writer and novelist, and Bailey White, a schoolteacher, have taken up the form. Its succinctness and the possibilities for the pure *sound* of language have proved especially appealing for poets.

Writing "out loud" can teach a writer word-discipline and the nuances of spoken—compared to written—narration. You get used to reading your work out loud, and the ear picks up awkward phrases, lapses in sense, and rocky transitions that your eye alone would never recognize. (For that reason, I now read everything I write out loud before sending it off to an editor.)

Pause and inflection are as much a part of the commentator's art as punctuation is for the written essayist's. And spoken out loud, even a mild moment of bad taste becomes magnified. Since the emotion is part of the audible presentation, flat writing often works better than sentences with a lot of modifiers, which can seem melodramatic. On the other hand, overly terse writing may have to be softened a bit so as not to sound like the hard-boiled voice-over from a '40s detective film noir.

For this reason, radio essays usually require some editing to make the transition into print. Irony that was obvious from the tone of the commentator's voice has to be made plain through style alone on the page.

"You don't need to be a professional-sounding radio person to do the commentaries, and in fact it might even be a handicap if one was," says Pinkwater, who regularly appears on *All Things Considered* and who refers to his own humorous commentaries as "Yiddish Dada" meant to divert and amuse listeners as well as to make them think. "There's a tendency to like—and I like them, too—people with regional accents, people with sloppy speech like me, people who sound not like somebody who gives you the news."

When I began writing for radio, I paid attention to guidelines developed by the staff at NPR, given to me by Jim Polson, our local producer. "Write the story the same way you'd tell someone who asked," they advised. "Tell the story as if you were telling it to a stranger over the phone."

Other bits of advice, many of them valuable when writing for print:

- Use simple sentences with only one idea.
- Use clear language and words that matter.
- Always write in the active voice.
- Find the element of surprise in the story and use it to convey information.
- Write descriptively, using visual and sound images so that listeners feel as if they were there.
- Allow your listeners the opportunity to discover the story with you.

One of the limitations, obviously, is that you have to establish an affiliation with a radio station that will air your pieces. Its programming becomes your magazine. "You must have a microphone, or it will not work," Pinkwater advises wryly.

One advantage to the form is that it can allow you to treat a subject that isn't big enough for either a lengthy article or a book. Another is that the reaction of your audience is immediate and ongoing—phone calls, letters, even on-air replies. Part of the reason for this is that your audience, even on a national broadcast, always includes your neighbors. And there is an immediacy to the spoken word that seems to spark reaction and reply rather than simple reflection. You shoot an arrow out into the world, and if it hits home, you'll know it.

CHAPTER SEVEN

TELLING A TRUE STORY

USING THE TECHNIQUES OF FICTION

story—I've been using that term a lot, and with good reason.

It's a term I first heard long before I had any ambition to write novels. In those days I was a newspaper reporter, working for a cranky editor who stood over my shoulder as I pounded out my sentences on a Royal manual typewriter, tearing out each "take" as I finished it and slashing it up with a blue pencil. He never sent us to get the *facts*. He always sent us to get the *story*.

Terry Tempest Williams observes, "In a good piece of nonfiction, there has to be a *story*. I don't know how many undergraduate pieces I've seen that have an epiphany around every corner, but what's it all mean? There's no story."

The journalist's definition of *story* is the crystallizing conflict that makes the facts come to life as human drama. For example: Suppose the facts are that the state highway department wants to build a super-duper high-rise bridge to a tiny island community that is served by an antique swing-bridge. Many of the handful of year-round residents on the island oppose the new bridge for various reasons.

Not a bad set of facts—two sides in opposition over an issue. But a bridge is after all just a bridge, and why should anybody outside the little community care about the outcome?

Let's pause here to consider a fairly traditional fiction writer's definition of *story*: A character we care about acts to fulfill his desires with important consequences. (Many contemporary fictions are about a character refusing to act—but that refusal itself is a kind of action.)

L. Rust Hills, longtime fiction editor of *Esquire*, in his excellent book *Writing in General and the Short Story in Particular*, claims that every good story contains a moment after which things can never be the same again. A moment of profound change: for the characters, for the reader.

Somebody is trying to build a bridge—but who? We need to personalize the ambition. Maybe it's a progressive politician in the mold of Huey P. Long, the legendary Louisiana Kingfish, who measures political success by grand public construction projects. Examine the desire—*why* does he want to build a bridge? Out of a genuine wish to make life better for the islanders? For personal glory? Or does he have some other kind of investment?

Usually when somebody wants something important, somebody else is determined not to let him have it—that's all that's meant by those old literary terms you learned in high school: *protagonist* and *antagonist*. You find both wherever you find a conflict.

Again, who? And why?

In this case, perhaps the person leading the opposition is a longtime resident who is worried that a new bridge will lead to an increase in summer tourists, along with more noise, crowding and crime.

Now, many stories have a coalescing element that is not obvious at first glance, and that leads you to the real subject underlying the apparent one. While everybody else is arguing about the merits of the proposed bridge, you visit the island and talk to some residents, among them a realtor who lets it slip that a sewer line will go to the island under the new bridge. The current swing bridge, of course, can't carry a sewer line, because sewer lines, unlike bridges, cannot be opened and closed for canal traffic. At present, the island is served by private septic tanks.

Since the zoning regulations (boring) are based on state restrictions about how big a dwelling can be built on a lot served by a septic tank (really boring), it now occurs to you that when the bridge brings the new sewer, high-rise hotels and condos may spring up, driving up property assessments (and therefore taxes: boring, unless they're your taxes), driving out longtime residents (not so boring), and utterly changing the nature of a quiet, quaint island.

The literal bridge now has become a figurative one as well.

So the story turns out to be exciting after all: the struggle for the soul of a community. If the writer can make the people seem real—if they become, in E.M. Forster's phrase, "round characters," capable of surprising us, people who are both likable and disagreeable, greedy and altruistic, admirable and ignoble—their lives will take on dramatic texture, we will recognize ourselves in them, and we will care about their fates.

Their story will carry implications for any community that feels invaded by the forces of change and that is struggling to maintain traditional values on prime real estate where there's big money to be made. The consequences will reach far beyond local interest. The bridge will become—like Ron Powers' Mark Twain Bridge across the Mississippi—a metaphor for a much older and much larger American story.

Three simple lessons emerge:

1. Every story is about people, even when at first it doesn't seem to be.
2. A seemingly boring set of facts, pursued far enough and with enough imagination, may yield a fascinating, dramatic story.
3. The value of a story is likely to be directly proportional to its consequences—for both the actors in the story and the reader.

When the people are interesting enough, when the struggle goes beyond local interest and resonates with some fundamental part of human nature, when the consequences are significant enough, the piece has a chance to become more than just a report of facts.

It has a chance to become a *story*, in the most lasting and literary sense of the word. And as Lee Gutkind puts it, "A reader doesn't want to hear what you have to say. A reader wants to hear a story you have to tell."

POINT OF VIEW: WHO'S TELLING THE STORY?

To tell a story is to make a series of choices.

The most important creative decision a fiction writer faces is choosing the most interesting point of view from which to tell the story, since that decision colors all other decisions about story craft. The point of view defines the scope of the story, the narrator's angle on the action, and how naive or well informed that narrator will be. In common usage, there are three: *First person, third person omniscient* and *third person limited*—also called *third person assigned*. A fourth possibility, *dramatic* point of view, is not much used anymore.

First person, of course, employs the "I" narrator—the witness.

Third person omniscient uses the third-person pronoun (he, she) and claims unlimited knowledge about the world and the interior lives of all the characters. Think of it as God telling the story—without mentioning himself. (A useful conceit, especially in nonfiction, since sometimes it turns out that what we thought all along was a third-person know-it-all account turns out to be a first-person account told by a narrator who has judiciously kept himself out of the story.)

Third person limited (or *assigned*) also uses the third-person pronoun, indicating the narrator is removed from personal witness, but claims the prerogative of entering one character's thoughts and feelings, to which the point of view is limited or assigned—hence the term *viewpoint character*. A novel may employ several of these by turns in order to discover nuances of perspective without having to be omniscient in every scene.

Dramatic tells the story as a series of exterior scenes, just as in stage drama (hence the term), revealing only what an onlooker could observe, hear or otherwise directly sense, without presenting the interior lives of any of the characters.

Nonfiction writers don't always start by reflecting on point of view, but if your aim is to tell a compelling story, you should. The same issues are at stake as for a fiction writer: How much scope will you allow the narrative? What is your angle on the action? How informed or naive will you be in approaching your material?

Journalism—basic reportage—has long prided itself on being objective or neutral: Just the facts, ma'am. No speculation, no dreams, no thoughts, no feelings, nothing that cannot be known from *outside* the characters and events by an observant spectator. This, more or less, mimics the dramatic point of view in fiction, which most storytellers have abandoned precisely because it is so limiting and flat. (Hemingway, who cut his teeth as a reporter, favored this stance in his early stories.)

The so-called "New Journalists"—people such as Tom Wolfe and Gay Talese—went off in precisely the opposite direction, applying the first-person point of view to journalism in a big way, interjecting themselves into their stories as narrators and characters, making use of their biases and opinions rather than hiding them, in a sense making the story happen as well as reporting it. All they really did was take the "we were there" stance long favored by war correspondents, radio commentators of the 1930s and 1940s, and eyewitnesses to disaster, heat it up stylistically, and put it into the literary mainstream.

The first-person point of view grants the narrator instant credibility of one kind—as an eyewitness—and also limits the scope and balance of his story. One great advantage is that the reader finds himself unconsciously saying "I" over and over again, thus identifying in a very profound psychological way with the storyteller. Its main drawback is that it can seem claustrophobic to the reader, who can feel trapped in one narrow viewpoint.

The two remaining points of view present challenges for the writer telling a true story about real people.

In fiction, the writer is allowed to invent what characters are thinking or feeling. In fact, most good fiction relies on making such interior lives "real" in order to create depth and resonance. But obviously, in real life nobody can say for sure what goes on in someone else's mind or heart, and to pretend that you can is to lie. So in nonfiction, a true omniscient or even third-person limited narrative is impossible.

The best the nonfiction writer can do is to present the *illusion* of interior lives, giving the reader insight and private information about real people, but stopping short of claiming to *know* what cannot be known—without making it up.

So a strictly omniscient point of view is out, as is a third-person limited point of view, because the interior life of the characters is unavailable. All nonfiction must be told in either dramatic or first-person point of view or it becomes, by definition, fiction. That's why Truman Capote's *In Cold Blood*—like other so-called "nonfiction novels"—crosses the line from nonfiction and becomes fiction: He not only presents facts and events he can verify, but also delves into the minds of his characters and invents extensive dialogue to show their personalities.

In practice, though, creative nonfiction rarely feels coolly "dramatic" in presentation. It almost always is told technically from the first-person point of view (the writer being the "I"-witness, whether or not he alludes to himself).

The first-person narrator (the writer) can obviously let us in on his thoughts, fantasies, judgments, dreams, wishes, etc. But if the writer does not want the feel of a first-person telling, it can be made to *seem* like an omniscient or a third-person limited point of view. That is, as readers we will get to know all the characters—or one character in particular—intimately and have the sense of being included in their story, rather than of reading a report.

The devices used to create this illusion give a well-told true story the feel of compelling fiction.

REAL PEOPLE ARE CHARACTERS, TOO

For a story to come alive, the people in it must come alive. They must be more than names on a page. Real people are characters, too, and they are not real to your reader until you make them real. The special requirement of nonfiction is that we must learn what is inside them through what we can reasonably learn from the outside.

The nonfiction writer can accomplish this using many of the same devices as the fiction writer:

• Physical description, including characteristic mannerisms (Charley Smith is never seen around the ranch without his Tigers baseball cap, which he uses to swat horseflies).

• Names and nicknames (Susan Jones, the highest-ranking woman in a billion-dollar-a-year company, insists that everybody call her "Pinky").

• The physical context of the character, including what he owns, his lifestyle, characteristic props (Old Flatwheeler slept in a cardboard-and-roofing-tin shack by the railroad and cooked his supper in a Maxwell House coffee can).

• Dialogue—what the person says and how, including favorite expressions repeated throughout the piece and the answers to your questions ("What's the diff?" she likes to say).

• The person's statements. If he confides he was "worried about his son," "euphoric about the promotion," "feeling nostalgic for Kansas," or whatever—and you trust that he is being candid—you can write that without having to quote it, the same way a fictional narrator would. This is one of the ways you have access to an interior life.

- The person's written words—in letters, diaries or journals, memoirs, reports, depositions, police statements, trial transcripts, manuscripts, published work. The written word may contain intimate and candid details that allow a window into a person's imagination and thought process.
- Any other artifacts created by and reflective of the character's essential qualities (a painting she has done, a schooner he has built, a nonprofit organization she has established).
- Actions and gestures—what the person does: not just during an interview, but at work, in the course of daily life, reacting to what others say and do, or during especially dramatic circumstances (While everybody else is watching the President, he watches the crowd).
- What the person *doesn't* do or say that a reasonable person might expect her to (It began to rain heavily, but she just sat there on the park bench, knitting, as if she didn't notice).
- Background and personal history—the person's resumé as it illuminates the concerns of the piece (By the age of twenty, she had already been a dog musher on two polar expeditions).
- Anecdotes that illustrate character traits (When the army failed to provide adequate food for his men in Cuba, Teddy Roosevelt bought provisions for them out of his own pocket).
- What others say about the person—out loud or in writing (One admirer has called her a modern Florence Nightingale).
- What others say *to* the person—and how they say it ("You're a jerk," she said, laughing, and bussed him on the cheek).
- How others react in the person's presence (The young hard hats grudgingly made room for Alvin at the lunch counter).
- *Your* reaction to the person (Smith was trying too hard to impress me with his knowledge of classical music).
- Juxtaposition—putting two disparate elements side by side (Rory slashed the man's tire with his Bowie knife. Later I saw him using the same blade to remove a porcupine quill from a stray dog's paw).
- Paradox and contradiction, often in juxtaposition (Her married son says he hates her, but her teenaged daughter clearly adores her). The two elements may also be presented at different places in the story.
- Metaphor and figurative language (Hap Jones drank whiskey like it was his job).

It's a little harder to establish character in nonfiction, because you have to rely on external cues rather than imaginative instinct. But using some combination of the above, you can draw a convincingly "real" character.

In *Going Back to Bisbee*, Richard Shelton recounts his first meeting with Molly Bendixon in the teachers' lounge of the Lowell Junior High School in Bisbee, Arizona:

> She was sitting at the table with her coffee and her ciga-rette, looking glum. I said "Good morning," got my coffee, and lit a cigarette, aware that she was staring at me all the time with an expression somewhere between irritation and amusement in her bright black eyes.
>
> "You a Mormon?" she asked with apparent disgust.
>
> What an incredibly rude and unobservant woman, I thought, to ask such a thing while I'm drinking coffee and smoking. And what business is it of hers anyway? "No," I said, bridling. "What makes you ask?"
>
> "You look so damned clean," she said, throwing her head back and exhaling a long breath of smoke as if to say, "Wanna make something of it?"
>
> Suddenly I realized that I was dealing with a woman of unusual dignity.

Shelton's scene reads like fiction, and by the end of it we have a strong, vivid impression of who this woman is. He doesn't describe her head-to-toe. Rather, he tells us exactly those physical details we need to get a fix on her character—the glum expression, the bright black eyes, the head thrown back defiantly, the long exhalation of smoke. The props—cigarette and cup of coffee—both set the context of the scene and help characterize her. We have something to watch as we hear her talk in a direct, almost aggressive way, even using a mild profanity. He confides to us his reaction to Molly Bendixon—including the figurative "Wanna make something of it?"—and the drama lies in the fact that, after only a couple of lines of shared talk, he changes his mind about her.

There has been movement in the scene, a heightening of aware-ness. And of course we're really learning about two characters, since the narrator is clearly an actor in the scene.

If you present a character well enough using such devices, the reader won't even notice that he is not privy to the character's reflections. You will have been able to demonstrate in other ways—as Shelton does—what the person is thinking and feeling, what she believes, what she cares about, who she really is.

DIALOGUE

Just as in fiction, in nonfiction dialogue—voices talking out loud on the page—accomplishes several important dramatic effects: It reveals personality, provides tension, moves the story along from one point to another, and breaks the monotony of the narrator's voice by interjecting other voices that speak in contrasting tones, using different vocabularies and cadences.

Good dialogue lends *texture* to a story, the sense that it is not all one slick surface. This is especially important in a blatantly first-person narrative, since it offers the reader relief from a single, narrow viewpoint. The voices in dialogue can enhance or contradict the narrator's voice and contribute irony, often through humor.

And dialogue offers the reader something else: white space.

A passage of dialogue is not as dense-looking on the page, and the effect of this seemingly insignificant detail of presentation is to make the pace quicken. The story seems to move faster through sections of dialogue. So use of dialogue is one way that a writer can speed up the story or slow it down to accomplish other effects, including a sense of action or reflection.

In nonfiction, writing dialogue is not, as in fiction, a matter of invention, but of *selection*. You can't just pour your interview notes onto the page. You have to choose carefully from everything your subject said and present his or her words in a dramatic context—which usually means in a different order from the one in which they were actually said. More often than not, you leave out much of the interview, choosing only the best, most telling lines. Otherwise the really eloquent, startling, informative or funny lines get lost in a thicket of background talk.

When Bob Reiss went to the Amazon rain forest to research *The Road to Extrema*, he didn't intend to write about the political murder of activist Chico Mendez. Mendez had been trying to stop the destruction of the rain forest to preserve the traditional way of life of rubber tappers, who harvest latex from wild rubber plants. He wanted to write about the ranches being bulldozed out of the rain forest.

"Unfortunately, the best spokesperson for the ranchers' point of view was the guy who everybody believed ordered his death," Reiss recalls. "As the story progressed, his quotes became more interesting, and I learned more about ranching—not through the facts about ranching, but through his passion for ranching—all the aspects of ranching that had been attacked in Washington. He put a human face on it. Nevertheless, everything he told me seemed permeated with this question of whether he killed Chico Mendez.

"And then one day João Branco and I were sitting in a bar, and finally I couldn't take it anymore, and I said to him, 'Well, did you kill Chico Mendez?'

"And he leaned over—and he had a really throaty voice—and he said to me, 'Look into my eyes and you will know the truth. I did not kill Chico Mendez.' And there I had that story. I had that line. Everything was going to revolve around that quote. Everything: how a ranch worked, how many cattle you can put on an acre, land fights between ranchers and rubber tappers, Indian deaths, quality of Amazon land, nutrients in the soil. Everything became connected to the question of whether one man had ordered the death of another man."

The quote—the last thing João Branco said to him—became the first line of his piece, "The Accused," which was a finalist for a National Magazine Award.

Dialogue in nonfiction is meant to convey accurate information as well as to present the illusion of warm, human conversation, connecting the people in the story with the reader. Ordinarily, you don't want the people in your piece merely to trade set speeches—unless speechifying is the character tendency you're trying to portray.

While the dramatic aim is to create a lively give-and-take, you cannot distort reality merely for effect, the way a fiction writer can. It may be, for instance, that, in preparing the piece, you heard no actual dialogue, except the ones you had with several people as you interviewed them. One tactic for simultaneously serving the truth and creating drama is to juxtapose several observations about the same person, place or issue, as John McPhee does in the following passage from *Coming Into the Country*, in which he describes Ed and Ginny Gelvin, who live in a cabin in the Alaska wilderness, by stringing together quotes from those who know them:

> "The Gelvins are here thirty years and they attack any project with the enthusiasm of a newcomer."
> "They leave a situation better than they found it."
> "They are modern-type pioneers. They do things the old way, they do things the new way. They are the kind that built this country."

You can do the same with several responses to the same question:

> Will the new high-rise bridge destroy an island culture that has survived since the days of Queen Elizabeth?
> "We'll be extinct, like the dinosaurs," Mr. Smith says.
> "It's progress, that's all—you're not against progress?" Mr. Jones says.
> Mrs. Washington asks, "Will we have to move the cemetery, do you think?' "

The passage looks like dialogue on the page, and the effect mimics the tension of dialogue, but the reader understands from the cues the writer has provided all along—as each person is introduced in a specific location and context and the structure of the piece becomes clear—that these people are not all sitting in a room together answering in turn.

YOU CAN'T MAKE IT UP—OR CAN YOU?

The hitch about using dialogue in nonfiction is the obvious one: You can't make it up. If you're quoting a real person, your obligation to that person and to your reader is to be as accurate as you can be, given the limitations of note-taking and tape recorders.

Two exceptions: First, in memoir, writing about remembered scenes, the writer usually has no choice but to re-create dialogue. You're trying to capture a flavor, to recover conversations long vanished into the ether. You may think you remember accurately, but probably you're fooling yourself, catching a gist, recalling some composite of many similar conversations. Your reader is reasonable about this, so long as you are candid in calling your piece a memoir and don't claim to be able to offer verbatim transcripts.

You also can construct *habitual* dialogue—the *kind* of conversations characters have (or had). You're capturing the essence of the sort of talk that went on, but you have to stop short of claiming that it actually happened in exactly these words at a particular time and place. You have to be clear about this with your reader and offer unambiguous cues (italicized):

> They *used* to sit late around the fire on those camping trips.
> Hugh would *usually* remark on the weather.
> "Rain's good for the crops," Dal *always* replied.
> *If* they played cards and Dal won, Hugh *might* say, "All my luck went south when Marnie left."

You're actually interjecting a carefully constructed piece of fiction within the larger nonfiction, to make a point, to capture a flavor. It's a trick, and whether it's a cheap trick or merely an entertaining one will probably depend on what's at stake in the story and whether you're using the device to unfairly slam a real person or to illustrate honestly the way he *usually* talks.

We're talking about *honesty*. Giving the reader clear signals about exactly what kind of truth you're claiming—literal truth of event, emotional truth, truth by hypothetical illustration, approximate truth of memory, or merely the truth of intuition guided by special insight. Always ask yourself two questions:

1. In what way is the reader trusting me in this passage?
2. What are the consequences if I convey a false impression of literal accuracy?

Be aware that you're dancing around that line dividing fiction from fact—which is fine, so long as you never forget for a moment where that line is.

BEGINNINGS AND ENDINGS

The opening and closing are probably the most important passages in the whole piece. The opening breaks the silence and captures the reader's attention, and the ending leaves a lasting impression that can crystallize the impact and leave your story lingering in the reader's memory.

You don't necessarily want to start at the beginning of events. You want the reader to enter the story at some significant moment that captures his interest both for itself and because it encapsulates the larger theme of the piece—in medias res, in the middle of things.

Edmund Morris' *The Rise of Theodore Roosevelt* covers Roosevelt's life from birth until 1901—yet it begins on New Year's Day, 1907, as TR is about to shake hands with a long line of ordinary citizens at the White House. It's a moment of high anticipation, causing a "shiver of excitement" among the thousands waiting four abreast outside the front gate: "The shiver is accompanied by a murmur: 'The President's on his way downstairs.' "

The moment also illustrates a key, paradoxical theme in Roosevelt's life—and Morris' biography: Roosevelt the millionaire had an extraordinary common touch. The opening gives the reader something to grab on to. He can then fill in the background details *after* he's caught the reader's interest, at the precise moments when the reader needs to know them. We'll return to this part of the storyteller's art directly.

The reader has plenty of other diversions vying for his time, and his implicit question is always, Why am I reading this? The author needs to provide an answer. Morris answers by giving us a glimpse of a remarkable man in action, inviting us to learn more about him, rather than boring us with all of Roosevelt's vital statistics—where and when he was born, who his parents were and so on.

Morris could have begun with the Rough Riders' melodramatic charge up San Juan Hill, but he saves that for later. If you begin on too high a pitch, the risk is that everything that follows will be anticlimax.

An ending derives from all that has gone before. It pays off the promise made in the opening. If you don't know how to end a piece, go back to the beginning: What did you promise your reader?

It is often useful to close on a resonant image, one that will call back the rest of the piece. So Morris' book closes with an image of Vice-President Teddy Roosevelt munching sandwiches on a mountaintop in New York as a forest ranger clambers up through the trees, "clutching the yellow slip of a telegram." Roosevelt knows—and so does the reader—what news the telegram brings: President McKinley is dead, and TR is headed for the White House, where he will begin the New Year's Day custom of shaking the hands of "all citizens who are sober, washed, and free of bodily advertising."

The story has come full circle.

In storyteller's terms, the ending will show us whether the character got what he wanted and triumphed, got what he wanted and was disappointed, got something else instead, succeeded only partly or was foiled altogether. Complete resolution is rarely possible, because real life is messy and hardly ever serves up a perfectly formed drama. Usually a true story can be resolved only approximately, loose ends still dangling.

Ted Conover's *Rolling Nowhere*, an unabashedly first-person adventure on the hobo railroad in which Conover aspires to become a hobo, finishes—as journey stories are wont to do—at the end of the journey. The narrator's lesson, "that the hobo is not 'one of them.' He is one of us," answers his original yearning to find out what their life is like.

Since I had begun my Hemingway piece, "I came to Paris to find Ernest Hemingway," I felt I'd better find him. I owed the reader a glimpse of the man, dead or not, and so I closed with the imaginary meeting in Harry's New York Bar.

CONFLICT AND PLOT

Plot is more than a series of events: This happened, and then that happened, and then something else happened. In storyteller's terms, plot is a series of events related *causally*: This happened *because* that other thing happened. Things were going along fine (equilibrium) till something happened to disturb the equilibrium (dramatic problem), one thing led to another, escalating the tension (rising curve of action), culminating in a dramatic confrontation (climax), and resolving things back to some new equilibrium (denouement).

We had ourselves a nice quiet island here, then some joker decided to build a high-rise bridge, and all hell broke loose. . . .

The defining metaphor of the last two generations is probably the conspiracy theory—the "plot" at its most sinister. Simultaneously, after a spate of World War II novels, literary fiction began a wholesale move away from the public arena (where such plots happen), away from plot itself as a literary device, and into the world of the dislocated, brooding individual: the household novel, the private fiction removed from any definite historical or political milieu, the contemplative monologue, the minimalist short story, the self-referential metafiction.

Into the void rushed nonfiction writers, taking on the great public subjects such as the space program, computer technology, nuclear physics, genetic engineering, the environmental movement, the politics of race and sex, and so on. And taking on also the great and not-so-great public real-life "plots"—Vietnam, the Kennedy and King assassinations, CIA coup-making, and assorted political shenanigans, investment scams and celebrity murders-for-hire.

Such found plots are a storyteller's dream—and you could make a pretty strong case that the explosive renaissance of creative nonfiction we talked about in chapter one came about precisely because nonfiction writers began doing the work that previously had been tackled by novelists. (Now fiction is moving back, often borrowing the documentary style of nonfiction, and the boundaries between the two genres are increasingly smudged.)

But again, in nonfiction, you can't make up a plot where none exists. You can't force real events into an artificial shape just for the sake of drama without doing violence to the truth—or at least to *truthfulness*.

You can be *artful*, which is not the same thing, and which is the reason for all this discussion about fictional technique. To be artful is to demonstrate coherence and meaning through how you arrange all the parts.

So not all nonfiction pieces have plot. A profile, for instance, is more likely to resemble a character sketch than a plotted story. The same goes for an interview. But all good nonfiction contains *conflict*—an opposition of forces that lends tension to the account.

It's no accident that the subjects that attract nonfiction writers most frequently are subjects rife with conflict.

Nature, for example. What we call "nature writing" is most often serious writing about the natural environment in conflict with the modern, technological world: the government-sponsored deforestation of the Amazon basin, the slow destruction of the Chesapeake Bay by development, or the reintroduction of natural predators such as wolves into tamed Western ranch country. It has an edge.

Even Henry David Thoreau's *Walden Pond* is no idyll of wildflowers and woodchucks; it's all about the conflict between civilization and a life outside of ordinary "civilized" conventions. The best nature writing captures this elemental conflict between the tame and the wild.

A profile can present contradictory sides of a single personality—

conflict. An adventure piece can offer the tension of physical challenge, even danger, just as a personal essay can take advantage of emotional or psychological uncertainty. A travel piece always holds an implicit tension of destination: Will we get where we're going, and what will we find there? A review carries the tension of judgment—thumbs up, or thumbs down?

An issue piece or essay of ideas treats the pros and cons of a given program, course of action, philosophical or ethical premise and so on, presenting not necessarily only two sides but many sides. The tension is the tension of argument, of reasoned debate, of making up one's mind. The choice is hardly ever between obvious right and obvious wrong, and the best choice is rarely clear—in fact, when it is too clear the reader is liable to lose interest. The harder it is for the reader to make up his mind, the more tension he experiences.

This tension, whatever form it takes, is the most important reason the reader continues reading. It is not necessarily unpleasant—it can be nerve-wracking, like the tension of waiting for a jury to return a verdict; but it can also be downright delicious, like the tension of a child waiting for Christmas morning.

We achieve it through *suspense*.

SUSPENSE

"The reader who is not turning the page to the next page, you have lost them. They're gone. They went someplace else, they're doing something else with their time," says Kevin Canty, author of *A Stranger in This World*, a short story collection widely praised for its unflinching look at the lives of characters on the edge. Canty also regularly contributes personal essays to *Details* magazine. "You can do anything else you want, but if they're bored, they're just not reading it anymore."

What usually keeps the reader from being bored is suspense, a widely misunderstood term. *Suspense* gets a bad rap because too many of us associate it only with pulp detective novels, horror movies and melodramatic thrillers.

But suspense lies at the heart of every good story. It is achieved through the artful combination of two elements: *conflict* and *delay*. We've already defined *conflict* as *forces in opposition*; *delay* simply means *making the reader wait for resolution*.

You don't make the reader wait simply to be perverse. You make the reader wait because, as he waits, he learns relevant information, the conflict becomes more clearly and profoundly defined, the mystery deepens, the anticipation builds, and the reader's investment in the outcome is heightened. The solution becomes more and more urgent.

It's the same reason we wrap a Christmas present—we promise a fine surprise and even show it to the reader, sort of, but we hide its exact shape and make the reader wait till the right moment and then struggle—just a little—with the ribbons and tape.

We use this tactic every day. Home from an errand, we usually *don't* say to our wife, "I saw your Aunt Maude at the video store making out with an eighteen-year-old bodybuilder." We say: "Guess who I saw at the video store." Now we've got her attention.

"Who?" she says.

We insist she make three guesses, then we say: "Your Aunt Maude."

We string it out: "You'll never guess whom she was with."

We want to arouse as much curiosity as we can, give her time to wonder, to anticipate, to make her own guess—but we've got to play it just right or she'll become exasperated with us, even angry: "You'll never guess what they were doing." Then we deliver the punchline. The payoff.

Telling stories is all about timing—and time. The order in which we tell a story—whether or not it is the order in which events actually happened—becomes for the reader the order of their happening.

The secret of narrative lies in deciding what to tell first, what to tell second and so on, right up to the ending.

Imagine how the little scene of his first encounter with the schoolteacher in *Going Back to Bisbee* would play if Shelton made just one small change in the order of telling, confiding to the reader, "I realized I was dealing with a woman of unusual dignity" *before* we get to witness their first conversation. He would be asking us to take his word for his judgment of her character, rather than letting us meet her along with him and make up our own mind, and we would balk. Gone would be the snap of irony, the humorous jolt of sudden insight. And everything she says in that sardonic exchange would seem less interesting because we would already be forced to color it with an assumption of her essential dignity.

With every fact you tell, every scene you present, you are raising questions, instigating local conflicts that all somehow serve the larger conflict, the over-arching question of the piece. The art of suspense lies in making your reader wait just long enough for the answers. You raise a question, and you answer it—but not before raising another, even more intriguing question. You keep on teasing the reader along, answering bigger and bigger questions, at long last resolving the question which formed the subject of the piece in the first place.

Make him wait too long or for too little payoff, and he gives up on the story.

In his instructional book *The Art of Fiction*, John Gardner claims that "the highest kind of suspense involves the Sartrian anguish of choice; that is, our suspenseful concern is not just with what will happen but with the moral implications of action." In other words, a reader is drawn into a story not just out of base curiosity about what will happen next—the kind of suspense we encounter most obviously in lurid melodrama—but out of an anxiety of decision shared with the character.

The question is not only, What will the character do next? but also, Will the character do the right thing? and all the attendant implications: How? What is the right thing? What will be the consequences? What would I do in his place? This is why you can successfully achieve suspense even when the outcome is already known, as all historical novelists realize—since all history has, by definition, already happened.

No matter how many times we refight the Battle of Gettysburg, the Confederates are going to lose. But in *Killer Angels: A Novel About the Four Days at Gettysburg*, Michael Shaara focuses our attention on the anxiety of decision—the choices that led to the debacle of Pickett's charge and the slaughter of thousands of men in gray. The eventual outcome hovers over the story like a great black shadow, but each choice made by every officer on both sides takes on the kind of Sartrian anxiety Gardner is talking about, and we as readers are forced to concur or disagree with each choice in the vivid context of the time in which Shaara has drawn it—not from hindsight.

As readers, we absorb facts and mull them over, watch a predicament unfold and worry about the fate of the character. Vicariously, we participate in the story—not just with our heads, but with our hearts.

It is as if we, too, are making the decisions.

EMOTION AND STYLE

Fiction writers have always known that the best stories have an emotional appeal. It may be unliterary to be *sentimental*—tossing in cuddly puppies and wide-eyed orphans whenever the story gets bogged down. But honest *sentiment*—true human feeling—is the most valuable literary commodity there is.

"What makes my stuff work if it does work—and I'm not sure that all of it does—is the ability to sometimes find an emotional core inside other kinds of material," Canty says. "You're trying to move the reader, as you would in a short story."

Suspense is both intellectual and emotional. The reader's curiosity is piqued—he wants to see where your argument leads, learn some useful and startling fact, solve a puzzle. But you can make him do all of that with his heart galloping, his pulse racing, his face flushing with anger or fear. Or laughing out loud. Or with tears streaming down his cheeks, his heart too full for words. Even if such extreme reactions are rare, you want your reader to feel *something* as he reads.

If you make your characters seem as real to the reader as they were to you when you met them, your reader will experience a real emotional reaction to them, an empathy that puts him squarely in their predicament.

If you tell the information and events in an effective order, creating suspense, your reader will feel an emotional engagement in the choices those characters make. The reader's reaction will be visceral—from the gut.

Long, convoluted, abstract sentences of the sort favored by academics (some, not all, since even epistemological writing is undergoing profound reassessment), full of unnecessary and redundant qualifiers and not unlike the sort of speechifying, hegemonic rhetoric engaged in by politicians (many of whom use too many parenthetical expressions and passive voice constructions to be truly—or shall we say fully—effective), not to mention clichés, lacking in focus and deliberately constructed with the utilization of large Latinate words where little Anglo-Saxon ones will do—like the sentence you have just read—tend to kill off emotion.

Jesus wept.

Clarity and focus matter. If the reader is confused or not sure what to be paying attention to, his only emotional reaction is going to be frustration at you, the author.

One stylistic rule of thumb for generating an emotional reaction: The more lurid your material, the flatter the writing should be. Tales of violent death, erotic sex, emotional trauma, war, heinous crime, etc., are best told with some control, rather than using loaded verbs and heavy-handed modifiers. The tension between the high-octane material and the understated telling will usually cause the strength of the material to work on the reader.

But if you insist too hard, the reader will resist.

The more complex the idea or technology you are trying to explain, the simpler, more straightforward the writing ought to be. Emotion requires a sustained experience with the writing, and if a reader is blocked by dense, obscure passages, stopping and starting and stopping again, it's hard to build emotion.

Conversely, sometimes the simplest, most obvious phenomena give you an opportunity for an exquisitely intricate, lyrical metaphor: Beauty always arouses emotion.

And if you want the reader to share your emotion, your passion, your best tactic is to let him also share the experience that aroused that passion in you. Don't just *tell* him about it—*show* him.

SCENE AND SUMMARY OR SHOW, DON'T TELL

Writing is about power—the power to capture your reader's attention, to occupy his mind and heart, to make him think thoughts and experience feelings he would never have on his own. The power to enlarge the reader's world, to make him look at things he would ordinarily not notice—and might even turn away from. The power to make him—however briefly—entertain a point of view different from his own, to consider a subject that would never have occurred to him otherwise, to live for awhile in a world of your making.

Even if it is the real world, it is still the real world as you have made it happen on the page. And your story doesn't succeed until it also happens in the reader's imagination.

Nonfiction is about persuasion. In a reasoned essay, the persuasion may be largely rhetorical, based on logic. You make a case, connecting fact to fact, premise to outcome, the way a trial lawyer or a debater does. The storyteller's method of persuading is more dramatic and emotional. He presents real people in action, and through their actions the issues of the story become clear, ideas and positions are tested, and we come away with a definite impression of meaning.

The two methods of persuasion are not as far apart as they might seem, though. Both depend on *showing*. Both depend on making the abstract somehow concrete. We don't really trust abstract pronouncements, in life or in nonfiction. We don't want to be told "I love you"; we want somebody to prove it.

Rhetorical persuasion—the success of, say, a movie review—depends on demonstrating abstract judgments (the musical score was inappropriate) with concrete observations (as a child is being murdered on-screen, we hear the Looneytoons theme). You're not asking the reader to take your word for it, you're putting the evidence of the film in front of him and proving your point. Even if he interprets the evidence differently than you do, he appreciates your candor and will trust you to show him more.

He senses you're not trying to put anything over on him—you are showing an essential respect for *his* judgment. You are allowing him one of the most delicious satisfactions of reading: the chance to make his own discoveries, including ones that you've missed.

How you arrange your examples—in escalating order of importance, ending with the strongest, most vivid one—will convince the reader far more effectively than insisting that he take your word for it, just because you saw the movie and he didn't.

Usually, your best chance at being original is to be as specific and as concrete as possible in illustrating your points. If the reader gets an exact and consistent sense of how you are coming to your conclusions, what sort of logic and bias you are applying to your subject, he will also stay in his seat to listen to the more abstract part of your tale, the *told* part.

A storyteller persuades by creating scenes, little dramas that occur in a definite time and place, in which real people interact in a way that furthers the aims of the overall story. Shelton's scene with Molly Bendixon in the teachers' lounge is a good example.

Then the storyteller connects the scenes by means of transitions—

filling in background information, setting us up for the next scene, *telling* us what cannot effectively be shown, such as the employment history of a character. Obviously, the narrator is *always* telling, in one sense, but sometimes the narrator backs away and lets someone else talk (dialogue), presents sensory data for us to enjoy firsthand (description), lingers on a particular encounter (scene), and all at once we forget that the story is being told at all. We are just watching and listening, as if it were happening right there in front of our reading chair.

That's the advantage of having a narrator, an advantage that the theater, for example, doesn't enjoy. The narrator can bring information and perspective, slipping facts and statistics into scenes quietly, without interrupting the flow of action and talk. Then, when we really need some guidance about how to interpret what we've just seen, the narrator can talk to us awhile, anticipating and answering our questions.

Telling is not always a bad thing. The trick is to find a balance and to achieve a sense of flow, of forward movement or *narrative profluence*. If you find yourself writing giant blocks of dialogue separated by giant blocks of narrative lecture, you may want to consider integrating the parts a little better, avoiding such "block writing," which can be jarring and discontinuous. You want one to lead naturally into the other.

This modulation between *summary* and *scene*, between telling and showing, is the engine that drives most stories, true or invented. We arc from one scene to another, like walking across stepping-stones, and the cumulative effect is one of scope, of largeness, of inclusion, of progress toward climax. The climax can be an actual scene, or it can be the coalescing of an impression or idea—like the punchline of a joke.

CONSEQUENCES—WHAT'S AT STAKE?

In a good story, something important is at stake. Remember our high-rise bridge? We weren't much interested in it so long as it remained a matter of a few local residents being inconvenienced. When the sewer line raised the ante, and the very survival of a way of life was threatened, it took an intriguing turn. It began to matter.

Some nonfiction stories—such as Williams' *Refuge*—are literally matters of life and death. In others, the stakes aren't nearly so high. But it's probably true that the more that's at stake, the greater our interest. Often, as with our bridge example, the consequences are not obvious. You have to teach your reader why the subject matters. Ask yourself, what is at stake here? For the characters? For the reader? Who is risking what? What's the most they can gain or lose in this story?

If the answer is "Not much," then find a better story.

VOICE

What distinguishes a competently told true story from a truly memorable one?

"One of the things that editors are looking for is a voice. They want you to sound like somebody," Canty says. "They don't necessarily want good gray reportorial prose. They want somebody who's going to have an attitude."

Voice is another one of those slippery terms that seems to have different meanings for different writers. It takes in style—the cumulative effect of the way sentences are crafted into paragraphs—but it is somehow more than style. Voice is what the reader hears in his mind's ear, the strong sense that the words of the story are coming from another living, human personality with a unique perspective on events. The sense not only that you are hearing a story but that *somebody is telling you* that story—somebody distinctive, somebody you could pick out of a crowd, somebody whose voice you'll listen for and recognize the next time you hear it. Somebody you can trust.

Voice is precisely what conventional journalists try to keep *out* of their stories, because *voice* is the opposite of impersonal objectivity. You, the writer of creative nonfiction, want to have a distinctive voice.

But here's the paradox: If you *try* to have a voice, you'll fail. Your written voice will sound as false as the stagy patter of a disc jockey.

You can't overlay it on the work. It is intrinsic in everything you do from the moment an idea occurs to you till you turn in the finished draft. It is part of how you go about researching a story, what questions you ask in an interview, what form you choose to write in and what words you choose. How you work from beginning to end.

Voice is instinctive. It is the hallmark of who you are.

That's why, way back when we were discussing subject, we began with that question: Who am I? And all the questions that went with it: Why am I writing this? What do I believe in? Where is my passion?

And that's why, when we discuss autobiographical writing in the next chapter, we'll never get far away from the question of voice.

Bob Reiss makes the point unequivocally: "In the end—and this is the scary thing about any kind of art, and this is where nonfiction *becomes* art—in the end, the story will sink or swim on your attitude, your perspective, what you do to the story. What *you* bring to the story—what *only* you can bring to the story. Your kind of sensitivity. Your kind of anger. Your kind of whatever the dominant thing is in you. Whatever that special thing *you* have is."

Your passion is your voice.

CHAPTER EIGHT

PUTTING YOURSELF
ON THE LINE

AUTOBIOGRAPHY, MEMOIR
AND PERSONAL ESSAY

A few years ago, I almost died by my own hand, and when I woke from that disagreeable event, I recognized for the first time that I was fully and solely responsible for my existence. . . . These essays enact that responsibility, however belatedly discovered, in the terms in which I can understand it: as a writer of my life."

So opens Nancy Mairs' collection of remarkably candid personal essays, *Plaintext*. The essays are as matter-of-factly intimate as the preface, chronicling her experiences, her not-always-successful loves, her mistakes and triumphs, and the household truths of her life.

"On Being a Cripple," for example, reveals what's it's like to endure multiple sclerosis—Mairs explains the symptoms of the disease, how it overtook her, her bleak prognosis, and how she has come to terms with it. Oddly, it's a very uplifting, even inspiring, essay—not because it offers false, feel-good platitudes, but because we're listening to the honest voice, tinged with humor, of a woman who clearly does not feel sorry for herself.

"People—crippled or not—wince at the word 'cripple,' as they do not at 'handicapped' or 'disabled,' " she writes, in heartfelt allegiance to accurate language. "Perhaps I want them to wince. I want them to see me as a tough customer, one to whom the fates/gods/viruses have not been kind, but who can face the brutal truth of her existence squarely."

Mairs thus displays herself—physically, emotionally and

stylistically—with dignity. Knowing that our first impulse upon glimpsing a cripple is to look away, she looks us square in the eye, inviting us to stare back without embarrassment. Her attitude, the very choice of the word "cripple," takes the fear out of the encounter.

This is the first-person voice at its best—a credible voice of witness speaking to us with warmth, humor and wisdom, free of bitterness or self-pity, inviting us to share an important confidence. That confidence may take the form of autobiography, memoir or personal essay.

By *autobiography* I refer to a long account of one's own life, encompassing a fairly complete lifetime, or focused within formative years or some other limiting time frame. It may be anecdotal, fragmented, jumping from scene to scene with large holes in the record, or it may be methodical. It is likely to be intimate and revealing, candid and self-conscious at the same time, and as a record of fact and event may be notoriously unreliable, for reasons we will get to presently.

A *memoir*, for me, strikes the same emotional note as autobiography—written memory—but is usually focused on some triggering person or event in the narrator's experience, so that a memoir is always a memoir *of* something outside the narrator's interior life. A memoir may be brief, and memoirs often wind up collected into a loose autobiography, though a collection of memoirs is liable to be as much about other things—a time in history, for example—as about the writer.

A *personal essay* is a story with a point, usually in the short form, but not always. The writer relates a personal experience that in itself does not necessarily matter beyond its private interest to the writer and then *makes* it matter to the reader, the stranger, by couching it in a greater context, so that the story becomes a demonstration of a larger truth.

Naturally a memoir contains fragments of autobiography, just as a personal essay is usually built upon a memoir, a remembered anecdote. However they are blended, the intimate first-person voice is the hallmark of all three.

Jan DeBlieu speaks with such a voice in *Hatteras Journal*, the memoir of her sojourn on a North Carolina barrier island. "It was like falling in love," she says, recalling how the natural, storm-washed landscape captured her imagination. "And you know how when you fall in love with somebody, you end up just wanting to tell them everything and portray them as honestly and poetically as you can to other people? That's what happened with me and Hatteras Island."

THE FREEDOM OF YOUR OWN VOICE

Writing about your own life can liberate you from the constraints of somebody else's style. We all learn to write—as we learn to cook, to play the guitar, to teach—by imitating those who seem to know how to do it well, whose style appeals to us. Sometimes we are also tempted to imitate their subjects; we naturally learn *their* recipes, *their* songs, *their* lessons.

Many of my students start out writing in first-person about famous paintings, Vietnam, the homeless and other unfamiliar, borrowed subjects with voices not their own, because they have a crush on a particular writer, a certain book. Once they are forced to address subjects closer to home, subjects that touch their own lives—their families, the pressures of job-hunting after college, the suicide of a friend— their voices take on a refreshing honesty. They know this life, this subject, and they must tell about it in their own words, according to their own sentence rhythms.

This does not usually happen on the first or even the second try. (I say "they," but of course they are only traveling over the same ground I traveled.) At first, they tend to lapse into clichés, both of language and of idea. They've picked up these clichés in a lifetime of living in a culture that substitutes pleasant euphemisms for hard truths, bureaucratic terminology for basic facts: "downsizing" for "firing loyal workers"; "causing collateral damage" for "accidentally bombing civilian hospitals."

Writing about growing up in a family in which the father beats the children, they will parrot pop-psychology jargon such as "dysfunctional," "self-esteem" and "enabling behavior." Largely without being aware of it, they will adopt a neo-Freudian stance: If only the right therapy could be applied, all would be well. In other words, they will fit their experience into a preexisting formula, complete with its own language bites—a simplification that does no justice to their tangled subject and does not begin to tell their story.

Or else, in a piece about the suicide of a friend, they will fall back on language that is romantically overwrought, full of shrill questions to God about *Why?* and embarrassing—and usually generic—

superlatives about the deceased: how nobody could make you laugh the way he could; how he always thought about others, never about himself; how he was the most talented and charming and idealistic person in the whole graduating class; and so on.

Language that is nearer to the TV melodramas they've watched all these years than it is to their actual experience, telling us about a person who was just too good to be true.

We don't believe it.

It's not that it isn't all true; it's just that the truth isn't in the writing yet. No doubt the poor kid who drowned himself was a nice guy and will be sorely missed—and I deliberately use melodramatic examples because it is often the melodramas of our lives that first turn us inward. Suicide is a common subject among student writers. But the writing keeps the writer from really engaging the truth. The stiff words, like the suit and tie dragged out of mothballs only for weddings and funerals, are false and unnatural. They formalize—and *formulize*—the truth and so keep it at arm's length.

Which may be safe—the writer can find reassurance in formulas and platitudes—but does not get him or the reader any closer to understanding the profound experience he is trying to relate. It mummifies the experience, wraps it in euphemism, pushes it away into the rhetorical distance, rather than bringing it to chilling and troubling life right up close.

Often the underlying problem is that the experience is still too fresh, too newly painful, too emotionally "hot," and all the writer needs is a little time for it to cool off.

It is only through crafting original language, which requires a certain emotional distance, that the writer can begin to capture the genuine feeling of the experience—in this case, the hollowing grief that comes with a preventable death. It will not be trite superlatives that endow the young man's death with dignity and meaning, but the flat language of everyday use, exactly applied.

We always write out of mystery, looking for an answer we don't have, trying to resolve what troubles us, to understand what seems beyond comprehension. To understand why a decent young man might end his life, we may have to confront our own temptation to suicide; our own fear of mortality; the guilt we feel at not recognizing how much more friendship he needed than we were willing to give; the profound despair and loneliness he must have felt—that we, too, have felt at times; his not-so-admirable qualities; our unsettling relief that it was him, not us; even our anger at him for acting with such finality.

To get it right, we'll have to lose some sleep over it.

When I encounter such a first draft, I usually put it aside and have the writer *tell* me the story in his own words. Or I will urge the writer to *talk* the story into a tape recorder, play it back, and then compare it to the written draft.

Two things usually happen. First, the generic information turns into specific detail: "committed suicide" becomes "stripped off his clothes and walked into the ocean on Christmas Eve." Second, the language, the very way of telling, turns genuine: "My dysfunctional family gave me low self-esteem" turns into "The first night I can remember not crying myself to sleep was the night I moved into my college dorm room, two hundred miles from home."

It's hard to look at unpleasant, frightening things head-on. But that's the writer's job, and he does it with words that go to the heart of the matter, that touch rather than push away, that clarify rather than obscure. Clear, direct language is a weapon against fear and despair. It can bring the monsters up into the light where they're not usually so terrifying anymore. And even if they remain scary, at least we can learn from them. And we can share with the reader the genuine emotions they evoke.

If you're writing the truth about your own life, you can't fool yourself. You can't hide behind data or interview quotes or pretty descriptions of a place. You have to put yourself on the line.

"The more honest sentiment that I can put on the page, the better off I am," DeBlieu says. "I was more inclined to hold back than I needed to be—as long as the emotion was honest and sincere. I was a little bit shy about putting myself on the line. I think that you need to be as honest with the reader as you possibly can be, but at the same time not self-serving."

You put yourself on the line by telling the story in your own words, discovering those words with precision in memory and experience, then recreating the memory and experience through those words.

DeBlieu found her personal voice with *Hatteras Journal*. In chapter seven, entitled "Loggerhead Rites," she relates,

> One July evening just before dusk I stood on a narrow, gently sloping beach two hundred miles south of Cape Hatteras with the hope of catching a glimpse of prehistoric times. A southeasterly wind tousled the sea oats, and a calm surf with thin coils of foam rolled across a mosaic of footprints in the sand. Next to me Cindy Meekins yawned, touched her toes, and did a spurt of jumping jacks in an effort to wake up. Behind us were two pale blue, woodframe houses with porches rimmed by short white railings, the kind of fusty, weatherbeaten retreats that tourist guides describe as charming.

The narrative voice is familiar and quietly arresting, inspiring immediate trust in the reader. "Before that time I had been working a lot on honing my basic skills as a writer," DeBlieu says. "I think the fact that I had spent years doing that enabled me to suddenly develop this voice. I guess the voice wasn't really developed suddenly—it grew out of those years of previous work and then an experience that really moved me."

When at last you are confronting the truth of your life honestly in words, you have found your voice. And with that comes a terrific freedom to write about anything else, too—anything else at all.

THE SEDUCTIVE EGO

The first-person voice is seductive, not only to the reader, but to the writer, and while that's a wonderful thing, it can also be dangerous to good art. It's easy to lapse into self-centered preoccupation that excludes the reader—to become stuck on yourself. Mere opinions and feelings, however strongly you hold them, are not necessarily significant. They may be of little of interest to anybody but you.

Think of the worst thing you can say about someone you've just met: "He wouldn't stop talking about himself." A self-centered ego can clear a room faster than a fire drill.

Trained since college as a journalist, DeBlieu has written for *The New York Times Magazine*, *Audobon* and *Smithsonian*, among many other periodicals, and her subject is most often the personal self coming to terms with the natural world. "I didn't write about myself at first at all," she recalls of her evolution as a personal essayist. "I think the fact was that I learned how to write by observing and trying to develop an eye for detail, and looking for good material, material that was interesting to me *and* to other people, that had some relevance to a wider audience. And then I slowly began inserting myself into the material, into my journalism back before I did my book on Hatteras, and finally inserting myself completely into the landscape in Hatteras because I felt so much a part of it."

The best memoir is informed by such close observation of the world, whatever world that is: the world of family, of workplace, of solitude. The best personal essays are usually about the self in relation to a world beyond the self. The friction between the personal self and the requirements of the world often—perhaps even most of the time—provide the dramatic tension in such a piece.

"The function of autobiographical work for me is not simply to be self-indulgent and it's not to presume that my life is inherently interesting to the world," Ron Powers says of the scenes recalling his childhood in *White Town Drowsing*. "It has a resonance with the rest of what I'm trying to write. It illuminates what I'm trying to write." His object was to contrast the Hannibal where he grew up to the grotesque parody it was being turned into by the Mark Twain theme park experts, so boyhood memories were crucial in making the town a real place where real little boys used to roam.

These days, it is standard practice in freshman English classes to begin the semester by having the students write a personal essay rather than, say, a third-person essay about a topical issue or a work of literature. The theory is that students are "experts" on themselves, and that this kind of writing is natural and nonthreatening. Having eased into writing about themselves, they can then move outward in ever-widening circles, addressing the rest of the world in more formal terms. This would seem intuitively right.

But years of experience have convinced me that this is exactly wrong.

Writing about yourself is hard, and not everybody is prepared to do it, as a first stage or ever. Many eminent writers never attempt to write nonfictionally about themselves, and the ones who do often come to it after years of writing about other subjects or in other genres. It is one important way to find your voice, but not the only way, and maybe not the first way.

Let's be clear: We're not talking about keeping a journal or diary, recording private thoughts as a form of self-expression, self-awareness, even therapy. Such writing may be wonderful for the soul but is engaging to the reader only by accident.

As soon as a writer is writing to be *read*, something has changed. Even writing a letter introduces a new anxiety that wasn't there when you were entering thoughts into your journal: You are imagining someone opening your letter at the other end, you're concerned that you come across well, that you set the right tone, keep the proper intimacy or distance.

No research paper in the world can make you sweat over it as much as a love letter to someone you're not sure loves you back, or a letter applying for a job you really want.

By the time you are writing even to a single reader, the act of writing about yourself is anything but natural. It requires selection, artifice and a qualified honesty—"qualified" because all of us need to keep some secrets. Though there are always exceptions—writers who take to the autobiographical voice as a natural way of talking—to my way of thinking, it's very hard to learn to write memoir or personal essay without first knowing how to write well, because you're trying to learn to do two things at once: write, and come to terms with your life directly. It's a very complex transaction, and everything we've said about emotional cost in fact-based writing is doubled.

I recommend this sequence: learn to write competently, write about the world for a while in third person, then turn to the first-person narrative, find your voice, take your writing to a new level of elegance and emotional honesty, turn that writing loose on the world again, and repeat the cycle continuously.

"Part of the problem of teaching memoir is that students often don't know the difference between memoir and psychotherapy," explains Norman Sims, chairman of the Journalism Department at the University of Massachusetts and the scholar who has done the most to define and analyze literary journalism. He's being deliberately wry about the danger of simply wallowing in the self, but his point is well taken.

"Sometimes we need to shut up and stop talking about ourselves," echoes William Howarth, who has written frequently for *National*

Geographic and *The New York Times*. In his course on environmental writing at Princeton University, Howarth doesn't allow students to write in the first person. He maintains, "We have an obligation to make them look outside themselves."

CREDIBILITY VS. NARROWNESS OF VISION

There's no denying the power of the first-person voice: As the reader hears it, he unconsciously repeats "I" and is tricked into regarding the experience as his own.

For sheer primary access to the truth of event and emotion, there is nothing to match a first-person account by an eyewitness. Paul Fussell, whose nonfiction book *Wartime* debunks many of the popular patriotic myths of the Second World War, writes about how unreliable were the newspaper accounts, movies and novels about the war: "One turns, thus, from novels to 'non-fiction,' especially memoirs, and especially memoirs written by participants not conscious of serving any very elevated artistic ambition. The best are those devoid of significant dialogue, almost always a sign of *ex post facto* novelistic visitation. Because forbidden in all theaters of war lest their capture reveal secrets, clandestine diaries, seen and censored by no authority, offer one of the most promising accesses to actuality. The prohibition of diaries often meant increased devotion and care on the part of the writer."

But the very thing that makes the first-person narrative compelling can also undercut it. Even when they mean to, not all witnesses tell the complete, unvarnished truth—and as readers, listeners to a voice telling us the story, it's exactly their biases we crave.

"It's very difficult to be accurate in memoir," cautions Sims, editor of *Literary Journalism in the Twentieth Century*. Even a writer trying to tell the truth often doesn't have much more to go on than memory, which is selective and prone to be self-serving.

We're all familiar with the *unreliable narrator* in fiction: the first person voice that doesn't always tell the truth, or the whole truth, or even deliberately lies. Think of Edgar Allan Poe's narrator in "The Tell-Tale Heart," who commits premeditated murder, dismembers the body, then pleads with us that he is *not* insane. Of course he is—crazy as a bedbug.

Or Nick Carraway, who narrates *The Great Gatsby*. At the moment, early in the novel, when he confides to us that he's the most honest person he knows, we start to count the silverware. We don't trust him, and immediately we begin to notice things he's conveniently left out of the telling.

In nonfiction, the first-person narrator works under a similar disadvantage: At any moment, the reader may find cause to dismiss his version as only *one* version and seek the truth elsewhere. This is especially risky in democratic America, where everybody's opinion has come to be regarded with equal weight.

In fiction, the effect of this can be a delicious irony, engineered by the author. His narrator is only a *persona*, an invented character impersonating the author, and part of our delight in reading the story is recognizing the discrepancy between what the narrator *tells* and the truth we discover through other clues. But in nonfiction there is no such ironic distance: If we don't trust the narrator, then we don't trust the author or the telling.

The first-person narrator must strive hard to gain the reader's trust but must not *seem* to be striving hard. Straightforward language and honest presentation can help. And he must establish his credentials to tell the story (remember that nagging question in chapter two: Who am *I* to be telling this story?). The personal essayist can take advantage of the same tools fiction writers use to calibrate the reliability of the narrator: Announce your biases to the reader up front; quote other people in the story as accurately as you can so their point of view is represented; use description and other kinds of "evidence" to convince the reader to trust your account.

A first-person narrator can use statistics, scientific data, historical information and dispassionate observation every bit as effectively as a third-person narrator. Describe your own actions without justifying them—let the reader judge them. That doesn't mean that you can't or shouldn't *explain*, retracing your motivation, your thought process, your feelings at a given moment of action.

As soon as the reader suspects that the narrator is making himself too perfect, too much the hero, or too much the advocate for a certain point of view, the story is likely to lose power. You can't afford to let the reader catch you in a lie, and there are many kinds of lies, ranging from outright untruths, to embellishment, to simply leaving out facts inconvenient to your case.

As a correspondent in the Second World War, John Steinbeck recognized the precarious position of the first-person narrator. In the introduction to *Once There Was a War*, his collected dispatches, he writes:

> All of us developed our coy little tricks with copy. Reading these old pieces, I recognize one of mine. I never admitted having seen anything myself. In describing a scene I invariably put it in the mouth of someone else. I forget why I did this. Perhaps I felt that it would be more believable if told by someone else. Or it is possible that I felt an interloper and eavesdropper on the war, and I was a little bit ashamed of being there at all. Maybe I was ashamed that I could go home and the soldiers couldn't.

MEMORY BEGETS MEMORY

In some sense, the writer is always the interloper, the eavesdropper, standing just outside the conversation, on the edge of the memory, participating in it but also already using it, and not always comfortable in the dual role.

We feel like spies in the family circle, looters of the family album, undercover agents recording the most intimate conversations of our friends. Informers on ourselves. We give up our lives to make words, telling as many of our secrets as we dare. We give up something—privacy, the freedom of anonymity, the freedom to forget and be forgotten about.

But, in the act of revisiting our lives, we also gain something important: We recover memory. And in so doing, we come to understand our own lives better. In the end, that may be the best—if most selfish—reason for writing memoir, autobiography and the personal essay.

"All my life, I had thought about ways to write about my father—every guy does," Powers recalls. "And I had memories, but the memories didn't add up to anything. They didn't seem to have the complexity of *story*. They were just personal memory fragments, and a lot of them were angry memories of a very forbidding, quiet, seemingly inexplicably angry man, of a diminished man, but I didn't know what to do with that. And when I wrote *White Town Drowsing*, I didn't even know my father was going to be in it."

Revisiting his native ground, Powers encountered all the ghosts of his boyhood. "I had to personalize it on behalf of the reader, so I started to remember the town as I knew it as a boy, when it made its own sense, worked according to its own logic, had its own economy, and I began to imagine my father at the center of all this—a Fuller Brush man in the 1930s. I learned from my uncle that his car didn't have any brakes and he zig-zagged down the hills by hitting trees and lightposts and fire hydrants, and that's how he got to the bottom of the hill.

"And as soon as I had that image, my whole perception of my father started to change. Suddenly he wasn't just 'Dad' anymore—he wasn't inexplicable Freudian Dad, he was a character in the town, and I began to see him through the town's eyes. And in the eyes of the town, he was a figure of affection."

Powers' creative reverie triggered memory—old stories he had long since forgotten, the way the Mississippi River smelled at night, the facades of missing buildings, and the faces of vanished friends. "Had I set out to write an autobiographical story, I probably would have remained angry," Powers says. "I started to like him for the first time in my life in writing about him as a figure of the town."

As a fiction writer, my impulse had always been to shy away from writing directly about my life, my family and close friends. But no writer can ever escape revealing himself on the page, so I'm sure my stories and novels are full of things I remember, experiences that changed me, people I've loved and hated, conversations that struck a chord in my heart. People who know me well often claim to recognize such moments in my fiction.

But that doesn't mean *I* recognize them. Fiction is a lens that distorts, combines, transforms, mixes things up, disguises real people as composites, cloaks real experience in the illusion of experience, blurs the hard edges of memory. If you write a fiction well enough, you don't remember which parts really happened and which ones you made up.

When I began writing personal essays for broadcast, I instinctively turned to the stuff of my own life. Even now, I can't say for sure why. Maybe it was precisely because it was material I had never addressed before.

Since I began vagabonding around America as a teenager, I have kept journals, some years more completely recorded than others. As a sailboat owner, I've kept ten years' worth of logbooks. But as I began to write personal essays, I realized an astonishing fact: It had been years since I had sat down and *deliberately* remembered my past. I had faithfully kept journals, but I had not gone back and read them. I had boxes full of old photographs, but what was in those boxes I couldn't say. My yearbooks and baseball card collection and letters from old friends were all somewhere, but where?

I began a kind of personal archaeology that is still in process, digging through the accumulated layers of my life, excavating telling artifacts among the litter, reading my life as I go.

Reading it as I write it.

THE CRYSTAL CAVE OF MEMORY

One of the best places my father ever took us when we were kids was Crystal Cave—a natural labyrinth of caverns and tunnels deep under the Pennsylvania hills.

Up above, it was a muggy hot day in July. Down inside the rock, though, the air was silky cool. The artificial light glowed weak and eerie—as if the rock were soaking it up. The walls were spangled with quartz crystals and crannied with secret nooks and crevices—who knew what spooky things lurked there.

Later, outside in the sunshine, with the entrance to the cave in the background, my father lined up us kids for a snapshot. He was something of a cubist with his Brownie camera—he often cut off arms and legs, severed heads at the neck, and sometimes disembodied arms and legs would show up inside the frame.

At Crystal Cave, he snapped a dozen shots to guarantee one good one.

A couple of weeks later, the developed snapshots arrived in the mail. My father opened the envelope and peeled them off one by one. There was the shadowy entrance to Crystal Cave, and there were the three of us brothers.

Except there were four.

Standing just to the left of my brother Paul, a crew-cut kid we didn't recognize stared into the camera. He was obviously posing as part of the group, but what was he doing there?

My father flipped to the next shot, and the next, and the next. The kid is in all of them. He's dressed like us in regular 1960s kid clothes—shorts, plaid sports shirt, Keds. We were snappy dressers in those days. But though we're all smiling for the camera, he has a sad, lost look on his face, as if something awful has just happened to him.

None of us, including my mother, always the most perceptive, remembered seeing him. Who was he? Some kid-ghost of the cave? For years, we made up stories about him—he was the lost boy, abandoned by his mother and father in the cave, coming back to haunt the tourists until they returned him to his parents.

We were kids. We were willing to believe anything.

I don't believe that anymore.

What I do believe is that we move about in the world pushing out space for ourselves the way a big truck barreling down the highway pushes air out of its way. The space is exactly our own size and shape. We're focused. A place exists for us so long as we're there, and when we're gone, it ceases to exist until the *next* time we go there.

We're each the star of our own moving picture.

The other people—the extras, the strangers in all the crowd scenes of our lives—seem to go about their business around us as if their function is to provide background for *our* lives. They linger just outside the edges of our family snapshots.

Sometimes, as at Crystal Cave, one of them slips inside.

Lately I've gone through all my old photographs. They've taken on an eerie quality. In the background of a shot of my brothers and me all dressed up for an Easter Sunday thirty years ago, a stranger ducks his head and hurries away.

In another, behind my aunt and all of us kids in Halloween costumes, there's a half-covered face at the window—who's watching?

And in all those shots of the first bicycle, the Christmas sled, the treehouse, there are strangers hidden within the scalloped frame: inside the flattened shapes of houses, behind the wheels of old cars, sitting in lawn chairs a block away, their backs to us, profiled in conversation with some offstage presence.

A snapshot, like a life, is all timing and point of view.

Like a story.

So now I think this about that little boy who was with me when I was a little boy at Crystal Cave and who now must also be a man in his thirties.

When he pulls out his scrapbook of childhood photos, does he wonder how three strange kids got into *his* picture? And does he wonder why, on a long-ago, forlorn day when his world is crashing down around him, we're all grinning like idiots?

What will his memoir say about me?

THE CONFIDENCE OF FAMILY AND FRIENDS

Remember when we talked about consequences? In nonfiction, they don't just happen to "characters," they happen to real people. And in memoir, the real people are often those whom we love most, whose opinion and affection matter to us far more than any abstract notions about the integrity of art. Art doesn't keep you warm on cold, lonely nights, or during long bleak months when it's always 3 A.M. in your soul.

When we write about ourselves, we write about all the ones who are a part of our story. Sometimes, as at Crystal Cave, we include them almost accidentally. The bigger the role they play in our story, the more we are compelled to write about them. We can't help it. We can't tell our story any other way.

"When writing about your family, both your immediate family and your extended family, the risk is always that they will see it as a betrayal," Terry Tempest Williams says.

It's an important risk, one you should consider when writing personal nonfiction—if only out of fairness to loved ones. You want to be prepared for what will happen when that story is published among strangers, because once the private story is made public, you can't call it back. It goes out into the world and takes on a life of its own. You may feel emotionally exposed, your soul laid bare. And if you feel that way, and you wrote the piece, imagine how ambushed a loved one may feel. Remind yourself that somebody will actually read what you write.

Imagine that reader a stranger.

Imagine that reader as the person who is most precious to you in this world.

I had written and broadcast radio essays for a whole year before I got my shock of recognition. My essays were mainly stories from my life, molded into meaning, or so I hoped—stories about my brothers, my parents, favorite students, childhood friends, my dogs. One day I was standing by my locker at the gym, completely undressed, when a stranger approached me. "Hey—you're Philip Gerard!" he said, apparently glad to meet me. I hate meeting new people when I am naked, but I tried my best to be nonchalant. He went on, grinning: "I know all about your childhood!"

My God, I thought, have I given away too much? And only then did I begin to reflect—with a certain amount of low-grade terror—on how my own family might react to having their most private foibles splashed across the airwaves of America.

Whenever we publish personal nonfiction, we are meeting new people, naked. And we're frequently undressing our loved ones, too.

Asked how her parents and sisters reacted to her memoir, *An American Childhood*, Annie Dillard responds, "I gave them every chapter, every page, to pass on, because they're in very good health and they have excellent lawyers."

Of course, her answer is ironic, but not entirely. She goes on to explain how family members can react in unpredictable ways to a memoir that includes them, even to passages that seem harmless from the writer's point of view: "I was telling a class the other day all sorts of strange things my parents didn't want me to put in there. My mother said that it wasn't her under the dining room table in the tornado, it was the maid; so I said, 'All right, Mom,' and I took that out. And my father said that I shouldn't put in a sentence about going boating on the Allegheny River in 1955 in Pittsburgh, that the water was dirty. And I said, 'Daddy! In 1955 in Pittsburgh the water was dirty? That's surely all right.' And he said, 'No, I've got to live in this town, and that really makes Pittsburgh look bad,' so I took that out.

"I had made some crack about the Pennsylvania Turnpike, which was one of the earliest big highways in the nation. I said it had been built in 1934 and scarcely improved since. And if you've ridden the Pennsylvania Turnpike, you know that's a really kind assessment. And he said no once again, that they had to live there, that I shouldn't say that. Lots of their friends use that road all the time. So I took that out, too.

"I gave my sisters all sorts of real good lines that I thought up while

I was writing the book, and they were happy. And my mother was happy. My mother said, 'Oh, it's going to just make me look so terrible that I didn't come and look at your amoeba under the microscope,' and I said, 'Mom, they're going to love you, take my word for it— they're going to love you, Mom,' and they did."

To honor her subject in *Refuge*, Williams had to write about the most intimate and private family moments, including the hour of grief—a trying time for any family, one which can be full of intense emotion as family members come to grips with loss, doubt, fear, guilt, anger, emotional exhaustion, uncertainty, depression and pain. Williams was also writing within the context of a very large extended family who have lived among one another for generations, within a very close-knit Mormon community in which the church plays a significant personal and public role, setting moral standards and placing a very strong value on loyalty to government and church, both of which she criticizes in the book.

It's a moral and artistic dilemma, one that has definite consequences: How do you write about living family members and other loved ones in a way that tells the emotional truth, yet doesn't cost you your place in their affections? No writer wants to destroy the precious community he finds so compelling in the first place.

Williams is clear: "The immediate concern to me was always my family."

Her practical solution was much the same as Dillard's: At every stage, she showed the manuscript to those whose good opinion mattered most, then made judicious changes to guard the family's privacy. "So when it was published, there were no surprises—I had the complete support of my immediate family. This was not the case with my extended family—they did view it as a betrayal of my mother, and of the Mormon Church."

As a practical matter, you simply can't show your manuscript to everybody who might have an interest in it, hoping for a collective imprimatur that will take away all the risk. As an artist, you may not want to—you and you alone are responsible for its truth. And showing your manuscript is not the same as soliciting approval—you may find yourself unwilling to make the changes that family members want you to make. In that case, you may only have focused their resistance, alienating you and perhaps—in rare cases—interfering with publication.

The implications can be legal—invasion of privacy or libel—but they are more likely to be ethical, artistic and personal. It's a hard choice. Not showing a manuscript prior to publication, a manuscript in which some loved one's private life is exposed, can be a kind of cowardice. I have been guilty of it.

"We're writing out of the truth of our lives," Terry Tempest Williams says. That lends our writing power—and risk. As a writer of conscience, you have to decide what is nonnegotiable. And telling your story to the world may come at a cost. Only you can decide whether to pay it.

EMOTIONAL COST

Unlike a fiction writer, the personal essayist, the author of memoir, has no buffer, no illusion of narrative distance, between himself and his subject. Whenever a student writes a really terrible short story, we can both sit in the clouds and move the characters around together, trying out new scenes, cutting and pasting dialogue, even throwing out the whole scenario and starting from scratch. The fiction writer's investment lies in the invention, and he can always invent something new. That's one of the reasons art is such an eternally hopeful occupation.

But if a memoir fails, if a personal essay seems dull and trite, I always have the awful feeling that I'm attaching an irrevocable failing grade to the student's *life*. We are who we are, and we've done what we've done. Mere technique can't change either one.

That's one way writing from personal experience can be devastating: You write your heart out, and nobody cares.

There's another way.

A graduate student of mine wrote a very eloquent personal essay about an event that happened while she was a teenager and her years of coming to terms with it: On a Sunday morning, her mother slipped out to the convenience store to pick up a bottle of milk. She walked in on an armed robbery, and the robbers shotgunned her to death. When the piece came to the workshop table, we were all at a loss. How could we possibly talk about such brutal, personal truth? Some of us broke down, and others of us simply clammed up. The writer, who was experienced and self-possessed, nevertheless had to leave the room to collect herself.

None of us—especially not the writer—was prepared for the cost.

That's the thing about writing your own life: It doesn't work unless you're prepared to come clean. But when you can take a deep breath and address the things that scare the hell out of you, that drive you to grief you thought was beyond words, that amaze and confound and baffle you, that keep you up at night and give you nightmares, that cause you joy so keen it begs to be expressed, you can come to terms with the truth of your own experience.

Most people never do. They're missing a primal human satisfaction: making memory into art.

Remember Socrates: "The unexamined life is not worth living."

CHAPTER NINE

MYSTERY AND STRUCTURE, STYLE AND ATTITUDE

D uring the challenger trials for the 1995 Americas Cup, on a clear breezy day off San Diego, syndicate *one*Australia's boat buckled amidships and sank in less than two minutes. A multimillion dollar investment, three years' worth of computer-aided design and tank-testing, space-age carbon-fiber spars and onboard computerized navigation systems—all disappeared in less time than it took to write these two sentences telling about it. Luckily the crew was rescued.

The boat was doing nothing very exotic. There was no tsunami or typhoon, no collision, no rogue whale or uncharted reef. The boat was simply trying to sail through the water.

It failed.

The boat was lovely to see—sleek and polished, with fair lines, a clean deck and towering rig. You did not have to be a sailor, you did not have to pretend to have the least interest in sailing or the Americas Cup, to find your eye arrested by it. But it didn't work.

What good is a beautiful sailboat if it can't sail?

The *form* was right, but the *structure* didn't hold up.

In engineering terms, the hull had no integrity. It wasn't enough that it look pretty. It was also supposed to *do* something.

What good is a beautifully written passage if it doesn't work?

Structural integrity in writing, as in boatbuilding, is what allows the thing to function, to do whatever exemplifies the essence of what it is. If it's a boat, it should sail without buckling in the middle. If it's creative nonfiction, it should tell a story accurately, deliver precise and crucial information, persuade the reader, move him to insight, tell him something important he doesn't already know and make him understand how urgent it is that he know it, capture his imagination in a way that is very nearly literal—and do all of these things in a manner that adds up to a complete, whole, satisfying experience.

It shouldn't buckle in the middle and sink without a trace. If it does, your characters will not be rescued.

I said before that writing is always a matter of character. *Integrity* is a good term to describe the convergence of the writer's character and the functional wholeness of the written piece. A good part of what makes for integrity is a commitment to good old-fashioned workman-ship—not cutting corners with materials or the way they are put to-gether; paying close attention even to the parts that don't show; being honest in setting up expectations for the reader; not leaving out any important pieces, even if you're sure the reader won't notice.

Structure goes to the heart of everything important about the writing. Structure isn't the glamorous part—the carbon-fiber mast, the spanking Kevlar sails, the snappy syndicate logo on the transom. It's usually the part the reader doesn't even notice: the hidden struts and braces beneath the pretty hull, holding it together; the abstract calcu-lations of load, drag and lift made literal in the shape of the thing; the wings and bulbs on the underwater keel that hold it upright; the pat-tern of connecting through-bolts and rivets; the deliberate balance of weight in the trim; the attention to details large and small; the attitude you bring to the work.

Structure is the arrangement of parts and all the techniques you use to hold the parts together and make it *do* what it is intended to do. Most readers never notice structure—until it falters.

In fact, one sign that you've done it right is precisely that the reader *doesn't* notice. All he sees is a boat under full sail sweeping along with a grace and power so breathtaking he longs to jump aboard for the ride, right now. Structure is the part for the person who doesn't care *how* a sailboat works, he just wants to experience sailing. If you don't get it right, you don't get anything right.

Writing is a mushy art. It's the only art form that cannot rely directly on sensation. That's why we reach for metaphors like sailboats, knowing that such metaphors are at best imperfect—they always break down somewhere—and at worst disastrously confusing. (I don't get all this sailing business. What's a rig? Or carbon-fiber spars?) We're trying to express the world of the senses through little black marks, and it's damned hard to do.

The word *sailboat* is just that, a word, and the writer's job is to put it together with other words so that it will explode with meaning in the reader's imagination.

Music excites the tympanic membrane of the ear; painting dazzles the rods and cones of the eye with the variant play of light and shadow; sculpture takes on shape and texture under the fingers; even the movement of figures across the stage in dance or drama plays to the peripheral vision, the acuity to follow and be excited by movement, that our hunting ancestors relied on for survival.

Each of the senses produces involuntary responses: emotions, physiological and chemical changes. We are startled, our pulse races, our palms sweat, we feel a surge of euphoria or panic. Whatever our philosophical position or politics, we respond in fairly primitive ways. This is not to say that we don't also have more cultured responses— an aesthetic appreciation for the lines of a drawing, or an acquired admiration for the athletic challenge of a certain brand of choreography. But you don't have to be a German intellectual to be stirred by the opening bars of Beethoven's Ninth Symphony, or a Renaissance aesthete to be awed by Michelangelo's David.

Writing, by contrast, offers no sensual experience. It touches the senses only indirectly, in a secondhand way.

Lincoln's Gettysburg Address is the same work of literary art whether it is presented in elegant handwriting on a sheet of linen parchment, in pencilled scrawl on the back of a torn envelope, or in the hypertext of a CD-ROM monitor. The handwriting and the paper, the typeface and the binding, are extrinsic to the writing. They're just the medium that allows the writing to go from the writer's head to the reader's.

And that makes structure paramount in achieving literary art. The art exists purely in the arrangement of words.

That's the single trick to which every writer is limited: You make black marks on a page. The marks, in our language, are always made in a line—from left to right, from top to bottom. There is nothing to hear, smell, taste or touch, and what is *seen* is purely an arbitrary function of one particular representation. But if you make the right marks in the right order, you can change a reader's life. Change enough lives, you can change the world.

Just ask Lincoln, or Jefferson, or the noble gentlemen who penned the Magna Carta. Or ask Mahatma Gandhi, who took a little essay by Henry David Thoreau called "On Civil Disobedience" and used it to liberate India and bring down the British Empire.

Remember, though, the story doesn't happen on the page. It happens in the reader's imagination. So the structure must happen there also. You have to make the *right* marks in the right *order* for the reader to reconstitute your imaginative logic.

That's the first and most important lesson about structure: It's always linear, even when we try hard—and succeed—to make it seem like something else. The line of words is the incarnation on the page of the underlying structure of the experience—the dramatic or persuasive logic by which the story moves.

The reader retraces your line, word by word. On both ends, it's a simple process, but a tenuous one. At any point, if the link between one word and the next is broken, the art is foiled. The story is aborted. The whole thing stops. Every space between words is a chasm between the part that has been written—or read—and the part that may never be written—or read.

That's where structure comes in. The form, like an announced subject or a title or an engaging first line, makes promises. Its big implicit promise is that this is all one thing—one particular kind of thing: a book, a memoir, a personal essay, an adventure in real life. The form promises that it will all, somehow, add up, even those parts that seem to digress.

Structure helps to make good on that promise: Here's the logic of chapters, here's the episodic diary format complete with dates, here's the anecdote and the turn into larger meaning, here's the setup and suspense and climax. At every turn, the structure reassures the reader of the wholeness of the work and reinforces the form: This part fits into a larger pattern.

Once we know from the title and subtitle that we are in for an adventure story, for instance, we automatically expect a dramatic structure. We are reassured that the information we are learning early in the piece will be useful when the moment of crisis comes and the storyteller—or some other character—is in jeopardy. If that moment of crisis, of danger, never arrives, then the structure has been violated, and with it the reader's trust in the wholeness of the piece.

If we expect an essay of ideas, we also expect, structurally, a sense of these ideas building one upon another and arriving at some break-through in the author's—and our—thinking. We expect illustrations, real or hypothetical examples to demonstrate the assertions. If we can't make the connections between the various ideas—if some strike us as trivial and others as profound, and we get them in no particular order of importance with no cues as to how to fit them together—then the structure has broken down.

We're not consciously aware of these expectations. When the right structure is in place, the reader just keeps reading. When the structure fails, the reader keeps wondering of both the individual passage and the whole work, "Why am I reading this?"

Whatever the formal shape of the piece and whatever the sup-porting structure, the reader experiences it word by word, sentence by sentence, not all at once. But he experiences the line of it in the context of its structure: a whole beautiful thing, moving forward.

If you want to learn how to write, pay attention to what happens in the act of reading. During the act of reading, the reader encounters words arranged visually on a page. The overall shape of the arrange-ment, which we can see without reading a word—a book broken down into chapters, a short article with subheadings in the context of a certain magazine—is a graphic representation of the form.

Within that form, the connecting parts—five sections, say, each subheaded with the name of a city, in a travel essay; or twelve chapters named for the months of the year in a book about a town in crisis—give a graphic sense of the structure. Again, we don't have to read past the table of contents to get a strong sense of the connective logic. In fact, structure is best noticed from a distance.

The structure that we see on the page, moreover, is only a represen-tation of the intellectual, dramatic or emotional structure that under-lies the arrangement, which is invisible, the pure expression of the writer's mind and imagination, and which will transfer across the medium of the page into the reader's mind and imagination. The structure is always moving the reader toward something—a point of view, an insight, an understanding of a person, an examination of conscience, a connection with a different way of life.

Structure is *dynamic*—it doesn't let the writing just sit there. It creates a sense of movement, of forward progress, what John Gardner calls *profluence*.

TIME

So structure, whatever else it is, is always a line, and that line always moves through time in at least four ways:

1. The chronology of events as you present them in the piece. This may or may not correspond with the order in which they happened in real life. *But the order of presentation becomes, for the reader, the order in which they first happen.* The order in which you line up your events is the basis for all narrative, all storytelling.

If you begin with a description of finding a murdered family, then retrace the six months leading up to the crime, the reader experiences the murder first and all the preceding events are already informed by the outcome, even though in real life no one could predict the outcome. Obviously this changes the focus of suspense. The reader already knows how the story will turn out, and the interest now is on *how* we get there.

This makes the reader's experience fundamentally different from the experience of those who witnessed the event in real life—who may have felt no suspense at all, if the crime was completely unexpected, or may have sensed a terrible foreboding about the direction in which events were heading, which the reader knows from the start.

2. The historical chronology: the order in which the events *actually* happened in real life. ("Historical" in this sense means only that something has already happened.) This often functions as a kind of shadow line that parallels the narrative line you lay down to tell your story; that is, the reader instinctively un-jumbles the fragments and re-creates the historical chronology, holding it in the back of his mind as he reads. He may do this deliberately or unconsciously.

So at some level, while he knows the story will end with the discovery of the murdered family, he pretends he doesn't know, and at times the narrative may trick him into forgetting what he knows, and he may even find himself illogically hoping events will turn out some other way.

As soon as you tell a story out of order, you are making the reader read at least two stories at once, and this discord between the *real* chronology and your *invented* one creates a delicious tension for the reader.

3. The time it actually takes the reader to read the piece. If the piece is a book, the reader will live with it for hours, days, even weeks, and the very duration of the experience will contribute to its artistic effect. Reading your story becomes part of the reader's life experience, situated in the context of who he is at the moment and what else is going on in that life.

Norman Mailer has always argued that his novel about a lost World War II infantry patrol, *The Naked and the Dead*, needed to be 721 pages long, or it would not have accumulated the intensity and power he was aiming for. In the same way, Lincoln's little speech at Gettysburg is memorable partly for the tautological reason that it is short enough to be memorized in its entirety.

4. The past time the reader brings to the piece—through memory and previous experience—as well as anticipation for the future and the subjunctive, wishing time of "what if" that includes dreams, day-dreams and fantasies. This is where resonance comes from—the writing resounding on the reader's own experience, ideas and memories in such a way as to intensify or clarify them and add energy to the work.

This is what makes a piece of writing immortal, timeless: its ability to hook up with the ongoing flow of other lives, both in memory and in anticipation of the future. In one sense, the writer has no control over this. But the writer does traffic in human constants, Faulkner's famous "eternal verities" that always somehow involve "the human heart in conflict with itself."

Each of us, as a reader, brings to someone else's story our own memories, idyllic or traumatic, as well as our own hopes and fears for the future. If a story works, it's partly because each reader places himself in the story and measures the experience of the story against the truth of his own life.

Most people will never, God willing, experience the murder of their family, but all of us have been afraid of losing someone we love to violence. In a book that broke new ground in melding fact and fictional technique, Truman Capote's *In Cold Blood*, it's not the act of murder itself but the primal fear of the act, the working out of a nightmare on the page, which excites a strong reaction in the reader.

Likewise, we don't all worry about whether we would be brave in battle, but many of us do wonder how much we can count on ourselves in a moment of physical or moral danger. It is not war but self-doubt that is the universal touchstone in Stephen Crane's *The Red Badge of Courage*.

In nonfiction, the reader's experience does not have to be exactly the one portrayed, only emotionally parallel. The reader's own life experience, in other words, actually helps create resonance with something that happened to someone else, that may never have touched the reader's direct experience at all. This is curiously like the fiction writer's relationship to his stories—the passion is real, but it comes from something different from the actual event invented for the story. When Civil War combat veterans asked Crane, who had never been to war, how he could so convincingly portray the psychology of men under the stress of battle, he replied that he had played football at the university.

Recognizing these human constants is crucial to the emotional structure of your piece—you deliberately lead the reader through moments of stress and anxiety, orchestrating the timing of each crisis, on the way to the end of the story.

Your structure must then take into account all these kinds of time. Mostly we do it intuitively. Knowing our book is liable to go long, we break it into chapters, sections, subsections, setting a long-distance pace. But first, perhaps, we tease the reader with a glimpse of how interesting things are likely to get, if the reader can go the distance, as Edmund Morris shows us Teddy Roosevelt first in the White House on New Year's Day, then backtracks through the stages of his developing career.

We are careful to focus suspense by telling a story somewhat out of chronological order, holding back important revelations for later, and we invite the reader by implicit and explicit cues to match it against his own life.

A very short personal essay, on the other hand, might begin with a first line that hits the reader right between the eyes, announcing that we haven't got a minute to waste.

Ernest Hemingway wrote to his editor, Maxwell Perkins, about the necessity for sound structure: "It wasn't by accident that the Gettysburg Address was so short. The laws of prose writing are as immutable as those of light, of mathematics, of physics."

LINCOLN AT GETTYSBURG

Abraham Lincoln's brief address on the occasion of the dedication of the National Cemetery at Gettysburg, Pennsylvania, on November 19, 1863, has been praised for its masterful use of classic rhetoric: all those ringing parallelisms straight out of Aristotle.

The form is the memorial dedication speech. We've all heard it at the dedication of a new courthouse named after a local hero, or of a scholarship fund named for a venerable alumnus. The usual, ceremonial structure is to greet those present, pay homage to the occasion, sort of explaining why we're all here, then conclude with some elegiac words for the dead and how they will live on in this memorial. The underlying structure is, as the form dictates, *memorial*—to move the audience to *remember* a person and thereby to honor him. That's the focus of the arrangement that guarantees wholeness.

But think of the Gettysburg Address for a moment not just as a rhetorical structure *in* time (the Civil War) but as a structure *using* time. Everybody at the dedication and everybody who has ever read the speech since knows that the occasion for the speech was to honor the dead from a great and decisive battle. But Lincoln doesn't start with the battle. He goes back "four score and seven years" to the founding of the United States, then works through the chronology— not of the battle, or even of the war, but of the national experience.

This is the inspiration that makes the Gettysburg Address more than just an "occasional" piece—a piece in time: He takes the underlying *memorial* structure further and deeper than it is usually conceived. What he wants to make his listeners remember is much more than they had expected to be reminded of, much more than the specific occasion of the battle or even the particular men who fought it.

Like every successful writer of creative nonfiction, Lincoln invents a structure to serve his piece. He doesn't invent it from scratch; part of such success is always that the structure is familiar enough to reassure the reader but new enough to recalibrate his expectations.

Lincoln traces the entire history of the Union, from its birth in revolution as "a new nation, conceived in liberty, and dedicated to the proposition that all men are created equal," through the crisis of the present: "Now we are engaged in a great civil war. . . . We are met on a great battlefield of that war."

Only then, in the context of the nation's provenance and founding mission, does he invoke the incredible three-day slaughter that broke the back of the Confederacy: "We have come to dedicate a portion of that field as a final resting place for those who here gave their lives that that nation might live."

It is the chronology in which he places the terrible fight at Gettysburg that lends dignity and hope to the sacrifice of all those thousands of blue and gray soldiers, the insight toward which his underlying structure is leading us.

He knew—as his audience knew, as his contemporary readers know—that there was an elephant in the room: all those graves. The temptation to begin in the moment, recognizing the powerful blood-consecrated landscape, must have been nearly overwhelming. But he began his speech in a different place. Instead of making it only a morbid, sorrowful occasion, and without sacrificing solemnity, he takes the occasion beyond the grave, envisioning a future in which the sacrifice will have inspired "a new birth of freedom."

He finishes with the strong invocation "that this government of the people, by the people and for the people shall not perish from the earth."

His speech is entirely chronological in telling events: past, present, future. But at the moment in which he delivered it, the nation itself, the crowd before the podium, was in medias res, in the middle of the drama of the Civil War. He adroitly backs out of the dramatic moment long enough to provide perspective, a sense of history and meaning, then propels his listeners forward into the future: "The world will little note nor long remember what we say here, but it can never forget what they did here."

And the scope of his chronology was striking and unexpected.

His listeners' chronology was roughly this: The Civil War began, the battle of Gettysburg was fought, and now our President is giving his little speech to honor the dead.

Lincoln's chronology: Our forefathers founded an experimental

Union in democracy, then the Civil War threatened to destroy all they had built, then Gettysburg tested the army of the Union against the army which aimed to end that Union, and now we are here to understand the judgment history will render on this event and these brave men, and I think history will enshrine it as a defining moment in our national story when our forefathers' plan was vindicated for future generations.

We, of course, experience his future as part of our national past—we know how the Civil War came out—adding our own resonance. But it's a planned resonance, as much as such a resonance can be planned. The very structure of his speech invites each person who hears it to meditate on the past and take responsibility for the future, filling in his or her own experience.

In other words, every generation will have its own Gettysburg.

It works because of the contrast between the grand, sweeping scope of his chronology and the short, spare, almost sketchy way it is rendered. We can almost imagine his listeners groaning at the first line, thinking, "He's got four generations to cover before he even gets to the battle." But then it's over almost before they know it—all 270 words. All two minutes. They're catapulted into the post-Civil War future bearing the legacy, not just of Gettysburg, but of Washington, Franklin and Jefferson.

Lincoln reconfigured the chronology everybody thought they already knew, and his address became a powerful template for seeing the Big Picture. In enlarging the chronology from the predictable one, he was defining the very terms of the dedication ceremony, placing it as one tragic scene in a longer play, changing its meaning profoundly from a eulogy to a national creation myth that must be revisited in sorrow from time to time to remain vital.

By changing the chronology, by manipulating time, he effectively took it outside of time.

One way to understand why a piece is successful is to imagine how it might have been written differently.

Imagine if Lincoln had begun and ended with an account of the battle, mentioning specific acts of heroism, selfless deeds, moments of courage. Most writers would probably have written it that way. A modern president would have focused on some fallen local boy who exemplified the virtues of the good soldier, maybe even invited his grieving widow or mother to the reviewing stand for a photo op and a sentimental plea for patriotism and solidarity. He would have been meticulous in citing details of the battle, careful not to leave anything out or offend any constituency, and his speech would have run on for hours and remained firmly dated in the present, now past. (The other politician who spoke that day did just that.)

And in so doing, he would have missed the story. The story wasn't the dead at Gettysburg; the story was the living. The story was their ongoing struggle with the idea of the Union—an idea so profound men were willing to die to test it, and must always be so.

In the Gettysburg Address, Lincoln tells the living story of a whole nation in crisis, and like all writers, in telling that larger story, he can't help but also reveal his own. He implicitly sees himself presiding over a historical moment every bit as profound as the one faced by those same forefathers, Washington, Jefferson and company.

And the story's success began with a decision about structure that required a large imagination—a creative decision.

MYSTERY

Another way to think about structure is to think about *mystery*.

Mystery is not just what we don't know; it's what we don't know *and really want to know*. Mystery is any unanswered question that piques our curiosity.

Think of structure as a string of mysteries organized in a deliberate order. The mysteries will be large and small, and the writer will make good use of this variation in interest, resolving the mysteries in escalating order, using smaller questions to lead into larger ones, saving the resolution of the biggest mystery for last.

Just the opposite, by the way, of the conventional "inverted pyramid" structure used by newspapers. In this structure, the "lead" (or "lede") sentence answers the most important mystery right off the bat. The second sentence will solve the next most important mystery, and so on, till the piece trails off in the least interesting detail of the story:

> President John F. Kennedy was shot to death today in Dallas. Police have arrested Lee Harvey Oswald for the slaying. Texas Governor John Connolly was wounded in the

shooting. Oswald is a former Marine who resided for a time in the Soviet Union. . . .

The practical use of this structure is apparent: An editor sweating out a deadline and cramped for space in the newspaper can edit from the bottom up without fussing with revision, cutting the last line, the second-to-last line and so forth, knowing that the most important questions will still be answered, and that he is only cutting ancillary information.

But it makes for dull reading, because the usual effect after the first sentence is anticlimax—the opposite of a dramatic structure, which introduces a character with ambition and the struggle against opposing forces to make that ambition come true, amid growing tension, with an outcome that remains in doubt till a climactic moment of crisis and resolution, followed by a slow return to a normal heart rate.

The inverted pyramid structure allows the reader no time to become curious, no time for that curiosity to build, no time for him to experience the anxiety of wondering what the outcome will be, or for hoping for a particular outcome. No delay to allow suspense to happen. He will read such a story with diminishing interest—exactly the opposite effect, in other words, from the one a writer aims for in creative nonfiction.

Imagine Lincoln's speech recapitulated in an inverted pyramid:

> At Gettysburg today President Lincoln expressed his hope that this nation would not perish from the earth. He dedicated a cemetery to those who died in last summer's battle in this ongoing civil war. He reminded his listeners that our forefathers founded this nation based on liberty and the proposition that all men are created equal.

Gone is the sense of purpose, of connectedness, moving from one point to the next with escalating urgency.

Now imagine Lincoln ascending the speakers' platform that cool November day. What can he possibly say under the circumstances that will not sound trivial in the middle of a graveyard full of thousands of brave men?

The first, little mystery.

The others, asked and answered, raising the ante:

Do you remember what this nation is founded on? Let's recall some first principles put forth by our forefathers.

What have our forefathers got to do with anything? Well, I'll tell you: They're the other ghosts on this battlefield—they have an interest in what happened here.

You remember what happened here? Brave men struggled in the middle of civil war—and by the way, remember that the "enemy" are also Americans and also brave.

How do we dare dedicate this place? Well, we can't do any better than they did. We aren't half as brave as they were, so let's be a little humble. Certainly nobody cares about my little speech. But we must remember that the struggle isn't over, and we've all got some fighting left to do with our own convictions.

What happens if we lose this war? We could lose everything, that's what, and so would all the generations after us. So we'd better make damned sure we don't lose it.

The big mystery is always the unanswered question that forms the subject that got us into the story in the first place.

Williams speaks eloquently about the mystery that first engaged her passion: "I wrote *Refuge* in response to a question that was turning over and over in my mind: how do we find refuge in change? I desperately wanted to make sense out of something that made no sense."

That's what Lincoln was doing at Gettysburg. That's why, finally, we write: to make sense of a world that does not always make sense. The less intuitive sense it makes, the more urgent the mystery, and the writing.

OUTLINING: LITERARY ENGINEERING

It's not usually considered literary to talk about outlining, and in fact there are plenty of writers who maintain that they never outline, that they work in a more spontaneous and less conscious way. "I once did an outline for a piece and it was a disaster," recalls Jan DeBlieu, who followed *Hatteras Journal* with *Meant to Be Wild: The Struggle to Save Endangered Species Through Captive Breeding*. "I have a very fly-by-the-seat-of-the-pants approach."

But what she says next is telling: "What I tend to do more than anything is to start with a collection of ideas, and then I use it almost as a collage. I start stringing some ideas together, then I'll move things around. Once I get on track, I think the outline evolves from pieces or notions that I've accumulated, so I have all these different subjects or points I want to make floating around in my mind. And I'll think of a couple of points that I want to start with, and then I'll start writing the beginning of the piece and then I'll say, OK, it makes sense to talk about this next. The outline will evolve once I have maybe a third of the piece written."

DeBlieu's intuitive working style is typical of many writers, especially those whose work habits have evolved out of long experience. The greatest challenge for any serious writer is to figure out *how* to work—designing the right system of habits with which to approach her art. What she is really doing is listening to her instincts and listening to the story as she is learning it, knowing by now she can trust the little voice in her head to arrange things on the page.

And how she goes about arranging her material will manifest itself in her style on the page, a style that turns back on itself with ideas and themes recurring, that doesn't seem like a line at all but like the living imagination of a thoughtful woman intensely aware of her environment at many levels—physical, emotional, societal.

In other words, she is just doing in her head what other writers do with a scratch pad and pen: outlining. Organizing everything she's found out, all that she wants to say, in a structure that will sustain the piece. And learning what to leave out.

"When you're doing nonfiction, you're always bombarded with a million facts—you're always going to have more facts than you want to put into the story," Bob Reiss, who spent months in the Amazon rain forest researching *The Road to Extrema*, explains. "And many of the facts can be superfluous to the emotional point of your story. And yet, if you are not in control of the facts, if the facts are in control of you, they will dominate you and ironically cause you to diffuse your own point. They'll confuse you. A good nonfiction story is a complicated story told in a simple way."

Structure—reflected in an outline of whatever kind—allows you to get control of the facts and present them in a coherent way.

A good working outline may be a scrawled list of the five big things you want to include in the piece, or the twenty-five scattered ideas you've jotted down in no particular order. Or it may be quite detailed, subordinating a set of ideas to a larger paradigm. It may be a dramatic plan, the classic arc of story with the climactic moment at the top of the arc, or it may be a short list of places, stops on the journey you're writing.

Several writers I know work with index cards, each card a piece of the larger work, shuffled and reshuffled until they've got them in the right order. Some writers draw a picture or diagram of a piece to see both the overall shape and the way the pieces connect to make that shape. An outline might be a circle, beginning with a certain scene, with points on the circle labeled with one-word reminders of the next four things that need to be told, as they accumulate toward meaning, and ending back at the beginning with some version of the opening scene, or the opening scene expanded with new information or quotes, or told from a different point of view.

An outline might be a "target" diagram of concentric rings, beginning at the outer ring and moving closer and closer to the bull's-eye, the focal point; each of the points is a satellite revolving around that focal point.

Or it might be a straight line of narrative action, a simple story of moving from point A to point B, pausing at key moments to interject background or information.

It all depends on how you think, how much you trust your memory, how your imagination best organizes material. And plans change. Outlines are meant to be modified, turned upside down, even abandoned. The outline is only a means to an end, a scaffolding that allows you to reach everything you need to reach. You discard it when the job is finished.

Generally, the shorter the piece, the less need for any kind of formal structural plan. It's possible to hold a short piece in your mind all at once. Once you know where it opens, you will quickly discover the ending, and in a couple of sittings you may write the entire piece— electricity arcing between two poles.

But an outline is also one way to gain control of time.

In a longer essay or book-length work, the writer cannot hold all of it in his mind at once. And he certainly can't keep it all there in clear focus over the time it takes to write two or three hundred pages. An outline can help sustain focus and aid the memory, reminding you of all those fascinating things you meant to include six months or a year ago when you started the project, and how each part relates to your subject.

And, as we'll see in chapter ten, an outline can be indispensable during the revision process—especially if you have that nagging sense that somewhere you got off the track.

My outlines tend to be lists of things I know that, somehow, I want to include in the piece. In the piece on Hemingway's Paris, it was a list of places in the city that had held significance for Hemingway and his crowd. That's one element of an outline: the highlights of content. The other element is order—what comes first, second, third, etc., and the resulting pattern they make. I wanted the reader's experience with those places to lead ever deeper into Hemingway's books, and in the end for the reader to discover the man alive in his style, which was most like Harry's Bar—thoroughly American and foreign at the same time.

So my outline was a list of places, which I rearranged many times. And at the top of the page, one word: Style, to remind me of the focus, the thing I was searching for in all those picturesque places. In writing *Brilliant Passage*, I solved the order by borrowing the chronological logbook structure of a passage from Halifax to Mystic, Connecticut. I had access to both my own private log and the ship's log kept by the captain. The content came in three kinds: first, the events of the actual voyage; second, the history and attributes of the boat; and third, my own interior journey.

Obviously, the events of the actual voyage could be neatly outlined from the logbooks, following the same structure and told in the same order. Each chapter could be labeled by navigational location, moving just as the actual passage had moved: "Brazil Rock to Cape Sable" or "91 mi. E. of Cape Cod to Nantucket." The interior journey could likewise be matched to the logbook structure during the segments that inspired them—many of the reflections came right out of my personal log anyway, and the others were triggered after the fact by specific occurrences on board.

Finding a way to integrate the history of the boat was trickier, and I solved it through another structural decision: not to present dry information in large chunks, but to deliver it in small helpings in the context of events during the voyage. My aim was to teach the reader certain things about the boat at exactly those moments when he would want to know them in order to appreciate the events of the voyage. I searched my outline for transitions—passages that could easily lead into background.

So the discussion of the schooner rig is matched to a section from my log that describes shutting down the diesel and raising all sail for the first time, so the reader can appreciate what an intricate and dynamic system those sails and rigging really are.

Each chapter would then have three elements: the events of the voyage, something new about the boat itself, and interior reflection to anchor it in a personal voice.

Outlines are sketchy, often messy, and always written in sand. No structure is likely to be perfect, but it has to make the piece move through the water without falling apart.

COMMON STRUCTURAL TEMPLATES

You invent the structure your piece requires.

But you invent based on common templates, the arrangement readers have come to expect. Not because some rule book requires that you do so, but because certain basic structures have endured as useful ways to deliver common forms, and you can use your reader's expectations to your advantage. They are only templates—no piece ever follows them exactly. But it's useful to observe how some frequently used forms find their expression in common structures.

Personal Essay. Since this form combines the dramatic urge of storytelling with the persuasive logic of an essay of ideas, the structure somehow must combine two elements: the personal experience, usually related as an anecdote that may or may not be a finished story, and the meaning, some larger context of ideas. One structure simply relates the story, using the typical dramatic structure of suspense-climax-resolution, with a reflective "denouement" added to the story. The writer tells a little story, one that perhaps may not seem all that significant, then reflects on what it means. Often this reflection comes as the result of retrospection—looking back through a lens of experience and wisdom the writer did not have at the time the event occurred. This is also how many radio pieces take shape, my own included.

To vary this form, the writer sets up an abstract context of ideas: "Fear of embarrassment accounts for most heroic action, a Vietnam infantry sergeant once told me." The writer may elaborate further, before telling the experience in light of that philosophical context, connecting with it again at the conclusion. Or the writer tells more than one story, either in sequence or cutting back and forth between them. The juxtaposition of the stories themselves may result in implicit meaning, or the writer may make the meaning explicit at the end, or by ongoing reflection throughout.

Profile. Often a profile is structured around a single significant encounter over a limited period, told more or less in the order in which it happened, interrupted by information inserted at strategic points that adds both heat and light to the encounter. These insertions may include background details of the individual, details of other encounters with that same individual told in scene or summary, interview segments with other people commenting on the individual, even experiences from the writer's life or from literature that on their face seem unrelated to the profile but in some way illustrate the personality that is the focus of the piece.

Issues Piece. Whether the issue is political, environmental, ethical, social, historical or some combination, the piece frequently begins with some dramatic illustration of the issue (a scene), so that it is not merely an abstraction but an interesting piece of real life that matters here and now: "Whiskey Creek runs so close to the Smiths' dining room window that they can hear it rushing softly over the mossy rocks during supper, when the traffic has stopped on Alden Parkway. But Mr. and Mrs. Smith never thought much about it until one afternoon last May when their two younger boys went swimming in it and got sick."

The structure will then take one of two turns: Either it will follow a story structure, following a suspenseful line to a moment of crisis and resolution, breaking in from time to time to inform events with outside statistics, quotes from experts, descriptions, technical detail, whatever is required, and thereby heightening the suspense as knowledge is added; or the story is used merely to set up a more intellectualized persuasive essay, an argument that will proceed from point to point, using the story of the Smiths as well as other stories, facts, quotes, observations and statistics to illustrate key points.

Sometimes, as with the personal essay, the author will tell a complete, single story (the story of the Smiths and their polluted creek) in tandem with a fairly elaborate persuasive essay, moving back and forth between one and the other, indicating changes of tack with space breaks.

Biography. One rather trite structure is the cradle-to-grave chronology, mimicked in some of Dickens' biographical novels, in which we relive the life in question in painstaking chronological order. More imaginative biographers are aware of why they are writing about a figure in the first place, and try to re-create the story of the individual's achievements. Ron Powers reminds us, "Biography flows from the early Sanskrit text, the sacred histories of Buddha, the legends of Mohammed, the New Testament that illuminated Christ's life in the four Gospels. It has as its ancient mandate the exemplary life of a sacred character whom mortals can then read about and emulate."

Obviously the subjects of biographies are no longer only the sacred, but the biographer must never lose sight of what it is that makes the individual special and interesting—worth emulating, in Powers' terms—and the structure must take this into account. So the best biographies borrow the structure of novels—though unflinchingly truthful and accurate, they nevertheless present selected scenes from the subject's life in a manner that builds toward some kind of defining moment. They may interrupt or shuffle the chronology in service of drama, or they may present the real-life chronology, but selectively, leaving out the trivial, skipping periods in which not much happens (even the Gospels don't say much about what Jesus was doing between age twelve and age thirty). And they reserve the right to fill in background, other critics' comments, and any other illuminating information, in the place where it will do the most good.

Book. You don't really write a book, even a biography. You write *parts* of a book—chapters, sections, scenes. Whatever your overall plan, once you have it you put it in the back of your brain, refer to it from time to time, and measure your progress and your finished manuscript against it. But the structure that engages you day by day is the structure of chapters and parts. Whatever structure the book has taken on, the chapters tend to mimic in microcosm. Chapters in particular must have a sense of wholeness, of movement.

The trick in structuring a book is to make each chapter discrete and whole without making it *complete*. That is, you don't want the reader coming to a full stop at the end of a chapter, but compelled to move on to the next chapter.

In a general sense, each chapter of a book answers a question, a mystery, and the mysteries take on more and more importance. But each chapter also asks a question, opens the next, more intriguing mystery, so the reader feels compelled to read on for a little longer. Just as the writer can write only part of a book each day, the reader doesn't usually make a conscious decision to read the whole book. Instead, he decides to read on a little longer, and a little longer after that, until you have brought him to the end.

In other words, all narrative books are mystery stories.

James Gleick's *Chaos: Making a New Science*, for instance, begins not like a treatise on theoretical physics but like a mystery novel: "The police in the small town of Los Alamos, New Mexico, worried briefly in 1974 about a man seen prowling in the dark, night after night, the red glow of his cigarette floating along the back streets." The man is not a shady denizen of the underworld but a respected scientist, conducting an experiment. But whatever else he is, the reader meets him as a man of mystery. The emerging science of Chaos is, for Gleick and his reader, a kind of high-tech detective story, and what follows is as suspenseful as any private eye tale by Raymond Chandler.

This is not to trivialize creative nonfiction but to recognize a structural similarity in all long narratives. The genre mystery novel is only the most exaggerated and blatant expression of that structure—the tricks are all out in the open. But finally we read and write, not because of what we know, but because of what we *don't* know, and a good storyteller recognizes that human fascination with mystery. Chapter by chapter, he leads us closer to the thing that fascinates us.

The examples above don't begin to cover the great range of nonfiction, but you can easily discern the structure of your favorite writing, the writing that moves and provokes you, the stories you remember, once you stand back and look not at the content but at how that content is arranged—the structure. You will see an overall pattern and the various devices, often repeated in some cyclical way, that support that pattern.

And one way or another, it will make use of story structure, piquing your interest through the interaction of human characters in conflict; adding dramatic and informational ingredients that create tension and the desire to find out answers; delaying resolution for the sake of suspense, coalescing in a defining moment; and finishing with some resolution that satisfies, as best it can, your curiosity and emotional investment in the outcome.

Setting off a chain of mysteries, moving through time and beyond time, never letting go of you.

ATTITUDE AND THE ACCIDENT OF STYLE

Student writers frequently ask, "How do I develop a style?"

My answer is, "You're asking the wrong question." Style is an accident, an artifact of the attitude you bring to the work, and the way that attitude translates into small-scale structural decisions.

What kind of an attitude engenders lasting nonfiction? Terry Tempest Williams gives the best answer I've ever heard: "Deep commitment, deep patience, and deep passion."

Your attitude sets the criteria for all the structural decisions that happen at the level of sentences and paragraphs, which then accumulate inevitably into a recognizable style.

Michael Rozek uses very long, uninterrupted, verbatim quotes from the people he interviews—for the sake of accuracy and out of respect for his subjects—and those long quotes become a hallmark of his style.

Your attitude is founded on a decision about what you value most in your writing. I value clarity, accuracy, compassion and respect for the reader above all else in creative nonfiction—in what I read, and in what I write.

For clarity, I often favor short paragraphs, active verbs and concrete rather than abstract nouns. For accuracy, I will use a technical term, even if that means explaining it, rather than a word that is not quite accurate. Compassion defines my attitude toward the people I write about.

Out of respect for the reader, I pay attention to how I compose sentences, writing and rewriting, reading them aloud for rhythm and sense, keeping an eye on focus, trying to let the emphasis fall naturally on the main idea. I use—perhaps overuse—fragments, because I'm fond of infinite-time verb forms—participles and infinitives, which don't always need a repeated subject, and which can connect several sentences into a complex but clear single "sentence."

Clarity

It's easy to be obscure, to throw words at a subject, to show off arcane knowledge and impress a reader, to stroke your own ego. It's tempting, and it's hard to root out, because a lot of the time you're struggling to express complex stories with limited gifts. But the virtue lies in striving to be clear, even if you frequently fail. My aim is to make the difficult seem effortless to the reader. If a piece of writing isn't clear, it can't be much else.

"If you start hooking yourself up with the ego, you're going to be really miserable. Hook yourself up with the work," Michael Rozek of *Rozek's* says emphatically. "The craft is what's important. Doing it properly is what's important."

Accuracy

Anne Matthews, whose work must measure up to the rigorous standards of top publications such as *The New Yorker*, maintains that laziness or fear—both character issues—lies at the bottom of many accuracy problems: Writers make excuses to avoid unpleasant situations or sticky issues, and instead of offering precise facts they wind up giving a vague gloss on the facts. She says, "Until a writer learns to be honest with himself or herself and the world, you're not going to get very good nonfiction or fiction."

Do your homework. Don't cut corners.

Accuracy also means, as Mark Twain remarks in his essay "Fenimore Cooper's Literary Offenses," a scathing and hilarious critique of Cooper's shoddy workmanship, "Use the right word, not its second cousin."

Flags are flown at half-*staff* on land, half-*mast* on a ship. A *podium* is a platform on which a speaker stands; a *lectern* is the upright thing he stands behind. *Disinterested* means neutral; *uninterested* means bored. Trivial examples, but multiply them by hundreds or thousands, and the result can be a piece of writing that is foggy and not very true. Elegant style begins in choosing the word: Get it exactly right.

Compassion

Don't confuse "compassion" with "sentimentality." Compassion is an honest portrayal of the people you turn into characters, not a hatchet job. It's easy to slam a person in print, much harder to present him as a complex individual with human failings and virtues. Compassion is respect for your subject and yourself.

Compassion requires humility, not ironic superiority, toward both my subject and my reader. It also means I agonize over descriptions of people and their behavior: Is someone's child "fat" or "stocky"? Is she being "sullen" or merely "quiet"? Is he "overbearing" or "imposing"? And when I quote what a person says, I want it accurately to reflect that person's attitude and ideas, not merely reinforce my own preconceptions.

Respect for the Reader

I believe the average reader is a lot smarter than many writers or editors give him credit for being, so I don't believe in "dumbing down" the prose. This book is a good example: If you're reading this, I assume you genuinely want to know not just some "how-to" formula for quick publication but what goes on down deep in a piece of serious writing. If I quote from somebody else's book, it's because I expect you'll want to find it and read it sometime. In the back of my imagination, you the reader are thoughtfully reading, mulling over what I've written, disagreeing with or raising objections to certain passages, in other places testing it and finding it true, and applying everything to your own ambitions as a writer.

My reader is as smart as I am—probably smarter—and I'm writing for the same reason he or she is reading: because I don't know exactly what I have to say or how this is going to turn out, and I really want to know.

I just might learn something important.

CHAPTER TEN

REVISING—WITH AND WITHOUT AN EDITOR

E ditor Lisa Bain tells a story about the time she worked with a piece by a very well-known writer. The piece was rough, and it needed a lot of editorial attention. Bain edited it heavily, then braced herself for the fallout—the writer would surely be miffed at being second-guessed by a young editor.

Instead, he sent her flowers.

Those flowers reflect well on the character of the writer, who appreciated her diligence and savvy, of which he was the ultimate beneficiary—his name went on the piece. And on Bain's competency as an editor—she made the piece better, and was willing to trust her judgment even in the shadow of the writer's reputation. They signify the crux of the editorial process: It's not always easy or pleasant, it demands professionalism on the part of both writer and editor, it requires an honesty that is not usually necessary in other aspects of life, and it results in a strange kind of intimacy.

Novice writers too often assume an editor—even a teacher-editor—to be an active adversary, locked in combat for the soul of their writing. But a good editor can be the writer's best friend. It's his job to help you do your job—to focus your conception of the piece, then to change anything that doesn't serve the work.

"I think that every writer needs an editor," Lisa Bain says, "and every writer deserves a *good* editor."

A good editor will grasp what you are trying to accomplish in a piece of writing. He or she will appreciate your style, since style is not ornamental, but reflects your deeply held convictions about how you go about discovering a story and putting it into words. A good editor will help the piece fulfill itself on *your*—not the editor's—terms, helping to bring out your distinctive voice, helping the piece become *more* your own.

THE WRITER-EDITOR DIALOGUE

So the process of working with an editor is a kind of dialogue, a give-and-take in which writer and editor "talk out" the piece, face-to-face or through phone calls, letters, e-mail or any combination.

The dialogue begins, of course, at the moment of first contact. Usually this comes in the form of a writer proposing a piece or a book, or an editor talking to a writer about a possible project. Sometimes it happens in an informal conversation about story ideas at a writers conference, long before the writer and editor will actually work together. If the writer has not published before, or if the editor simply doesn't know his work enough to hang a proposal on it, the dialogue may begin when a writer first shows an editor a piece of writing, hoping to place it.

For writers serious about their craft, the "first draft" that an editor sees is almost never a true first draft; it has gone through many layers of edits. The routine, rough-draft sloppiness is gone. The prose is clean. The thing is already breathing on its own.

The second important element that makes this dialogue possible is a maturing of the writer's idea of *self*: I tell my students over and over that they must stop thinking of themselves as "student writers" or "novice writers" or "unpublished writers" and simply start thinking of themselves as *writers*.

No qualifier.

They will recognize the moment: It will happen when their ambition for the *writing* becomes more important than their ambition to become *writers*. They will make the transition from daydreaming about being published to a more prosaic, critical kind of daydreaming. In this daydream, they are an editor, a reader, looking over the piece with their own name on it, comparing it to the best writing they know, and dispassionately deciding whether it makes the grade—and if it does, how it can be made stronger, clearer, better. And if it doesn't, what they can do to make it come closer.

Editors can recognize either ambition at a glance. It's in the writing—even the query letter.

I'm not suggesting that simply calling yourself a writer somehow magically transforms you into a writer. But when you assume that identity, you also take on the responsibilities and habits of the serious writer: a relentless commitment to craft, an honesty about subject matter and research, a large curiosity about the world you don't know, a subordination of your ego to the work, an active respect for your reader, a determination to meet deadlines come hell or high water, and, perhaps most important of all, the willingness to listen to hard criticism and not be wilted by it—instead, to learn from it, holding your own work to a more rigorous standard, and doggedly to move on to the next project.

The third element is obvious, but seems to elude many young writers: Editors are editors because they love writing, and they are as eager to find you as you are to find them. Once you've found each other, the dialogue begins.

Remember: The writing is ultimately your responsibility, not the editor's. A good editor usually will make astute observations about the writing and is often uncannily accurate in pointing out awkward passages, faulty logic, flawed structure, weak transitions, confusing descriptions, fuzzy focus. But even the best editors, I've found, are better at identifying symptoms than prescribing remedies. If there's a problem with the piece, your editor will talk it out with you, but it's up to you to write your way into a solution.

THE LARGE VIEW

There are no great writers, only great re-writers—so goes the axiom. Revision is both an art and a process, and it's essentially the same whether you're working alone or with an editor.

The impetus is the same. Unlike the dilettante, the serious writer, the artist, the pro, is not easily pleased and satisfied with his work. On one level he is satisfied at what he has so far, but he also feels the urgent need to rewrite: to get it precisely, exactly, perfectly right.

When it comes to revising, there are generally two breeds of writer. The first fusses with every sentence, polishing it to perfection before moving on to the next. This writer revises constantly. The method makes for slow going, but it has the virtue that the next line is always built on a clean line of sentences that say exactly what the writer wants them to say. The drawback is the obvious one: How does the writer know yet what he wants to say? How does he know he will not throw out all those beautiful sentences when he sees where the story arrives? Without knowing the larger pattern, how does he even know *how* to revise them?

There is no "best" sentence. There is only the sentence that best advances the aims of all the other sentences.

I always think of the climber in that TV commercial who struggles across raging rapids, through dense forest, and up the sheer rock face of a mountain, only to discover a restaurant at the top. Apparently there was a faster, easier way to get there.

This doesn't mean that his way was not more interesting, but the honest question is whether the interest lies in the process—the writer's heroic climb—or the finished product—the successfully achieved destination. The writer cares about the one, the reader about the other. Don't invest too much in writing that you may throw away.

The second kind of writer doggedly follows the line of the story from here to there, and the first-draft prose may be ragged and sketchy, rough around the edges, full of mushy spots, passages the writer had to put down on paper to get to firmer ground on the other side. But once the distinct shape of the thing emerges, that writer goes back and does what the other writer was doing all along: cleans and sharpens the prose.

Most writers I know do both at once, more or less: They forge ahead trying to craft a completely shaped piece, while pausing along the way to hammer the worst of their sentences into some pleasing shape. The danger with this combination is that the writer may be lazy about revisiting those sentences later—they're pretty good as they are, he thinks, and perhaps they'll do.

But of course, they won't.

Revision—the third in our list of maligned literary activities, after researching and outlining—is more than just changing a few commas and running a spell-checker. It is *re-envisioning* your work. Stepping back from it in light of what you know now, what you have written, and determining if you have done what you set out to do. Just because the piece occurred to you a certain way and you wrote it that way doesn't mean that was the only way, or the best way, to do it.

What does your instinct tell you now?

Remember: You may change your mind in the process of writing and revising. You're a different person from the one who began the piece—if the writing is any good, it has changed you, just as you expect it to change your reader. You know things you didn't know before. Books especially, simply because of their length and the time it takes to write them, often leave the reader feeling that the writer who wrote chapter one isn't the same person who wrote the finale.

Reading your own first draft of a book, you may not recognize yourself in the opening chapters. This is normal and good—if you don't feel at least a tinge of personal vertigo, that's a sign that the book didn't grow, that you as a writer haven't grown either. The challenge is to keep on *enlarging* the piece—in resonance, depth and impact—without making it *longer*.

So revision begins with the large view and proceeds from the outside in, from overall structure to paragraphs and finally sentences and words, toward ever more intricate levels of detail. In other words, there's no sense in revising a sentence to a hard shining beauty if the passage including that sentence will have to be cut.

Are all the big pieces here, and have I arranged them in the right order?

What is the arc of story? Check your opening sentence against your final sentence in the piece. Then the whole opening paragraph against the closing paragraph. The first is the promise, the last is the payoff. Do they connect? Is there a spark across that gap? Did you move the reader from here to there? Does the overall persuasive or dramatic logic hold up? Is the voice consistent?

Now look at structure. What is the shape of the piece? If you were after symmetry—parts of matching emphasis playing off one another—did you achieve it? Or did one part end up too short, too long, in the wrong place? If you started out by telling a story in parallel with making an argument, does either the story or the argument trail off halfway through because you lost sight of it, or lost interest in it?

This is the moment to resurrect your outline, which is after all a fairly clear picture of what you intended to do—the large view with which you began. Retrace your decisions, the turns you made. If you got seriously off track, follow that line of story back to the turning point and rewrite from there.

How do you retrace your decisions? One easy way is to "rubric" (literally if archaically, "to adorn with red," in the manner of sacred medieval manuscripts) your paragraphs: In the left-hand margin of each, write a single word or phrase that best describes its focus. You can then read down the margin and discover, graphically, the two essential ingredients that went into your outline: content and order of delivery.

It's like doing a math proof backward.

Unless your outline is a cathedral of exquisite detail, it will probably resemble your list of rubrics. Compare. Play that little kindergarten game of "alike and different": of the following ten items, which two don't belong in this essay?

Sometimes your structure suffers simply because you've got certain paragraphs in the wrong order. Your list of rubrics will display an inherent logic—or illogic—in its progression.

Even if you ventured far afield from your outline, at least you can revisit your creative decisions—which were probably made intuitively in the heat of the writing—and with a colder eye figure out why you made them, what you might do instead. You can try on various solutions in light of your blueprint, satisfying yourself that your choices were sound ones.

TECHNIQUES FOR REVISING: INTERNAL LOGIC

Take the most recent piece you've finished. After you've determined that its overall structure is sound, that it moves from a promise to some kind of satisfying payoff for the reader, take a paragraph at random. Read the first sentence—what your freshman English teacher called the "topic sentence"—aloud. Now skip to the last sentence in the paragraph and read it aloud.

Juxtaposed in that fashion, do they complete a thought? Do they make connective sense?

If the leap is too large for the paragraph, one solution is to break the paragraph at the point where a new idea comes in or where it turns in a radically different direction. If that doesn't work, reread the sentences slowly, in order, aloud, and your ear will probably catch the instant when the paragraph takes a turn away from its opening.

In other words, each paragraph ought to mirror, on a smaller scale, the logic of the overall piece. It should move the reader through the content of the story and push him out on the other side, interest heightened, accurately oriented, eager to read on. If the reader instead stops, scratches his head, and rereads simply to figure out what he missed, then the whole piece has stalled. It may never move again.

Now read the last sentence of any paragraph—aloud—followed by the first sentence of the next. Does the transition make sense?

If it doesn't, usually you have two options: one, write a transition that does make sense, bridging the imaginative gap; or two, remove that paragraph and set it down in a place where it makes better sense. You can determine whether this is a useful option by pretending it isn't there and matching the last sentence of the preceding paragraph to the first sentence of the following paragraph, in effect "jumping" it altogether. If the transition works without it, that's a sign the paragraph may be unnecessary, or in the wrong place.

Work through your entire piece this way. It will be tedious at first, but after you've done it once or twice you won't need to do it so deliberately again, unless you find yourself in obvious trouble. You will internalize the structural logic of the writing, and the way you build and order your paragraphs will reflect your clarity of thought.

Remember when I said I have an old mechanical Corona, but that I prefer working on my notebook computer? One reason is that it's quiet. Late into the night, when my wife is asleep in the next room, it's like whispering the story onto the page. The page doesn't exist yet—the page itself is an optical fiction, a backlighted high-resolution field. The words don't exist as permanent blots of ink yet; they're only transitory runes in the ether of cyberspace. It's pure, as if you were watching the sentences actually scroll across the retina of your mind's eye. You're staring through a window into your own imagination.

Then you "save" it, and all the sentences go somewhere—somewhere invisible, but safe. To a memory more reliable than your biological one.

But there's another practical reason: If you're working in this ethereal medium of electronic blips, the story stays alive, doesn't freeze into a hard shape, until you print it onto pages—"hard" copy. So you're free to take advantage of the most useful function of word processing: "cutting and pasting" electronically.

You can mark paragraphs with your cursor and move them around, change the order as many times as it takes to get it right. This is another reason to write in reasonably short paragraphs: It will make editing for order much easier.

The two things I do most in a revision are reordering paragraphs and cutting sentences, both easier with a computer, because you can try out different versions until you get the piece exactly right.

THE SENTENCE

So if you've done all the above, the structure is sound. The paragraphs are all there and in their most effective order. The internal logic of each paragraph is satisfied, and the last sentence of one moves you into the opening of another, breathlessly.

Now it's time to become a stonecutter with the sentences.

Read each one aloud, listening for a well-modulated, flowing rhythm—does it sing? Some sentences in the Gettysburg Address are almost perfect iambic pentameter—blank verse: "Now we are engaged in a great civil war." Actual poetry, song.

Listen, too, for unintentional rhymes that will cause your reader to laugh in the middle of a poignant moment: "Her lover in the RAF was shot down over Dover."

Listen for shifts in diction, a voice that cracks: "General Lee's tired army marched all night to Fredericksburg, then in the morning they really kicked ass."

Sometimes it's best to let someone else read your sentences out loud, listening for stumbles, confusion, misconstructions, giggles. Or at least to read out loud to an audience: "While playing cricket, one mustn't allow oneself to get pissed off." Does the tone-joke work?

You're going to hate what I have to say next: Learn to diagram sentences.

A sentence diagram is exactly that—a *diagram*, a picture, of a sentence. It shows how each part is related to the central "core"—the subject and the predicate (verb). Again, sentence structure mirrors, in microcosm, story-logic or persuasive logic. Diagram your sentences, and you will see a clear image of your style. Do your sentences clop-clop along, subject-verb, subject-verb, so that your story also marches forward without surprise? Or does the focus, the main idea of the sentence, get lost in a tangle of modifiers, phrases, wordy clauses, leaving the reader baffled about where his interest lies in the sentence, the story?

Diagram a long sentence by Faulkner and a long sentence by Hemingway, and you will see at a glance two very different imaginative logics at work.

Faulkner's sentences tend to be *complex*, intricate webs of subordinate clauses, turning back on themselves over and over with nuances of connection, meaning and qualification. He uses polysyllabic abstract Latinate words to capture the deep ideological foundations of the culture that is his milieu and subject. A single Faulknerian paragraph may cover a full page with its lush tangle of prose.

Hemingway, by contrast, works mostly in short, straightforward declarative sentences, or in *compound* sentences—bare clauses linked as equals in an associative logic, leaving it to the reader to sort out which ideas are trivial and which profound. He uses modifiers sparingly and prefers short, concrete, Anglo-Saxon words. The effect is a flatness, a bare realism, a kind of *prose noir*.

Both re-invented the American sentence, and both did it from radically different creative points of view. Their respective story-structures, their ways of seeing the world and telling its truth, are contained in the grammatical essence of any of their sentences.

The subject is the character. The verb shows movement, which is always a vector: It has direction and magnitude.

The story always lives in the verb: Jesus wept.

One of my favorite classroom exercises, especially with advanced writers who are pretty sure they know how to write a clear sentence, is to ask them to go on a verb hunt. We take a sentence and count the verbs: "Waiting for the concert to begin, Mack felt he had decided too impetuously to perform in a theater that had cancelled his program two years before." We find, in this case, six: a present participle, "waiting"; an infinitive, "to begin"; a past tense verb, "felt"; a past perfect predicate of a subordinate clause, "had decided"; a second infinitive, in the same clause, "to perform"; and another past perfect predicate in a second subordinate clause, "had cancelled."

Having a lot of verbs in a complicated sentence is not necessarily a flaw, but you can't decide whether it's a flaw until you recognize how many times you are asking the reader to shift focus. Whenever we perform the exercise, almost nobody recognizes all the verbs on the first pass.

Modifiers add dramatic detail and background information: "Tom was an old stove-up rodeo hand with sunken eyes and a rusty knife in his pocket."

Compound subjects and verbs can offer the tension of choice or confrontation: "Baseball players and owners met Thursday."

Or they can diffuse your focus: "The angry crowd surged and moved forward."

Compound sentences can be miniature dramas, full of tension and irony: "A stranger comes to town, or someone goes on a journey."

Complex sentences can offer dramatic development, extending a metaphor, as Melville's Captain Ahab reminds us: "The path to my fixed purpose is laid on iron rails, on which my soul is grooved to run."

President Kennedy knew how to use the power of rhetorical structure: "Ask not what your country can do for you, ask what you can do for your country." Diagram that sentence and you'll find that the subject is not even stated; it is only *you* implied. The subject is not what's important—*you* are not what is important, the whole point of Kennedy's speech. Stop being so damned narcissistic, he sternly admonishes us, and pay attention to serving your country.

Grammatically, we say such a sentence is in the *imperative* mood—the verb gives a command or an exhortation. The grammatical structure of the sentence, emphasizing duty over the individual "you," mirrors the greater logical structure of the speech, as a rousing call to selfless action closing on "country," and serves its content in a way another structure would not. Imagine the line written another way: "You should ask what you can do for your country, not what your country can do for you." The sentence begins by emphasizing "you" and returns to that emphasis at the end in an anticlimactic negative; the sentence now carries a whining tone, not the ringing timbre of leadership.

Kennedy learned a few tricks from Lincoln.

Just as narrative is built on the order in which you tell events, a sentence achieves part of its power by what you tell first and what you hold back for last: "At sunrise, they led him to the scaffold." The sentence sets up an expectation, achieves suspense, then delivers the news.

"They led him to the scaffold at sunrise"—altogether different emphasis. If there is any suspense, it must be because we didn't expect him to be led away till noon or 3:15 or whenever.

Pay attention to the parts, to the way those parts are arranged in syntax.

For years I made the mistake of trying to rescue a mauled sentence by changing a word here, a comma there, and I wound up with a good many presentable cripples. Now if I discover I've written a truly ugly, unwieldy sentence, I put it aside and start over. What is the point of the sentence? How does it further the point I just made and lead to the next thing?

There are many kinds of sentences, and if you're serious about writing you'll have to get serious about the craft of writing sentences. Try this: write a fairly long, involved sentence. Then write it at least five other ways—not the same words, but the same thought, with the same complexity of nuance.

Then diagram all of them.

ELEMENTS OF STYLE: DETAILING THE PROSE

Once you are satisfied that the structure is sound, the arc of story is complete, all the sentences are there in more or less the most effective order, the real revising begins. Prose writers tend to paint with a broad brush—we rush through paragraphs and pages, whole chapters and books, our eyes straight ahead, fixed on the outcome. Which you have to do, if you're going to maintain any sense of continuity and coherence over the long haul.

But now that logic is satisfied, we have to satisfy beauty: by sculpting paragraphs, honing sentences, fine-tuning phrases, testing words for clarity, hardness, originality.

Detailing the prose.

Finding the exact word, excising the redundant one. Modulating the rhythm of a sentence and offering a variety of sentence rhythms. Finding fresh language to tell old truths.

I urge my students to read all the good poetry they can get their hands on. A poet will spend days sweating out a single word, weeks constructing a line, years arranging a dozen lines into a coherent poem. Not even a great poem—it's just as hard to write a mediocre poem. I envy them their word-discipline, a care worth emulating.

CUTTING

You write your words, then you love them. Unreasonably, with the unqualified love we usually reserve for children and pets. It hurts to slice them away. To push the "delete" key and watch them disappear into cyberspace. It's also hard to write short. Hard to make perfect choices. Maybe we didn't communicate it clearly enough for the reader. So instead of choosing, we hedge. We say it again. We add a modifier.

Then we have no choice but to cut.

Cutting is easier after a little time has passed, after the heat of creation has cooled. The only way I know that works is to set an arbitrary goal—I'm going to cut this manuscript by 20 percent. Five hundred words, a thousand or five thousand.

Then take a mildly sadistic joy in every word you zap.

Sometimes, the chore is easy: It becomes apparent that a whole paragraph is redundant, or a whole chapter is irrelevant.

Zap. Fifty words. Three thousand.

But more often, it's a matter of meticulously operating on a passage sentence by sentence, excising a word here, a phrase there. The words add up quickly. Count them—you'll be amazed. You can make it easier by not trying to revise an entire long piece at once. Select a short passage. Then another. Take it on in small, manageable bites.

And before you write again, try this: Write a description of an actual person performing some task. Loading a moving truck, say, or preparing supper. Something you can observe carefully and write about completely, that includes several actions.

Then take what you have written and excise every adverb and adjective.

Whenever I pull this on my students, they panic. Then, with a lot of head-scratching and giggling, they attack their paragraphs and, on average, cut out every third word.

Next, write a new paragraph, using no modifiers, only nouns and verbs.

Somewhere between the two extremes of overmodified prose and bare clauses, you'll start to figure out just what kind of sentence you need to write to convey clear action with an interesting gloss. Then you won't have to cut so much later.

WHAT IS NONNEGOTIABLE?

The relationship between writer and editor is a creative dialogue, but there's a catch: In the end, the writer's name goes on the piece. The editor languishes in obscurity, his only satisfaction that, if the dialogue has worked, he has pushed the writer to better work than the writer alone would have been capable of.

That doesn't mean editors are timid, self-effacing creatures. The ones I know approach their work with passionate professionalism. They can be dead wrong, but they, like writers, are working from a creative philosophy arrived at over years of experience. They too have strong convictions about what makes good literary art, and they are energetic advocates for their readers. Lisa Bain, like all the best editors I've known, takes seriously her responsibility to every manuscript that comes under her hand. She says, "I feel that I have the right to do anything that makes the piece sing."

A good editor pushes a writer, and the best editors expect the writer to push back. The writer-editor dialogue can become heated. It can even reach an impasse: The editor insists on changes you can't or aren't willing to make.

In my experience, this doesn't happen nearly as often as nonwriters generally believe. Sometimes, the editor is merely testing the depth of your convictions. That's part of the editor's job: to ask hard, probing questions, usually beginning with *why*. And to force you into an examination of your literary conscience: Am I merely indulging my ego, or is this really necessary to the piece?

And persuasion works both ways. It's frequently possible to bring an editor around to your point of view. But in the end you, the writer, must decide what is nonnegotiable in your own writing—which part, if altered or cut, will destroy its integrity.

We're not talking about titles, which customarily are the editor's prerogative. But the thing that lies at the heart of the piece may seem, on the face of it, equally trivial: a single quote, a narrative idiom, an anecdote within the larger story, or even a single word.

As Maxwell Perkins wrote to F. Scott Fitzgerald during the revisions of *The Beautiful and Damned*, "Dear Fitzgerald: Don't ever *defer* to my judgment. You won't on any vital point, I know, and I should be ashamed, if it were possible to have made you; for a writer of any account must speak solely for himself."

If you write and publish long enough, sooner or later it will happen. The price for sticking to your guns may be that your book or essay will not be published by that editor—maybe never will be published. But a writer is not an artist until he is unwilling *to be published at all costs*.

It's not worth fretting about until it happens. You'll lose enough sleep over it if and when that day comes, especially if there's money or prestige involved—both have a way of clouding judgment. In any case, if you have been rigorous all along pursuing your research and your craft, you will have already answered all the questions that matter in making the decision: Who am I? Why am I writing this? Where does my passion lie?

Then you take the only course open to you. When the thing is nonnegotiable, you don't negotiate.

CHAPTER ELEVEN

LAW AND ETHICS

W riting is a mystical art.
    At the dawn of Western Christendom, it was a sacred art: The first writers were holy monks, cloistered behind high walls to keep out the barbarians, working by lamplight in dim, stony scriptoria, copying out the word of God in elegant calligraphy on vellum and parchment for sacred libraries as closely guarded as the secrets of the priesthood.

Writing *was* a kind of priesthood. Initiated into the secret, wonderful code by which a finite system of marks penned in variable patterns represented precise ideas and made pictures in the head, writers were the first humans to save the Truth in a medium that freed it from the whims of individual memory and allowed it to last beyond a personal lifetime. The written word became a collective public memory, one that could be consulted in perpetuity. A more accurate and durable memory than the oral tradition, which depended on an unbroken chain of generations learning exactly the same stories, and which could be interrupted by a single untimely death.

The written word could survive famine and plague, war and diaspora. It offered a chance at immortality, a glimpse of eternity—if you knew the "code," and not many were allowed to. The written word also became a tool for preserving power.

It codified law—canon law at first: the word of God transformed into rules. Then secular law: the statutes by which local magistrates and assizes adapted church law to common moral and civil practice, settling disputes over contracts and property and trying accused criminals in matters of life and death.

Written documents became the foundations of great governments, from the Magna Carta to our own Constitution.

With the printing press, the doors to the library were flung open: The written word was democratized, and pamphlets could be circulated by dissidents and radicals just as easily as by a ruling class of initiates. Literacy blossomed. More and more people understood the "code." "Creative" writers got into the act, saving oral tradition into a written public memory, but one that carried the name of an individual author, a "creator." We started signing our work.

Then writers began creating public memory out of their private imaginations, and what had begun as sacred stenography brought us—by way of Dante and Chaucer—Shakespeare, Melville, Twain, Truman Capote and Janet Malcolm.

I offer this admittedly half-baked version of literary history to remind you of an obvious point, since it always seems to be the obvious points we forget: Writing is the place where priest and lawyer meet creator on the playing field of the imagination, and the encounter results in words on a page.

The act is public, the document is durable, and the consequences are not always predictable. But they are always partly spiritual, partly legal and partly artistic.

And writing occupies an implicit and distinct moral dimension. It carries moral consequences—for the writer, the subject and the reader. We pursue it according to our own code of behavior and bring to it our deepest beliefs and our most ardent faith—or lack of faith.

Writing also carries consequences under the law. It can make law— as Melville's *White Jacket*, an exposé of a seaman's life aboard an American man-of-war, persuaded Congress to reform the navy and to outlaw flogging.

It can also bring the process-server to your door.

Our moral, spiritual impulses seem to abet the imagination, but the law is a brake on creativity. The law demands proofs as irrefutable as mathematical sums.

Out of the tension of three disparate impulses—the encounter between priest, lawyer and creator—we craft our art.

THE LAW: LIBEL

Aside from plagiarism—stealing the expression of someone else's ideas—or otherwise infringing on copyright, there are mainly two ways a writer can get into trouble with the law: libel and invasion of privacy.

Because U.S. law is based on precedent—previous decisions in similar cases—it changes constantly. What the Supreme Court allows today, it may rule against tomorrow—and in five years it may reverse itself again. So unless you plan to devote your life to the study of literary law—and you can't if you've already decided to become a writer, which is a full-time vocation—the best you can do is be alert to situations that may hold the potential for lawsuits, then do the smart thing: Consult somebody who *has* made the law his or her life's work.

Such experts rarely include other writers, and I'm no exception. The law is complex, intimidating and distracting—if you meditate on all the ways you can get into legal trouble by writing about real events and living people, you'll never write a word. Your job as a writer is to be inquisitive, bold, imaginative, and if you work from a reliable moral compass with a little common sense, you'll stay out of trouble.

In my experience, writers hold widely divergent views on what constitutes libel and invasion of privacy, and you can get into trouble relying on such "barracks lawyers." That's why we have editors and real lawyers—they stand at some distance from the process, and, because they are more attuned than writers to the business side of things, certain situations send up red flags that they spot immediately but that are invisible to the writer hot on the trail of art.

Writers are amateurs at law. What we need to know is not the intricacies of the law, but when to consult someone who knows the intricacies of the law.

When does an editor consult in-house counsel?

"When I think that there's somebody who is identifiable in the piece, and I'm nervous about what we're saying about them," Lisa Bain says. "I have an essay right now, which actually I haven't bought yet, which is about this guy's girlfriend who was sexually harassed at work. Red flags go up because, since his name is on it, anybody who knows him knows who she is and knows where she works, and the guy is identifiable."

The issues, in this case, include both invasion of privacy and libel. Bain explains, "The person does not have to be named to successfully sue us for libel, so we have to be very careful if we see a trace of that."

Rule of thumb: Whenever you will be presenting a real person in a bad light, double-check your sources, your interview notes and your motives; then talk it over with your editor. This doesn't mean you collapse into a legal huddle every time you write less-than-flattering observations. But your nervous stomach will tell you to flag those pages for your editor and ask, "Do you see any problem with how I've handled this?"

Publishing contracts routinely indemnify the publisher against libel claims that result from mistakes made by an author, but in the event, everybody can and usually does get sued. So your editor and publisher have a strong vested interest in making sure your piece is based on solid fact, well documented.

The Associated Press Stylebook and Libel Manual remains the best, clearest reference for nonfiction writers concerned about the legal consequences of a story. It is updated regularly based on current case law and is useful in part because it addresses the working press, hard-news reporters on deadline dealing with controversy, crime and politics and likely to encounter every conceivable legal situation as a matter of routine and without the time for leisurely analysis.

You need to have this book on your writing desk, within reach of your keyboard.

The AP *Libel Manual* offers crisp definitions: "Libel is injury to reputation."

It goes on: "There is only one complete and unconditional defense to a civil action for libel: that the facts stated are PROBABLY TRUE." Do your homework, get it right, cross-check every important fact and keep good records, including notes and tapes.

There are other elements of libel law, including "absolute privilege," that apply to certain individuals under specific circumstances. Elected public officials, for example, may speak their minds in legislative session without fear of suit. This makes for lively debates in Congress and your local statehouse, because it doesn't matter if the speeches include false or malicious information.

So-called "qualified privilege" may or may not extend to you if you decide to quote the politician or judge or mayor in question. AP warns:

"Privilege can be lost if there are errors in the report of the hearing, or if the plaintiff can show malice on the part of the publication or the broadcast outlet."

Sound Reporting: The National Public Radio Guide to Radio Journalism and Production, another useful reference, defines "malice" as lawyers understand it: " 'Actual malice' is a legal term that has little to do with the common usage of the word 'malice.' Instead, it means that the reporter or the news organization had actual knowledge that the published statement was false, or had a reckless disregard for the truth or falsity of the statement."

Still with me?

It gets muddier. Whether you must be proved guilty of malice or only of negligence or "gross" negligence to be found libelous will depend partly on whether the person you're writing about is a public figure or a private individual. And that definition is itself tricky, since a private person may become a public figure for a limited time under certain circumstances, and then whether or not he or she remains a public figure will be partly a function of whether he has voluntarily placed himself in the limelight or only happened to be connected to a newsworthy event, which will cease to be newsworthy at some point.

In general, a public figure has a harder time bringing successful suit.

As you can see, libel is not a clear-cut matter. And its nuances are complicated by the myriad of differing state laws governing which proceedings are or are not official, which records become part of the public record and at what point, and so on.

The best you can do, again, is to make sure of your facts, make sure you can *prove* your facts if you are called upon to do so, and honestly appraise your own motives: Being fair to your subject— rather than *setting out* to cast him or her in a bad light—will result in better art and fewer legal problems.

Two odd features of libel law: First, you can successfully defend a piece that includes errors if you wrote and published falsehoods about a public figure having very good reason to believe them true; that is, what you wrote was untrue but not, in the legal sense, *malicious*— you did not write it with reckless disregard for the truth, but the "truth" you obtained turned out to be false, and any reasonably careful writer might have made the same mistake. On the other hand, if you quote someone else making a libelous statement, you may open yourself to a libel suit, by repeating the libel.

Under a legal doctrine known as "fair comment," reviews, editorials, opinion columns and criticism containing defamatory matter usually are not held to be libelous unless the writer makes errors of fact or writes maliciously. This holds true, however, only if the writing focuses on matters of interest to the general public, such as government proceedings.

Of course, even careful writers can make mistakes, and malice is a matter of interpreting whether you acted with reckless disregard for the truth: Did you take reasonable steps to ensure the accuracy of your information, and did you write anything *knowing* it was not true?

You can see that we are dealing with some fairly slippery terms, even in the law, and that the law may vary a lot from state to state. Anybody can try to sue you for any reason—that doesn't mean every suit has merit, just as it doesn't mean that a nuisance suit, or the threat of one, won't stop a timid publisher in his tracks, even if you're right. You can't go around worrying about every word you write, timorously shying away from anything that might provoke a lawsuit. But your editor and the publisher's legal counsel can help you address the risk.

Take comfort in this: Most writers are never sued. If you have any doubts or anxieties, talk to your editor. Make them known. Deal with them up front. Get expert advice.

Again, we live by our habits: If you are in the habit of doing careful research and keeping accurate notes, if you are in the habit of approaching a story with an open mind, if you are in the habit of conducting your business with an editor as a good-faith dialogue between two equals both invested in making the work the best it can be, you can solve most of these problems before the piece ever reaches galley proofs.

As Anne Matthews reminds us, "Accuracy is an art."

THE LAW: PRIVACY

Most of us don't write about private individuals who don't want us to write about them. We respect their privacy out of common decency, and so satisfy both our own sense of ethics and the law. As Anne Matthews reminds us, even though we may very much want to interview a person, "People say 'No' all the time." She herself says she never agrees to be interviewed—a matter of personal preference.

By way of illustration: I am quoting, with her permission, remarks Matthews made during a panel session at the 1995 Associated Writing Programs Conference. Since the conference was open to the press, I probably do not need such explicit consent, but why not be as gracious and forthcoming as she was during her talk?

Were she a private individual talking not for a public audience but for, say, a gathering of friends at home, I would have gone further and obtained written or tape-recorded permission, to avoid any claim of invasion of privacy. That's the simplest way to avoid being sued for invasion of privacy: If a person agrees to your interview knowing you plan to write about him, or agrees in general to "access," he has no claim against you later. He has, by cooperation, implied consent.

This applies to tape and video recording as well. If the recorder is visible, and the subject has consented to be interviewed, he is in effect consenting to be taped, too.

Telephone conversations are trickier. Says *Sound Reporting*, "The federal government and most states allow the taping of a call when one party (i.e., the caller) consents. Eleven states, however, require the consent of *both* parties." Remember that one reason you will conduct telephone interviews in the first place is that the subject is far away—in another state—and you will have to take *that* state's law into account. If you're recording for broadcast, the Federal Communications Commission requires that this be made clear to the interview subject.

In an age of "ambush interviewing," undercover reporting and hidden cameras, National Public Radio's policy is unequivocal: *"The person being recorded is always told. There is no surreptitious recording."* [italics theirs]

The best practice under any circumstances is simply to ask, on tape, for consent to record the conversation.

Sound Reporting defines another kind of invasion of privacy—*intrusion*: "Regardless of the story that is broadcast, *the act of reporting* may be an invasion of privacy if it involves trespassing or otherwise intruding into a plaintiff's reasonable realm of privacy." [italics mine]

If a person is a public figure—voluntarily in the public eye—you may write about him whether he consents or not. If you're not sure a certain person can be deemed a public figure, talk to your editor.

If you reveal private information about a public figure—unflattering personal details not obviously related to public performance or taxpayer-sponsored duties—you can be held liable unless you can demonstrate that these are of legitimate public interest—the so-called "newsworthiness" defense.

If the public figure claims that such information casts him in a false light, the defense is the same as for libel suits: truthfulness and lack of malice. But "truthfulness" alone may be a weak defense, because verifiable facts presented out of context *could* cast him or her in a false light.

Memoir or autobiography is a kind of black hole of privacy rights. You can share your manuscript with living people whom you can find and ensure their consent. But twenty years after the fact, you may not even know if the people about whom you're writing are still alive, let alone where to find them to obtain consent. You have two basic choices:

1. Figure out some stylistic strategy for protecting their privacy, such as giving them fictitious names or no names at all, or changing details about the place or circumstances—all tricky devices tending toward fiction.

2. Simply write what you want to write and hope that, wherever they are, they will be, like most of us, happy to be remembered in print.

ON THE RECORD OR OFF?

"An unwritten journalists' rule is, if somebody tells you something's off the record *before* an interview, it's off the record," Bob Reiss says. "If someone tells you something's off the record *after* the interview, it's not. Well that's great when you're dealing with a politician. But it's not so great when you're dealing with an air traffic controller who's been abused by her father and never dealt with a journalist before, and it didn't occur to her until forty minutes after she started talking to ask you to keep this stuff quiet."

The standard rules of journalism don't begin to cover the ethical dimensions of the art of nonfiction. Sometimes the solution is to change the name to protect the identity and privacy of an individual whose specific identity is not, in itself, important to the piece.

How about changing the name of a public figure whose identity may be crucial to the story?

Jan DeBlieu cautions, "If you are for some reason changing the name of the character to protect them, that's fine; I think you need to spell that out to the reader, if you are writing nonfiction." I agree. In nonfiction, your reader has the right to know unambiguously the degree of accuracy you are claiming for your piece.

Lee Gutkind, founding editor of *Creative Nonfiction*, doesn't ever change names: "Once I do, then my reader has a right to doubt my credibility. Once you change a name, what else have you changed?"

ETHICS: WHEN IS NONFICTION FICTITIOUS?

Because creative nonfiction relies on the techniques of storytelling—the tricks of the fiction writer—the lines between the two genres can blur. We've all felt the temptation to stretch the facts, to "heat up" the actual events, to exaggerate or overdramatize. You have to draw clear lines for yourself, decide how far you can go in dramatizing, telescoping and reordering events, selectively presenting some scenes but not others, arranging dialogue, changing names.

"At the rubbing points between fiction and nonfiction, you find interesting debates about what we should or should not do," Norman Sims says. "You can 'create' a scene and still be accurate."

Most writers agree that making up a "composite"—a character invented out of parts of several real people but not himself a real person—crosses the line.

"The idea of composites is absolutely verboten," DeBlieu says. "Are you writing nonfiction, or are you writing fiction? You need to make a choice. You have to decide which one of these genres you are writing in—you can't mix and match. If you're writing nonfiction, doing a composite town or a composite character is not cricket."

Gutkind agrees emphatically: "Because there's no way in the world you can write something that's true if you start with people who are not true," he explains. "Composite characters will give you composite situations."

Which is a pretty good definition of fiction.

The governing ethic of the nonfiction writer—however you long for the malleable and perfectible drama of fiction, however much you are tempted to make the story turn out the way it *ought* to have rather than the way it *did* turn out in real life—must be this: You don't make it up.

"It's so much harder to do it right—so much easier to take liberties and do it not-right," Gutkind says. "There's something to lose in every line you cross."

You're stuck with what happened. But Matthews reminds us that nonfiction takes its power precisely from this limitation: "Fact well arranged can be art."

ETHICS: ACCURACY OF FACT AND LANGUAGE

Matthews quotes Walt Whitman: "Any poet worth his salt must be a good reporting journalist." Extend that to any prose writer trying to make art out of facts.

Making up scenes out of whole cloth, distorting facts to serve a political or personal agenda, and inventing composite characters are the most blatant sins against the craft of nonfiction. Other, less egregious inaccuracies—changing a private individual's name, leaving part of a sensitive conversation off the record—may be excused as judgment calls in the name of compassion, of a higher ethic than the journalist's mandate to tell all, regardless of who gets hurt.

There are, however, more subtle issues. Let's look at a few.

Most of us do not speak in complete, grammatical sentences. We repeat ourselves, stammer, interrupt our first thought with a digression, use slang, mix tenses and numbers, inadvertently drop a profanity, and sometimes simply misspeak. Conventional practice is to "clean up" the quote, making it more or less grammatical and clear. We do this out of respect for the person we're quoting—he's given us his time and cooperation, sincerely spoken his mind, and implicitly trusts us not to present him as an illiterate buffoon. In other words, we do the editing that we could reasonably expect he would want us to do to capture clearly and accurately what he was saying—not a verbatim, warts-and-all transcript.

But we can go too far. Such seemingly cosmetic changes can sometimes distort rather than clarify the original remarks. And there are certainly times when a crude way of talking or a habit of infinite digression is a hallmark of the person about whom you're writing, and you want to capture it for artistic reasons, as well as for the sake of accuracy.

You'll notice that throughout this book I have used fairly long quotes, partly because the writers and editors I'm quoting can address a given issue far more articulately than I can, and partly because of my sincere wish to present their viewpoints accurately, which means letting them have their say. Not all quotes come in pithy sound bites.

I've tried to tamper very little with their grammar. I've left in fragments and repetitions, because I'm trying also to capture distinctive voices. I hear their voices on my tape recorder and in my head, but it's hard making them come across on the page.

And I know, despite my honest efforts, that the best I can do is *approximate* their voices and their attitudes. Someone among them— maybe a lot of them—will feel that I should have used a different or more extensive quote, cleaned up their words more or left them completely and raggedly verbatim, or provided a clearer context. Since I was not always able to use a tape recorder, it's possible I missed something in my note-taking.

And even if I have quoted them with unerring accuracy, how they come off depends on the whole book, the overall context of the work in which their words appear. Did I present their remarks in the right chapter? Juxtaposed with another quote, does theirs come off— falsely—as argumentative, arrogant or less profound? Did I make them appear to agree or disagree with a point, when in fact they hold the opposite position? Perhaps I got their words exactly right, but I misunderstood their deeper implications or misread their tone. And so on. They are real people. I respect them all. I want them to feel well served. It's a humbling and nerve-wracking process, but it's essential to ask such questions.

Sometimes we paraphrase more colorfully or succinctly what someone actually said. We do this for the sake of economy (a worthy goal) or to liven up a piece (a dangerous practice). We also do it when we have no exact record of a conversation, as when writing memoir or recalling conversation that happened in the heat of action. Ron Powers says, "I have strong feelings about the ethics involved in paraphrasing dialogue, of inventing dialogue, attributing dialogue to others that you're not sure of, so I don't do it. I have to be certain. On the other hand, I understand that there are times when that's unavoidable, and you can make an ethical allowance for it."

A less subtle issue involving quotation is selectively presenting only those remarks that leave the reader with a deliberately false impression. Simple: Don't do it. You have to quote a subject based on the sense and tone of the whole interview and try your damnedest to present the person—as well as the words—accurately. "Accuracy is largely a problem of how you arrange your material," William Howarth says, and that includes the things that real people say.

Failing to define your terms is another concern. "By not asking the right questions, a nonfiction writer can cause people to die—that's not an exaggeration," Reiss says. "By allowing the interviewee to dictate the vocabulary you're talking with, and to not challenge basic presumptions, a nonfiction writer isn't living up to what he should be."

He cites two compelling examples, both from the American rescue mission to Somalia, exhaustively covered by major magazines: "The first thing was, well the Marines would say, in their daily reports of their progress, 'Today we reached northern Mogadishu.' And the press would say, 'The Marines have reached northern Mogadishu.' Mogadishu is a *city*. That's like saying, 'We landed on Forty-second Street and we've reached Seventy-second Street.'"

Congress and the President base national policy on the version of the truth they read. "And of course a couple of months later you've got Marines naked being dragged through the streets, killed, because 'northern Mogadishu' was a city. And we should have been covering how tough these people were—that should have been challenged right away.

"Also the definition of who was running the opposition. A *warlord* is what we called Aidid, and the press dutifully recorded that word, 'warlord.' Well, what is a warlord? What you think of when you think of a warlord is a kind of renegade bandit, who if you eliminate him everything will be OK.

"Well a couple of months later, after he was winning, he stopped being a *warlord* and he started being a *clan leader*. Now, a warlord is very different than a clan leader. A warlord is a bandit. A clan leader is a rightful ruler of whatever clan he has. And the difference is, if you're stepping in against a *warlord*, you're stepping in to sort of clean up a situation; if you're stepping in against a *clan leader*, you're stepping in between the Hatfields and the McCoys."

Which pretty well describes the Marines' predicament in Somalia.

"They're not just words—they're whole ways of looking at things. And it's crucial for nonfiction writers to make their own vocabulary and not let other people control it."

How could so many conscientious writers be guilty of such a lapse in defining the basic terms of the story? Reiss' answer: "They probably said, well, isn't Mogadishu a city? Like maybe that sounded dumb, or maybe they don't understand Mogadishu, or what exactly is a warlord? Because maybe they felt stupid saying it. The truth is that *nobody* knew. And because nobody knew, people got killed. You shouldn't be ashamed of looking bad."

If you don't define your terms and insist on the accuracy of the language being used to tell the story, you may inherit language that makes a true story false. Don't be lazy: Truth lives in precise, right words.

BIOGRAPHY—THE GHOST IN THE ROOM

The art of the biographer is in some ways a special case in the realm of creative nonfiction. The subject is usually deceased, so he or she can't sue you for defamation or invasion of privacy, and in any case you wouldn't be writing about a private individual of no public interest.

But biography presents other challenges, both legal and ethical.

At the 1994 Bread Loaf panel on biography, David Nasaw, biographer of William Randolph Hearst, read an abridged version of Henry James' short story, "The Real Right Thing," to illustrate those concerns. In the story, "the great man" Doyne, now deceased, has become the subject of a biography commissioned by Doyne's widow. Withermore has been chosen to write the biography because the widow Doyne believes he can be manipulated into writing a hagiography that will show her late husband in an unblemished, heroic light. During the course of Withermore's earnest research, he encounters both increasing resistance from the widow and the ever-stronger influence of Doyne—first as a vague presence, finally as a ghost standing at the top of the stairs, barring Withermore from his study: not with him, but firmly against him.

"I tell this story," Nasaw explained, "because it represents, much better than I can I think, the dilemmas of the biographer and the unholy and impossibly uneasy relationship between the three principal characters in every biography: three, the writer, the subject, and the spouse or literary executor."

The biographer requires access to archives, often privately controlled. And he handles memories, private and public, that affect living relatives.

Nasaw: "Perhaps, of all the people to rail against the art of biography, the craft of biography, James has done it the most effectively, telling us biographers that not only do we corrupt, debase, degrade the lives that we write about, but that if we continue to do so, we will be visited by ghosts, that the ghosts are there, whether we see them or not, and that we should stop and desist at once. What, then, do we do if the great man is right? We should all give up now. But he's not right."

Powers asks the question that every biographer must answer: "Why do you intervene? How dare you intervene in a life, and by what fiat and with what goal?" Powers recognizes that arriving at a single absolute Truth is beyond the ability of even the most talented and conscientious biographer; instead, he aims at *truthfulness*, relying only on facts that can be recovered from the record, not inventing but interpreting: "If you frame it as a biography, then you must work against the temptation to interpret beyond the evidence."

But the biographer's ethical obligation, he maintains, goes much further: "In biography, you do gain possession of a life, and it's a terrifying possession that you have. You are entitled to walk around inside the life and the experiences and the memories of someone who had a great deal of influence in the world. I think we always ask ourselves, what is the moral accountability to that life? And what is the moral accountability to the people who survive the deceased and who are affected by interpretations of that life?"

Robert Houston, a fiction writer whose novels are often based on biographical research, is always conscious of the writer's hand in bringing the real-life figure to life on the page: "Whether we are fiction writers or biographers, we have to acknowledge, I think, honestly to ourselves, that we're making it up. And there is always that element of fiction in biography."

But the conscientious biographer does not invent dialogue. Like the historian, he cannot present the inner life of characters except through external evidence derived from the archival record—diaries, letters, memoirs. And even that may be suspect.

Paul Mariani, literary biographer of poets John Berryman, William

Carlos Williams and Robert Lowell, remains deliberately inside the boundaries of the archives, yet achieves living personalities on the page. One way he does this is by very consciously choosing the language with which he will tell the story of his subject. "For me, the language itself—I see language in a biography as a character," he says. "So that I can, in a sense, fill in the blanks with the language that I'm creating, without having to create dialogue."

Mariani strives for truthfulness. "Obviously I can't give you the life of Lowell, I mean the living life of Lowell," he explains. "That was lived by Lowell, right? OK. The best I can do then is to give you 'the life' of Lowell, which is itself a fiction. I'm aware of that. But at the same time my contract is to give you nothing that I haven't been able to uncover. And, yes, to shape that into a narrative.

"Now, 'uncover.' Does that mean that every single witness that you've gone to is equally reliable? Obviously not, right? And there are times when you've got directly contradictory evidence of the same party, say, or the same event. And then you have to make your own choices and shape it."

It is the surviving family members, or other custodians of the deceased's property and papers, who can deny access. Who, as ancillary—and perhaps now wealthy and influential—characters in the biography, can initiate lawsuits.

But the very integrity of a biography demands that it be written by someone outside the family circle, as Nasaw pointed out in his talk: "Just as Withermore always has Doyne looking over one shoulder, the ghost on one shoulder, and the wife looking over his other shoulder, so—though many of us don't feel the presence of the ghost—we all feel the presence of the families. They're always there. And the reality is, I think, that they don't know, they're not the ones who should be writing these books. And certainly the great men themselves and women should not be writing their own books—autobiographies do not come closer to what Ron [Powers] calls truthfulness than biography. And yet there is this uneasy aspect about writing a biography. I mean, you feel unholy, unclean, or you're made to feel as if what you're doing is not only lesser art but lesser truth."

A good biography is founded upon truthfulness. It probes the mystery of great personal achievement, and sometimes uncovers a monster or a saint.

More often, it simply celebrates the extraordinary drama of a single remarkable, flawed human life.

THE WRITING LIFE

Writing is no less mystical because we are chronicling the behavior of our fellow humans rather than ciphering out the codes of the angels. It's no accident that serious writers pursue their craft with the zeal of medieval scribes: We consider it a vocation. Writing is not just a livelihood or even a career; in some fundamental way it defines who we are all the time, even when we are not writing. It colors how we see the world, which in turn colors the way we write, which sends us back into the world for a fresh look.

Writing is a way of life.

It uses all of your talent, your energy, your passion, even your doubts and failings. It is a complete use of your personality. Writing well is the hardest thing I know, and it offers the most complete satisfaction I know outside of love and friendship.

It's not fun, exactly: It's difficult, soul-searching work of the most exacting kind, yet you do not think of it that way. You feel the tug of the words and you revisit them every day. You lose yourself in the act.

Creative nonfiction is stories from real life, stories that carry both literal truthfulness and a larger Truth, told in a clear voice, with grace, and out of a passionate curiosity about the world.

Your working habits reflect your identity in a very profound way. They are the practice of your ethics, your protection under the law, the outward evidence of your character and attitude, and the foundation of your style. All a writer has are passion and time, and if he is true to his passion and jealous of his time, he can leave behind words that will be the measure of a life well spent.

Writing is a transaction: It goes from your imagination into the reader's.

The more I write and the more I read, the more the two processes converge. I write for the same reason I read—to find out what happens next.

I linger over the final chapter, the closing sentence, the last word. When I write, as when I read, I hate for the book to end.

BIBLIOGRAPHY

In doing my best to show while telling, I've quoted from and referred to a whole lot of good books, some of them single narratives, others collections of shorter pieces that first appeared in magazines. My list is not meant to be inclusive—undoubtedly I've overlooked many fine works, or else I've used another, more convenient piece to make a certain point. But it's not a bad reading list for a sojourn on a desert island, and two things are true about it: First, the books taken together demonstrate a broad range of style and subject matter; and second, each book is *literary* in the best sense of that word—of enduring value, showing serious attention to craft and respect for the reader.

Abbey, Edward. *Desert Solitaire: A Season in the Wilderness.* New York: Bantam, 1985.

Atwill, William D. *Fire and Power: The American Space Program as Postmodern Narrative.* Athens: University of Georgia Press, 1994.

Bain, David Haward. *Sitting in Darkness: Americans in the Philippines.* New York: Penguin, 1984.

Bledsoe, Jerry. *Bitter Blood: A True Story of Southern Family Pride, Madness, and Multiple Murder.* New York: Dutton, 1988.

Capote, Truman. *In Cold Blood: A True Account of a Multiple Murder and Its Consequences.* New York: Random House, 1965.

Conover, Ted. *Rolling Nowhere.* New York: Viking Press, 1984.

DeBlieu, Jan. *Hatteras Journal.* Golden, CO: Fulcrum, 1987.

Dillard, Annie. *The Writing Life.* New York: Harper & Row, 1989.

Fallaci, Oriana. *Interview With History* (trans, John Shepley). New York: Liveright, 1976.

Fussell, Paul. *Wartime: Understanding and Behavior in the Second World War.* New York: Oxford University Press, 1989.

Gerard, Philip. *Brilliant Passage.* Mystic, CT: Mystic Seaport Museum Press, 1989. (I make no claims about the virtues of this book, but I include it because I alluded to it in the text.)

Hawley, Richard A. *Boys Will Be Men: Masculinity in Troubled Times.* Middlebury, VT: Paul S. Eriksson, 1993.

Hemingway, Ernest. *A Moveable Feast.* New York: Charles Scribner's Sons, 1964.

Hersey, John. *Hiroshima.* New York: Alfred A. Knopf, 1988 (this edition has a new final chapter).

Hills, L. Rust. *Writing in General and the Short Story in Particular.* New York: Bantam, 1979.

Horton, Tom. *Bay Country.* Baltimore: Johns Hopkins University Press, 1987.

Keneally, Thomas. *The Place Where Souls Are Born: A Journey to the American Southwest.* New York: Simon & Schuster, 1992.

Lopez, Barry. *Arctic Dreams: Imagination and Desire in a Northern Landscape.* New York: Charles Scribner's Sons, 1986.

Mailer, Norman. *Of a Fire on the Moon.* Boston: Little, Brown and Company, 1969.

Mairs, Nancy. *Plaintext: Essays.* Tucson: University of Arizona Press, 1986.

Malcolm, Janet. *The Journalist and the Murderer.* New York: Knopf, 1990.

McPhee, John A. *Coming Into the Country.* New York: Farrar, Straus and Giroux, 1977.

Mitchell, Joseph. *Up in the Old Hotel and Other Stories.* New York: Pantheon, 1992.

Morris, Edmund. *The Rise of Theodore Roosevelt.* New York: Coward, McCann & Geoghegan, Inc., 1979.

Powers, Ron. *White Town Drowsing.* Boston: Atlantic Monthly Press, 1986.

Reiss, Bob. *The Road to Extrema.* New York: Summit Books, 1992.

Shelton, Richard. *Going Back to Bisbee.* Tucson: University of Arizona Press, 1992.

Stein, Harry. *Ethics (and Other Liabilities): Trying to Live Right in an Amoral World.* New York: St. Martin's, 1982.

Steinbeck, John. *The Log From the Sea of Cortez.* New York: Penguin, 1977 (this edition contains "About Ed Ricketts").

—*Once There Was a War.* New York: Viking, 1958.

—*Travels With Charley: In Search of America.* New York: Viking, 1962.

Talese, Gay. *Fame and Obscurity, Portraits.* New York: World, 1970.

Terkel, Studs. *Working.* New York: Pantheon, 1974.

Terry, Wallace. *Bloods: An Oral History of the Vietnam War by Black Veterans.* New York: Random House, 1984.

Thomas, Elizabeth Marshall. *The Hidden Life of Dogs.* Boston: Houghton Mifflin, 1993.

Updike, John. *Hugging the Shore: Essays and Criticism.* New York: Knopf, 1983.

Vidal, Gore. *United States: Essays 1952-1992.* New York: Random House, 1993.

Wheelock, John Hall (editor). *Editor to Author: The Letters of Maxwell E. Perkins.* New York: Charles Scribner's Sons, 1979.

Williams, Terry Tempest. *Refuge: An Unnatural History of Family and Place.* New York: Pantheon Books, 1991.

Wolfe, Tom. *The Right Stuff.* New York: Farrar, Straus & Giroux, 1979.

Wolff, Tobias. *This Boy's Life.* New York: Atlantic Monthly Press, 1989.

ABOUT THE AUTHOR

Philip Gerard directs the Professional and Creative Writing Program at the University of North Carolina at Wilmington. He has published fiction and nonfiction in numerous magazines, including *New England Review/Bread Loaf Quarterly* and *The World & I*. He has scripted shows for *Globe Watch*, an international affairs program, for PBS-affiliate WUNC-TV, Chapel Hill, North Carolina, and some of his weekly radio essays have been broadcast on National Public Radio's *All Things Considered*. Gerard is the author of a memoir, *Brilliant Passage* (Mystic, 1989), and three novels, including *Desert Kill* (William Morrow, 1994).

INDEX